Sendivogius making gold

Jacques Sadoul

Alchemists and Gold

*Translated from the French
by Olga Sieveking*

G. P. PUTNAM'S SONS
NEW YORK

FIRST AMERICAN EDITION 1972

Copyright © 1972 Neville Spearman Limited

This book appeared under the title
Le Tresor des Alchimistes in France in 1970

SBN: 399–10990–0

Library of Congress Catalog
Card Number: 72–85242

PRINTED IN THE UNITED STATES OF AMERICA

Contents

Contents

To the Seeker

Let him forbear who believes that Alchemy is
concerned solely with the mundane, mineral
and metallic nature of things.

Let him forbear, who believes that Alchemy is
purely spiritual.

But those who understand that Alchemy is
but a symbol used to reveal by analogy the process
of achieving "Spiritual Realisation"—in a word,
that man is at once the prime matter and the athanor
of the Work—let them pursue it with all their might.

Claude d'Ygé,
New Assembly of
Chymical Philosophers

Foreword

"Life is not easy in the New World, even for an apothecary," reflected Mr. Starkey, who had emigrated from England to America in the early seventeenth century.

He took down the placard "Apartment to Let" that had been affixed to his shop-front. The new lodger, one John Smith—no doubt a fictitious name—was a man of medium height and unremarkable appearance, whose age was difficult to guess, but who was certainly an educated person.

He gave no trouble to his landlord, unlike the drunkard who had pestered the neighbour's daughter during the past winter.

Mr. Smith was, in fact, a model tenant, and Starkey had almost forgotten his existence, when one day he asked permission to make use of the small laboratory attached to the pharmacy. He explained that he wanted to try out a new tincture. Mr. Starkey agreed but, thinking that it seemed an odd request, he suggested to his son George to keep an eye on the proceedings through a chink in the shutters.

The young man took up his position and saw Mr. Smith go into the laboratory carrying a small bag that was obviously very heavy. From this he picked out pieces of some dull grey metal, probably lead, that he put into a crucible, under which he lit a very hot fire. When the metal reached melting point, the man brought out of his pocket a small box containing a reddish powder. George saw him mix a speck of this powder in a lump of wax and throw the pellet into the cauldron with the metal. Then he sat down and waited. After a good quarter of an hour had passed, George watched Mr. Smith pour the molten metal into a mould. The young man's eyes nearly started out of his head when he saw that the metal had turned yellow with a greenish sheen—that it had, in short, taken on the colour of molten gold.

At that moment the alchemist—as he must be called—turned to

where George Starkey was standing and said: "Come in, young man, if you are interested in what I am doing."

Mr. Smith did not appear to be put out at having been watched, and made his hosts a present of part of the product of his transmutation. On the other hand, he refused absolutely to initiate them into his Art, saying to George, who was more importunate than his father: "My young friend, if God has destined you for this Art, He will in His good time accord you the opportunity of learning it. But if in His wisdom He judges you to be unworthy to exercise the science, or if He sees that you would make a wrong use of it—well, a man who furnished arms to anyone capable of bringing harm to his fellows would indeed be blame-worthy!"

Mr. Starkey left a description of the episode, in which he says: "I admit that this sermon on the Divinity did not please me."

The alchemist, noting his vexation, continued: "You must know that we are bound by the most solemn oaths never to impart a knowledge of our Art to anyone who because he had this knowledge might possibly bring misfortune into the world. The Adept who was thus indirectly the instigator of any resultant evils would be answerable for them all before God."

"I understand, Sir," replied the father. "But at least you will allow us to know your name?"

"I am called Eirenæus Philalethes, English by birth, a denizen of the Universe."

This story is taken from *The Marrow of Alchemy* by Eirenæus Philoponas Philalethes, published in England in 1655 and now kept in the British Museum. George Starkey wrote an introduction to it under the pseudonym Egregius Christo.

AZOTH,

OV LE MOYEN DE FAIRE
l'Or caché des Philofophes.

De Frere Bafile Valentin.

Reueu, corrigé & augmenté par Mr. L'agneau Medecin.

Senior   Adolphus

A PARIS.
Chez PIERRE MOET, Libraire Iuré, proche le
Pont S. Michel à l'Image S. Alexis.

Azoth, or the method of making Philosophers' Secret Gold

By Brother Basil Valentine

Book I

The Hermetic Art

1. A First Contact with Alchemy

During the severe winter of 1956 I was caught in a snow-storm which obliged me to take shelter in a bookshop in the rue Saint-Jacques in Paris. It was a shop specialising in occult works on magic, astrology, clairvoyance and alchemy.

My attention was caught by a book on a shelf devoted to this latter subject, first because I liked the mediaeval-looking design on the cover, and then because of its curious title: *The Twelve Keys to Philosophy*.

To avoid being thrown out by the shop-keeper, who looked a formidable type, I decided to buy the book.

I must admit that my first contact with alchemy was disappointing. The preface, by M. Eugène Canseliet, seemed to be erudite to a degree very far beyond the comprehension of a neophyte such as I was; and the book itself, by Brother Basil Valentine of the Order of Saint Benedict, by no means lived up to its opening words, which read: "In my preface, Oh very dear friend and lover of the Art, I am offering to you and to others burning with the same fire, the prospect of learning by diligent study the potentialities of Nature; and to those who seek more deeply, of finding the corner-stone, the very foundation of the Art, as it was taught to me from on high. I will show you how our Masters of old brought forth the Stone, as they learnt from the All Highest, in order that it might be used for health and comfort in this earthly life."

This sounded very promising. But the text that followed was so obscure that I understood absolutely nothing. As for the drawings of the "twelve keys"—though from an artistic point of view they were quite delightful—they taught me even less than the Master's writings. They depicted various richly dressed personages, some more or less fabulous animals, and certain instruments such as crucibles and retorts, which did seem to be more nearly connected with alchemy. M. Canseliet's explanations certainly indicated the abstruse

15

symbolism, but the whole thing appeared to me to be addressed to readers who were already initiates. For instance, this is how he begins his commentary on the first illustration: "The King and Queen of the Work, that is to say the *philosophic gold and silver*, are exemplified in alchemy by the wolf (Note: =*molten metal*) and the great *ball* over the dome. This last and the chalice in the midst of the flames clearly indicate the *hard way*, in which the *secret fire* plays an important part."

I admit that, far from dispelling my confusion, such explanations only increased it. Nevertheless, the strange ideas of Basil Valentine came to have an irresistible fascination for me. A longing to make my way further into this occult world obsessed me, and I went back to that bookshop in the rue Saint-Jacques. I asked for something that could be understood by a beginner, or for some popularised version. The bookseller replied with a hint of condescension that the two most recent works of this type had been published in 1860 and 1891 respectively, and that they had been virtually out of print ever since. He added that nowadays only two kinds of books on the subject were published: one sort being reprints of alchemical treatises of past centuries, and the other modern studies analysing the psychological or psycho-analytical causes of what they called the "alchemical phenomenon", the latter always being written by people who, according to him, combined incompetence with fatuousness. Noticing my troubled face, he went over to a shelf and picked out a volume which he handed to me.

"Here," he said, "try this one. The author is a colleague of mine who specialises in the Hermetic Art; I mean alchemy," he added, seeing that I looked puzzled.

This work bore the title *A New Assembly of Chymical Philosophers*, and had been published in 1954, that is two years previously. I ventured a question:

"What does the curious title mean?"

"Alchemists are called Hermetic Philosophers or Philosophers of Chymistry, with a y—it's a traditional title. As for *New Assembly*, that is probably quoted from the ancient work *Turba Philosophorum* which should be translated as an 'Assembly (or Convention) of Philosophers' and not, as it sometimes is, a 'Rabble'!"

Feeling that I was rather out of my depth, I paid for the book and lost no time in beginning to study it. It was not exactly a book for beginners, but the author managed to make it clear enough for it to be understood by a serious student. It was the sesame that opened the first door to the Hermetic Art for me.

*

It was more than a year before I managed to procure the twenty or so basic works necessary for a study of the subject and as I proceeded I found that my first impressions were gradually modified. At the beginning I thought, like everyone else, that the whole of alchemy was included in the definition Louis Figuier gave in his book *Alchemy and the Alchemists*, published in 1856: "The object of alchemy is, as everyone knows, the transmutation of metals, changing base metals into precious metals, making gold and silver artificially. Such is the purpose of this curious science, which has been practised for at least fifteen centuries."

I had in fact read that the practical work of alchemy, called the Magisterium or Mystery, aimed at the production of a strange object known as the Philosopher's Stone, which was capable of transmuting into gold any molten metal whatsoever. Did not the English monk Roger Bacon, in his *Mirror of Alquimy*, say "Alquimy is the science that teaches the preparation of a certain medicine or elixir which, if it is poured over base metals, brings them on the instant to a state of perfection."

A warning against this misconception was given me by the learned Grillot de Givry in his book *A Museum of Sorcerers, Magi and Alchemists*, where he says: "Many people who have not studied the subject, think that alchemy is no more than a farrago of visions and fantasies, the result of men's vain attempt to produce gold artificially, to which they are impelled either by plain greed or by the megalomaniac hope of becoming equal to God. Those who enquire more deeply into the science, however, very soon discover that, over and above baser motives, there is an indescribable fascination in the work; and within the shadowy confines of mediaeval sciences this radiates like the great, peaceful rose windows that, far from the trivialities of life, bathe the transepts of our slumbering cathedrals in an ineffable light."

I began to wonder whether the stress laid upon the transmutation of metals was not a kind of dust thrown into the eyes of non-initiates, to prevent their understanding the secret truths of alchemy.

For yet another reason gold is still believed to be the ultimate objective of the Hermetic Art. In addition to alchemists properly so-called—and usually referred to as Adepts or Artists (that is, those who have mastered the Art)—there are two other categories of persons who have attempted the transmutation of metals: first Puffers and second Archimists, the latter being nearer to our own day. There has always been a tendency to confuse these individuals, whose only purpose is the manufacture of gold, with true Hermetic Philosophers.

An excellent definition of Puffers is to be found in René Marcard's book *A Short History of Chemistry and Alchemy*:

"On the circumference of the Great Art, Puffers formed a secondary circle that swarmed with charlatans, quacks, dreamers, magicians, fortune-tellers, purveyors of charms, cranks, imposters of all sorts, and more especially uninspired 'labourers in the fire', who hoped to steal some part of the secrets or a spark of their genius from the true Seekers. Magical practices, and the brewing of poisons, which at one time had a certain vogue, were the sources of their scanty income. Being convinced that a powerful elixir could be concocted by using animal matter, they experimented with the most extraordinary substances, and sometimes the most repugnant. The blood of young children was used all too often in experiments such as those which blot the name of Gilles de Rais, and which did not encourage the Law to be lenient to true practitioners of the Great Work.

"Claiming to imitate Nature in its slow evolution, alchemists carried on interminable operations, which might last for months or even years; so much so, that not seldom an Adept who had undertaken to consummate the Mystery died of exhaustion in the course of the work, leaving his disciples to dispute the honour of completing it. Puffers, people without self-respect or pride in their work, driven by a squalid lust for gold, could not bring themselves to face such delays; in their ignorance they thought to substitute the heat of their furnaces for the slow operation of time; so it often happened that an explosion put an end to their efforts, setting a period to the experiment at the same time as to the life of the would-be thaumaturgist."

Marcard's description is not in the least exaggerated. Three secret elements are, in fact, necessary to the production of the Philosopher's Stone: the *prime substance*, an irreducible element on which the alchemist works and which he exposes to the action of the *secret fire* (also called *prime agent*), and *philosophic mercury*. Puffers, not knowing to what these symbolic names referred, put all manner of things into their crucibles and retorts. In this way they made a number of important chemical discoveries, some of which unfortunately proved

Early Puffers (Egypt, *c.* 1450 B.C.)

fatal to them. At one stage of the Master Work, they might put a mixture of charcoal, sulphur and nitrate into the pot, a combination which comes dangerously near to being gunpowder!

René Marcard was therefore perfectly correct in observing that the career of many a Puffer had ended in a big bang. Here is an example, taken from *Memoirs of the New Atlantis*, written by Mary Manley towards the end of the seventeenth century:

"A lady of quality, being passionately interested in Alchemy made the acquaintance of a man who claimed to have the power of changing lead into gold—which is to say, in alchemical language, that he could convert base metals into precious metals. This Hermetist asked only to be provided with the necessary materials and the time to carry out his undertaking. He was invited to stay on the lady's estate, where a large laboratory was built for him and, so that he might not be disturbed at the work, the strictest orders were given that no-one should intrude. He arranged that the door should turn on a pivot, so as to ensure that nothing should disturb his high thoughts, and meals could be delivered without his seeing or being seen by anybody. During the two years he spent on the estate, he spoke to no one whatever, not even to his trustful patroness. When at last she was admitted, she looked with an agreeable sense of awe at the alembics, the enormous cauldrons, long tubes, forges, furnaces, and three or four scorching fires blazing in various parts of what felt like the interior of a volcano. With no less veneration she observed the smoke-grimed face of the physicist, pale, emaciated, worn by daily labours and nightly vigils. He told her in his unintelligible jargon of such successes as he had obtained. She looked around, expecting (vainly) to see little piles of gold spread about the laboratory. The alchemist had frequently asked for new alembics and vast quantities of charcoal.

"Realising now, however, that she had spent a large part of her fortune in supplying the demands of the philosopher, the lady began to subordinate the flights of her imagination to the counsels of wisdom. Two years had passed, enormous quantities of lead had been supplied and still she saw nothing but lead. She told the scientist how she felt about it, and he admitted frankly that he was surprised at the slowness of his progress, but said that he would redouble his efforts and would venture on a particularly difficult operation to which until now he had hoped not to be obliged to have recourse. His patroness left the laboratory, hopes and golden visions revived. One day not long afterwards, as she sat at dinner a frightful shriek was heard, followed by an explosion like the firing of a cannon of the largest calibre. She and her servants rushed to the laboratory, where they found that two of the biggest retorts were shattered and a great part of the building was in flames. The experimentalist himself was a charred corpse."

*

Nowadays it is not thought that modern chemistry derives from the traditional art of alchemists, but rather that it has resulted from the empirical work of Puffers. As we said above, a large number of chemical reactions and also of new substances were discovered by some of these pseudo-alchemists who pursued systematic investigations with anything that came to hand. The true Adept knew exactly what were the natural substances required for making the Stone, and so he was very seldom obliged to undertake purely chemical research. It is true that some alchemists—Basil Valentine and Paracelsus, for example—enriched the range of chemistry with new and highly important concepts, but this resulted from secondary experiments not bearing directly on the philosophic mystery.

We come now to Archimists, independent investigators who were working at the end of the nineteenth century and the beginning of the twentieth. They asserted that the transmutation of metals was perfectly feasible by ordinary chemical means, that is to say by using methods other than the liberation of the tremendous nuclear energies made possible by modern physics. Tiffereau and then Jolivet-Castelot were well known for research along these lines, but official science never admitted the validity of the transmutations they claimed to have effected. It must be confessed that the quantity of gold obtained in such experiments was so minute that it might have come from impurities in the substances used. One such case, rather an amusing one, occurred in Germany in 1931, when Professor Hans Miethe said that he had transmuted mercury into gold. An analysis of his procedure showed that the traces of gold found in the mercury at the end of the experiment actually came from the frame of the Professor's spectacles, which had been affected by the mercury fumes.

Moreover, after the 1914 war, at the very time when M. Jolivet-Castelot was President of his newly-founded Alchemists' Society of France, contemporary Adepts refused to allow that his experiments were alchemical. An article published in 1926 in a special issue devoted to Alchemy of the magazine *Le Voile d'Isis* (*The Veil of Isis*) by Auriger, one of the Adepts, will prove what I say. Here is an extract from the article, entitled *From Alchemy to Science*:

"M. Jolivet-Castelot will, I am sure, allow me to make one remark about the use of the word 'alchemical' as applied to his experiments. It would have been correct in the days when only alchemists undertook this kind of work; but nowadays the materials and methods derive from the domain of chemistry pure and simple. If they were alchemical in the true sense of the word there would be, as far as I am aware at any rate, not a single Professor at the Sorbonne, however learned, capable of verifying them. Besides, since M. Jolivet-Castelot asks for verification only by chemists, it means that the transmutations he claims have been achieved by chemical means and in no other way."

This quotation seems to me to sum up the situation perfectly, and no more will be said here about Archimists, who have no real connection with the Hermetic Art.

*

Once having decided to confine my study to true Artists, in the highest sense of the word, I tried to find out from their works how much importance they actually attached to the transmutation of metals. This has proved to be a real Labour of Hercules, to use the name Adepts sometimes give to their Mystery, for—even confining oneself to the most famous of the treatises—it is impossible to draw any general conclusions, since the methods vary so enormously from one author to another.

The diversity is due not so much to differences in routine as to the circumstance that the treatises practically never seem to cover the same part of the Work. There is, in fact, not a single case in which the process is described chronologically from the beginning—that is to say from the *raw material*, which will become the *proximate material* of the Stone, before being transformed in the last stage to the *rebis* (from the Latin *res bis*, double substance) or consummation.

The expression *raw material* is used in the treatises to mean three completely different states of matter; and ambiguities in the various meanings for "mercury" are innumerable. Each philosopher appears to speak of things without the slightest relevance to anything his fellow-practitioners have said, because, although he is referring to the same Work, he is describing a different phase of it. This is one of the first and most serious difficulties.

The second lies in the incredible obscurity of the texts and especially in the terminology, so that the same substance may be called by more than a dozen different names. The celebrated naturalist Buffon writes in the article on gold in his *History of Minerals*: "One can only say that nothing is to be gathered from alchemical books, nor from the Emerald Table, nor the *Assembly of Philosophers*, nor Philalethes. And some others that I have taken the trouble to read, and indeed to study carefully, have afforded me only obscurities and unintelligible processes."

One may well ask why Hermetic Philosophers have always taken so much trouble to conceal their meaning. One possible answer is that of Louis Figuier, the mid-nineteenth century scientific writer, who says: "Alchemists had an excellent reason for adopting obscure and ambiguous language. They had nothing to say about the art of manufacturing gold, since all their efforts in this direction were vain." This opinion is an exact reflection of the scientific spirit of the nineteenth century, which believed itself to have discovered everything and to have left nothing for the twentieth century to do but to calculate further decimal figures.

A second and more accurate reply is given by the Arabic alchemist Jabir, in his *Sum of the Perfections of the Mystery*: "I declare here that in this book I have never taught our science explicitly. Had I described the order of its development, ill-intentioned persons might have understood it and have used it for pernicious ends."

Persuaded of the validity of their Work, Adepts considered themselves to be responsible for the occult powers they released, and they therefore reserved to themselves the right to refuse the Master's degree to any whom they considered unworthy. No alchemical treatise, therefore, must be regarded either as a manual of initiation or as a scientific communication addressed to other philosophers. Such treatises are reserved solely for a third category of readers—those who are *initiable*, as René Alleau terms people who are capable of mastering the Art for themselves, without the help of a *guru* (guide). The comparison is made in Alleau's book *Aspects of Traditional Alchemy*, where he contrasts the system with that of the Hindu disciplines, in which initiation by a Master is the sole and invariable method.

Besides the answers to our original question given by Figuier and Jabir, there would seem to be a third possibility. Alchemical writings

23

may appear incomprehensible to us at this time simply because certain ideas current in the days when the science was instituted have now been forgotten. For example, Jacques Bergier, a contemporary scientific writer, recently spoke to me of a technical work about television that described the principal types of receivers, and he said:

"If ever in the future such a manual comes into the hands of someone brought up in a civilisation based upon a technology different from our own, the apparatuses described will seem like so much nonsense to him, because the author has not explained that they have to be connected to an electric current before they will function. It was so obvious to him that he did not think it nescesary to mention."

It is not altogether impossible that the same may be true of alchemy, and that certain incomprehensible texts and gaps in the explanations refer to ideas so familiar to scientists of those days that they never thought of mentioning them.

Personally, I incline to Jabir's reply, which I believe to be sincere, though incomplete. "Ill-intentioned" people have other means of procuring gold than by manufacturing it artificially! The conclusion that seems inescapable is that what alchemists had to conceal was something more important than secret formulae for making precious metals. But the question is, what was it? Perhaps a rapid survey of the history of Hermetic Philosophy may enlighten us.

2. Hermes and the History of Alchemy

Where did it all begin?

It is very difficult to give any date or the name of any particular place. China, Egypt, the Middle East and Greece can all claim to have seen the birth of alchemy.

I propose simply to follow tradition and make the Hermetic Art start with Hermes himself, who was one of the gods or a pre-Pharaonic king. Several alchemical treatises are ascribed to him, among them the famous *Emerald Table*, which contains the shortest extant epitome of the Great Work, if not the clearest. One legend has it that the text was found by Alexander the Great's soldiers in the Great Pyramid at Gizeh, this being none other than the tomb of Hermes himself. He personally, it is said, graved the words upon an emerald plaque with a diamond stylus, whence its name.

I am quoting it in its entirety, because it shows how difficult alchemical texts are, although I have expressly chosen a translation by the contemporary Adept Fulcanelli, which seems to me to be considerably clearer and more concise than most others.

"This is the truth, the whole truth, and nothing but the truth:— As below, so above; and as above, so below. With this knowledge alone you may work miracles. And since all things exist in and emanate from the ONE Who is the ultimate Cause, so all things are born after their kind from this ONE.

"The Sun is the father, the Moon the mother; the wind carried it in his belly. Earth is its nurse and its guardian. It is the Father of all things, the eternal Will is contained in it. Here, on earth, its strength, its power, remain one and undivided. Earth must be separated from fire, the subtle from the dense, gently, with unremitting care. It arises from the earth and descends from heaven; it gathers to itself the strength of things above and things below.

25

By means of this one thing all the glory of the world shall be yours, and all obscurity flee from you.

"It is power, strong with the strength of all power, for it will penetrate all mysteries and dispel all ignorance. By it the world was created. From it are born manifold wonders, the means to achieving which are here given.

"It is for this reason that I am called Hermes Trismegistus; for I possess the three essentials of the philosophy of the universe.

"This is the sum total of the work of the Sun."

Hermes Trismegistus

*

Just as the Egyptians were interested in alchemy from remotest antiquity, so, curiously enough, were the Chinese on the other side of the world. In fact, the most ancient texts in the Celestial Empire —the Tsai-y-Chi and the Tao—were already full of speculations about the constitution of matter and the possibility of transmuting metals. Yet in China, in the Tao period, nothing was known about the use of powerful acids as solvents for metals, which makes it the more remarkable that experiments in transmutation had already been undertaken on much the same lines as those of our own mediaeval alchemists.

Nevertheless, the actual cradle of alchemy, at least as we know it today, seems to me to be properly sought among the Greeks, the

Arabs and the Byzantines. The principal Greek school for the Art was founded in Alexandria by Zozimos the Panapolitan towards the beginning of the fourth century A.D. A number of his works have come down to us, in particular his treatise on furnaces, in which he describes the glass vessels used for distillation well before the Arabs mentioned them. Democritus, one of his disciples, refers to the existence of two kinds of transmutatory powder, one white and the other red. The famous woman alchemist, Mary the Jewess (sometimes mistakenly said to be a sister of Moses), lived at the same period. The "bain Marie", still used in our kitchens, is attributed to her. She also invented the *kerotakis*, a sealed container in which minute metal shavings were exposed to the action of vapours; and the aerometer, also said to have been evolved by her, is exactly like the one in use today, which was re-discovered by Baumé in the eighteenth century, after it had long been forgotten.

In the fifth century alchemy moved from Alexandria to Byzantium, where it achieved some distinction, before passing to the Arabs, who thus reaped the harvest of all the Egyptian and Greek work. Then from the seventh to the eleventh centuries alchemy was introduced into all the countries that the Arabs conquered by force of arms, Spain especially becoming one of the great Hermetic centres in an otherwise unenlightened Europe. Arabic influence on the Hermetic Art was considerable, keeping its importance at least up to the days of Albertus Magnus and Thomas Aquinas. Numerous Arabic words have passed into modern usage from those times—elixir, for instance, alcohol, alembic, and so on. The word alchemy itself comes from the Egyptian *khemeia* with the Arabic article *al*; and it literally means "the science of black earth", or prime matter.

The greatest of the Arabian Adepts was undoubtedly Jabir, whose most important work is mentioned above.

Jabir, whose full name was Jabir ibn Hayyan, lived in the eighth century A.D. He was the pupil of a celebrated Islamic Master, the Imam Jaffar, and in his turn became a famous scientist. In particular, he explained how to prepare nitric acid, nitro-hydrochloric acid (aqua-regia), and other chemical substances entirely unknown at that time to western scientists. Since he attributed many of his discoveries to his master Jaffar, it is clear that the Arabs must also have achieved some remarkable results in the seventh century. Perhaps one should not be surprised to find that certain western historians went to considerable lengths to prove that Jabir's works were very largely later forgeries, that he himself was never an alchemist, not even a chemist, and that anyhow he probably never existed. But since then a number of Jabir's works, of undoubted authenticity, have been discovered in the libraries of Cairo and Constantinople. They contain particularly interesting notes on "natural philosophy" (physics), on methods of foretelling the future, and upon the chemical composition of natural substances. Some doubts remain, however, about his *Sum of the Perfections*, because the Arabic text is lost, and the earliest known version is a translation dating from the end of the thirteenth century. There was, therefore, nothing to prevent the translator from introducing discoveries dating from the twelfth or thirteenth centuries, in order to bolster up the authority of Jabir. Not but what the question is purely academic today.

*

This brief historical survey of alchemy has brought us to one of those problems about the authorship of the treatises which are the joy of pundits. It seems worth remarking at this point that, throughout the present book, it will be found that practically all the great Adepts have had doubts cast upon the paternity of the works which bear their names. Thus, if historians (or some who claim the title) are to be believed, Albertus Magnus never wrote a line on alchemy, any more than did his pupil Thomas Aquinas—although the latter included a lengthy dissertation in his *Summa Theologica* on the question whether it was dishonest to sell Hermetic gold. Similarly the works attributed to Arnold of Villanova, Raymond Lully, Pope John XXII, and many others are said to be forgeries; and when it comes to celebrated alchemists like Basil Valentine or Nicholas Flamel—well, they never existed, although in the case of Flamel, there are plenty of legal documents referring to him, and there still is in Paris a perfectly well authenticated house in which he undoubtedly lived at one time.

All such arguments seem to me to be pure quibbling. Certainly, Basil Valentine was an assumed name. But it would never occur to anybody to say that Molière did not exist because that was not his real patronymic. There is no doubt whatever that someone existed who, under the name Basil Valentine, wrote alchemical treatises in which, for the first time in the history of western science, some most remarkable discoveries were described that are still often quoted in modern books on mineralogy. Let us just glance for a moment at the case of Raymond Lully (we shall return to the matter more fully later). Why are all his works said to be apocryphal? Principally because they were published after his death. Now it happened that Lully lived in Palma in Majorca, that is to say quite near to Spain, that very Catholic country, and it is highly probable that he felt it wiser to leave his Hermetic works to be published by his disciples after his demise.

It is for this reason that I do not propose to enter into academic discussions about the attribution of the books to anyone other than those whose names they bear. I admit freely that in some cases it is by no means certain that the name which appears on the title-page is really that of the author; but after a lapse of three or four hundred years, what does it matter?

One point that all the older philosophers stress is, however, worth noting. As I had suspected, the majority of them are much more concerned to emphasise the medicinal virtues of the Stone than its powers of transmutation. In the quotation I gave at the beginning of this book, from the *Twelve Keys*, we have already seen that Basil Valentine adjures his readers to use the Philosopher's Stone for the benefit of their health, and elsewhere he insists: "In this treatise I have done my utmost to impress upon you that the Stone of the Ancients was most assuredly bestowed on us by Heaven for the health and comfort of men in this vale of woe, and that it is the greatest of earthly treasures."

None the less, several points were still unexplained. Why, for instance, should it be said to be *essential* to effect transmutation? And what was the difference between the panacea (universal medicine), drinkable gold, and the elixir of life?

Clearly, it was necessary for me to study the principles on which the Hermetic Art was founded, if I were to find the answers for which I hoped.

3. The Principles of Alchemy

People are apt to speak of alchemical *theories*, but this term is repudiated by alchemists themselves, who regard it as too academic, too scholastic an expression. Their Art consists above all in a personal relationship with Nature, a relationship that varies from one Adept to another. Nevertheless, they all hold certain principles in common, and it is these which we propose to examine here.

The first and most important of the principles is insistence upon the unity of matter. Thus, in his *Triumphal Chariot of Antimony*, Basil Valentine writes: "All things derive from the same source, all are ultimately born of the same mother." Although in an allegorical form, this idea is also found in the *Emerald Table* in the phrase "As above, so below", and Raymond Lully sums it up definitively in his *Testament*, with the formula *"Omnia in Unum"*.

It is surprising to find so modern a concept in the Middle Ages; but it must not be forgotten that alchemy is first and foremost a traditional science, and that the Platonic teaching had been passed on uninterruptedly through all periods of history. Everyone knew that Plato had caused the following words to be carved on one of the steles in the temple at Sais: "I am all that has been, that is, and that is to come. None among mortals has ever drawn aside the veil that covers me."

Again, alchemists held the belief that metals, far from being simple substances, were compound and included the three elements, only in varying proportions—that is to say, *philosophers' mercury, philosophers' sulphur*, and *salt* or *arsenic*. It should be stressed that it is absolutely essential not to confuse *philosophers'* mercury with *philosophic* mercury. Many Puffers came to grief through identifying the two substances, though the only thing they have in common is that neither has any connection with chemical mercury! Nor do sulphur and salt correspond with the chemical substances whose names they bear. All three names are symbolic.

Applying this principle, alchemists reckoned that copper, for example, was composed of equal parts of sulphur and mercury, with only an infinitesimal admixture of salt. As regards gold, this is how two famous Adepts saw it: the eighth century Arab Jabir says in his *Sum of the Perfections of the Mystery*: "The Sun (*gold*) is composed of a very subtle mercury together with a small amount of very pure, homogeneous, limpid sulphur, of a clear red tint; and since sulphur is not always of exactly the same shade but may vary in depth of colour, so gold may be yellow to a greater or less degree." Roger Bacon, the English monk writing in the thirteenth century, declares in his *Mirror of Alquimy*: "Gold is the perfect substance, composed of mercury that is pure, homogeneous, brilliant, red; and of equally pure, stable, red sulphur that is incombustible. Gold is perfection."

So, although the two alchemists lived at different times and under different cultural systems, their views are identical.

It must be emphasised also that the names sulphur, mercury and salt were not mere abstractions but represented very definite characteristics of matter. Mercury, the feminine element, symbolised the actual metallicity, the cause of the lustre, ductility and malleability of metals. Sulphur, the male element, indicated the degree of combustibility and the colour. Salt (or arsenic), instead of being a third element, represented the means of union between the other two.

It is obvious that such a concept fully justified the idea of transmutation. If all metals were composed of identical elements, though in differing proportions, it was logical to suppose that the proportions might be changed by the use of a catalyst—the Philosopher's Stone. Jabir was the first to promulgate this "theory", though he did not claim to be its originator but attributed it to the Ancients.

From this, alchemists argued that there was in Nature a single prime substance. Furthermore, they considered that the formation of minerals and metals from this prime substance was in all respects comparable with the development of a foetus in the womb of living creatures. Hence, there must be a metallic seed, just as there are seeds of vegetable and animal life. One of the aims of the Hermetic Art, therefore, was to discover this seed; and even the expression "mineral sperm" was not unknown.

*

The old theory of the four natural elements, inherited from ancient times was not discarded by Hermetic philosophers, who simply adapted it to their Art. According to this theory, the universe was composed of four elements only—earth, air, fire and water. They were distinguished from one another by their weight, earth being the heaviest, then water, followed by air, while fire was by far the lightest. As a consequence of their weights, the first two were attracted downwards, and the other two upwards. Aristotle formulated this theory, and showed that the four elements were linked by their characteristics—heat, dryness, humidity and cold, the opposites (heat and cold, or dryness and humidity) being incompatible. This produced four unions that finally gave birth to the four elements:

Heat + dryness = Fire
Heat + humidity = Air
Cold + dryness = Earth
Cold + humidity = Water

Thus no element contained anything that was not partially contained in others, which made it possible to combine them.

The adaptation of this old classical theory was very well described by Albert Poisson towards the end of the nineteenth century:

"To an alchemist all liquid is a form of Water, all solids are Earth in the last analysis, and all vapours are Air. This is why all the old treatises on physics said that water changes into air when it is heated. They did not mean that water was changed into the breathable mixture that makes up our atmosphere, but that water, which started as a liquid, was changed into a volatile liquid, later called a gas. The elements did not only represent physical states but by extension of the meaning, also qualities."

Poisson concludes his study with a table of correspondences, which is as follows:

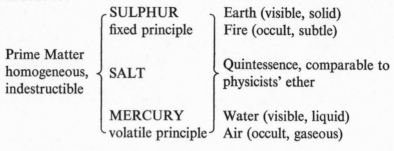

Prime Matter homogeneous, indestructible

SULPHUR fixed principle — Earth (visible, solid) / Fire (occult, subtle)

SALT — Quintessence, comparable to physicists' ether

MERCURY volatile principle — Water (visible, liquid) / Air (occult, gaseous)

*

This seems a suitable place to recall the connection that has always existed between alchemy and that other ancient science, astrology. Not all authors mention it, and it may be that great Adepts such as Nicholas Flamel or Philalethes regarded astrology as totally extraneous to Hermetic Work. On the other hand, alchemists who lived at times as far apart as Zozimos the Panapolitan, in the fourth century A.D., Basil Valentine, in the fifteenth, and Paracelsus in the sixteenth, always attributed great importance to it.

In an alchemical manuscript by Nicholas Valois the following words occur: "Know then, my son, and dearest of my children, that the Sun, the Moon and the stars perpetually shed their influence upon the centre of the Earth." In fact, from the very beginnings of alchemy, metals and planets have been closely linked, and the following correspondences were established:

Sun	— gold	Moon	— silver
Venus	— copper	Mars	— iron
Jupiter	— tin	Saturn	— lead
Mercury	— quicksilver (nowadays called mercury)		

*

This review of the main alchemical concepts brings us naturally to the Philosopher's Stone, which results from the sum total of the principles and is the pre-eminent vindication of the Work.

This is how the contemporary Adept Fulcanelli describes it: "The

Philosopher's Stone is presented to us in the form of a clear, crystalline substance, red in the mass, yellow when pulverised. It is dense and highly fusible, although solid at all temperatures, and its substance makes it penetrating, fiery, invariable, and incombustible."

The Stone, it should be noted, has of itself *no transmutatory power* —it makes possible the preparation of the *precipitate powder* which is the actual transmutatory agent. The Stone, in solid form, was fermented by direct fusion with purified gold or silver. The powder used to transmute a metal into gold was red in colour; for silver it was white.

The process of transmutation into gold has been described a number of times, but the proportion of powder used with any metal varied according to the potency of the Stone made by the alchemist. For example, one part of powder might be put to one hundred parts of the metal; when the metal reached melting point, the powder was added, wrapped in paper or a lump of wax lest the fumes of the hot metal should destroy its transmutatory power.

After about a quarter of an hour, the whole of the metal would have been turned into gold, with no loss of weight.

Almost all extant alchemical studies state that the Philosopher's Stone was equally efficacious for the preparation of "drinkable gold" or the universal medicine, and the elixir of life. But this statement has the facts quite wrong. It is nonsense to say that the Stone can be used for the transmutation of metals *and* for making the universal medicine *and* the elixir of life. The Philosopher's Stone is intended *only* for making the universal medicine, which *is* the elixir of life.

But, it may be asked, what about transmutation? Actually, the transmutatory powder was simply *an experiment* carried out at the end of the Master Work, to make certain that the substance manufactured was indeed the Philosopher's Stone. This is the essential point of the Hermetic Art: alchemists had no desire whatever to change metals into gold as was generally thought; they only wanted to achieve a transmutation to assure themselves of the quality of the Stone they had produced. This is the reason why very few of the Adepts made fortunes. They might carry out one or two or three transmutations at most, as for instance Nicholas Flamel says, purely for the sake of renewing their store of the elixir. Never had the possession of worldly goods, and of gold in particular, been the goal of true alchemists.

Their aim, after having transmuted a metal, was to transmute themselves by swallowing a homoeopathic dose of the Stone twice a year. There are very few treatises that explain the stages of the physical and intellectual transformation of an Adept, and the few that do exist remain as manuscripts in the dark maws of great libraries. It is through the kindness of M. Bernard Husson, a learned and enthusiastic student of the Art, who has spent over twenty years investigating unpublished Hermetic texts, that I am indebted for the following details.

Dosing with the Philosopher's Stone begins with the elimination from the body of all toxins, such as disease germs. Quite suddenly the Adept loses his hair, his nails and his teeth, but they grow again later, and are stronger and healthier than before. All natural elimination whatsoever is thereafter effected solely through the sweat glands. Very soon food becomes unnecessary. So the picture of an alchemist eating only just enough to keep himself alive is quite false. In fact, the higher Adept eats only for enjoyment, because he is no longer subject to natural needs. The influence of the Stone is not confined only to the body; it increases intellectual and spiritual powers tenfold, and is a means of access to true wisdom. Every dissertation stops at this point, for an ordinary person could no longer follow the elect into their new universe.

I would like to give a recent example here. A contemporary alchemist—I know of a dozen or so in France—was initiated into the mysteries of alchemy by an Adept full of years and knowledge who suddenly disappeared one day. Lately this alchemist met his Master again; it was forty years since they had seen one another. The difference was that now the Master looked much younger than the pupil. . . .

"All fairy-tales," say matter-of-fact people; "these supposed transformations only happen in the disordered imagination of your alchemists, and there are no proofs of what they say."

Well, there *is* proof of the reality of physical transformation and therefore of the efficacy of the elixir of life. Among the family papers of the Saint-Clair Turgot family, Bernard Husson found the story of an extraordinary event that occurred during the life-time of one of their sixteenth-century ancestors, who was a Councillor of State. The account was written by the personal physician of this Councillor, and was certainly not intended for publication, nor is there any reference to alchemy elsewhere in the papers.

The Councillor was carrying on a liaison with a lady who visited him at his private house every afternoon, and had done so for almost ten years. By way of safe-guarding her reputation, she was always accompanied by an elderly equerry, Maître Arnaud, who used to wait for her in the shop of a neighbouring chemist, with whom he struck up a friendship. This chemist had for over twenty years been experimenting in alchemy, and one day when Arnaud came into his shop, he rushed to meet him, exclaiming:

—"I've got it! I've got it!"

—"What have you got?"

—"Why . . . the Stone. Arnaud, the elixir! This morning I transmuted a dozen old tin spoons to gold. And here's the elixir of life. (He brandished a phial containing a colourless liquid.) Let's drink some of it at once, old friend; at our age one can't have enough of this sort of thing!"

He poured out a spoonful of his elixir and swallowed it; then he invited Arnaud to do the same. But the latter felt some hesitation and took only a few drops on the tip of his tongue. He was saved further embarrassment by the arrival of a servant who told him that his mistress was leaving and that he was wanted. Arnaud returned the elixir to the apothecary and went off as quickly as his old legs would carry him.

On the way home he suddenly broke out in a cold sweat, followed rapidly by a sensation of burning fever. The lady, anxious for the life of her faithful servitor, sent one of her lackeys to fetch the apothecary. The man came back alone and told her that the chemist had died suddenly.

The equerry soon recovered, but he had lost his hair, his nails, and even his teeth. Saint-Clair Turgot, hearing the extraordinary story, questioned him personally. He bought up all the apothecary's stock from the heirs, but neither he nor Arnaud was able to identify the elixir, because there were hundreds of similar phials in the shop, none of them labelled.

Many years later the Councillor told the story to his personal physician who, after Saint-Clair Turgot's death, wrote down the full details. He made particular mention of the fact that Arnaud's hair, nails and teeth had all grown again and that, at the time of writing, the equerry was in excellent shape, despite being one hundred and twenty-three years old . . .

4. The Work

Having skimmed through the outstanding points of the alchemical doctrine, it will no doubt be of interest for readers to get an idea of how they were put into practice. A short treatise entitled *The Principles of Philalethes* explains briefly, but quite clearly, how the Master Work was accomplished.

Its author, Eirenaeus Philalethes, one of the greatest of Adepts, introduces himself at the beginning of the best-known of his works, *The Open Door into the Secret Palace of the King*: "I am a Philosopher, an Adept, and I use no name but Philalethes, a pseudonym which means *Lover of Truth*." Further on, writing of research carried out in his laboratory, he adds: "These are not fabrications; they are genuine and successful experiments that I have myself witnessed and of which I have certain knowledge, as everyone who is a philosopher will immediately recognise when he reads this."

The Principles of Philalethes was written towards the middle of the seventeenth century, and was translated from Latin into French by Guillaume Salmon in 1672, among his collection of alchemical treatises called *Dictionary of Chymical Philosophers*.

THE PRINCIPLES OF PHILALETHES

Directions for carrying out the Hermetic Work, by Eirenaeus Philalethes, English by birth, a denizen of the Universe.

1. Never rely on the advice of the ignorant or upon sophistical books when you undertake the Great Work; and never lose sight of the fact that the goal at which you are aiming is Gold or Silver; Gold and Silver must be the sole objectives for which you will work through the instrumentality of our mercurial Fountain that will be prepared for their cleansing; and this will require your full attention.

2. Do not be misled by those who tell you that our Gold is not natural gold but artificial gold. It is true that ordinary, natural gold is dead but our operations will revive it, just as a grain of wheat revives when it is planted. After six weeks, gold that was dead becomes live, vigorous and fertile through our Work, because it is planted in the right soil—I mean in the compost we prepare. We may therefore fairly call it *our* Gold, because we unite it with a substance that brings it to life, just as, in an opposite sense, a man condemned to death is called a dead man, because he will soon be one, even though he is still living.

3. In addition to Gold, which is the body and the male element in our Work, another sperm is needed, which is the spirit, the soul, or the female. This element is fluid Mercury; it looks like ordinary quicksilver but is purer and more tenuous. Some people use all manner of liquids instead of Mercury and call them philosophic mercury. Take no heed of their fine words, and do not follow their advice: it is worthless. You will reap only what you have sown. If you sow the Gold that is your seed in an earth or a kind of Mercury that is not metallic and does not accord with metals, instead of in a metallic elixir, the result of your operation will be a piece of useless dross.

4. Our Mercury is a substance similar to ordinary quicksilver, but its nature is different, being empyrean and fiery and of great potency—qualities that accrue to it from the manner in which we prepare it.

5. The secret of its preparation lies in using a mineral that is of the same type as Gold and Mercury. It must be impregnated with volatile Gold that emanates from the body of Mars (*Note: Mars is the symbol of iron.*), and by means of it the Mercury must be purified at least seven times. This done, it is ready to be used for the Bath of the King, that is to say, of Gold.

6. By being worked upon from seven to ten times the Mercury becomes increasingly pure, and also becomes more potent, being animated by our living Sulphur; but if this number of operations or sublimations were to be exceeded, it would become too fiery; and instead of dissolving the substance it would coagulate, and the Gold would neither fuse with it nor dissolve in it.

7. The Mercury, worked upon in this way, must be further distilled two or three times in a glass retort, because some few atoms of the original substance might have remained in it despite our efforts. After this, it must be washed in vinegar and sal ammoniac (*ammonium chloride*); it is then ready for our Work, which must here be taken metaphorically.

8. For the Work, you must always use Gold that is pure and unadulterated. If it is not so when you buy it, purify it yourself in the usual way. Then reduce it to a fine powder, by filing or otherwise, or laminate it; or, if you prefer, calcinate it with corrosives. It does not matter what means you use, as long as the result is extremely fine.

9. Next we come to the compost: take an ounce or two of the prepared substance, and two or three ounces at most of the Mercury, modified as I explained above. Combine them in a marble mortar, heated to the highest possible degree with boiling water; pound and triturate them until they are completely mixed, then add vinegar and enough salt to purify it; after which it must be sweetened with hot water and dried thoroughly.

10. I assure you that, although what I have just said may seem enigmatic, I am being quite frank, and the method of which I am telling you is the one we use ourselves; also that all the old philosophers used the same system, which is unique. Our sophistry lies only in the two kinds of fire used in the Work.

The secret, hidden fire is the instrument of God, and its qualities are not perceptible to human eyes. We often refer to this fire in a way that might make it appear that we were speaking of external heat: it is on this account that the errors arise into which sham philosophers and imprudent people are liable to fall. This fire is a graduated fire, while external heat is almost constant, steady and uniform throughout the Work; even during the White phase of the Work it is constant, save that for the first seven days we keep it lower. But the experienced philosopher will not need to be given this information.

As regards the regulation of the external fire, it must be adjusted gently from hour to hour; and, since it is daily quickened in the progress of our Work, its colour changes as the compost matures.

I have hereby unravelled a very complicated knot for you; bear it in mind, and be careful not to be entangled in it in future.

11. You will need a glass crucible or matrass; without it, you will not be able to carry out the Work. It should be oval or spherical in shape, and of a size to contain your mixture easily—which means that it should be large enough to hold double the quantity that you put into it. This is called the philosophic egg. The glass should be thick, very transparent, and unflawed. The neck should be at most six inches long. When your substance has been put into it, seal the top of the vessel hermetically, so that no aperture

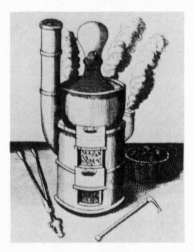

The hermetically sealed vessel being heated.

whatever is left, because the smallest perforation would allow the spirit to evaporate and vitiate the Work.

To make certain that the vessel is properly sealed, the following test is infallible. Allow it to cool, then apply your mouth to the seal, suck as hard as you can, and if there is the slightest leak you will draw out the air from the matrass; and when you take the vessel from your mouth the air will go back through the puncture with an audible whistling sound. This experiment has never failed.

12. A furnace will also be needed, that is called an athanor by philosophers; the whole of your Work will be carried out in it.

For the first part of the Work, everything should be so disposed as to provide a moderate or low heat, as you prefer, and so that when necessary it may be kept uniformly at its highest temperature for at least twelve hours. When it has reached this, there are five conditions that must be observed.

First, the capacity of your furnace should not be greater than is required to hold your crucible with about an inch of space all round it, so that the fire which rises through the vent may circulate freely round the vessel.

The second is that it should not hold more than one crucible matrass, or egg, with embers about an inch deep between the edges of the furnace and the bottom and sides of the vessel. And always remember the words of the Philosopher: one vessel, one substance, one furnace.

The opening should be so sited that it comes exactly over the draught, which should be only about two inches in diameter, allowing the emergence of an oblique tongue of flame that will always reach to the top of the vessel, surround the base, and keep it continually at the required temperature.

The third is that, if the bottom of the furnace were too large, since its cavity must be three or four times as deep as its diameter, the vessel could never be maintained at the precise and uniform heat that is needed.

Fourthly, if the position of the crucible is not some six inches from the fire itself, the ratio is wrong, and you will never be able to adjust the heat properly; while, if you exceed the distance, and allow the fire to flare, it will be insufficient.

Fifthly and finally, the front of your furnace must be firmly closed, leaving only a hole just large enough to permit of refuelling with philosophic charcoal, that is to say about an inch across, so that it may the more strongly reflect the heat from below.

13. Everything being thus prepared, put the egg containing your substance into the furnace, and give it the amount of heat required by Nature, which is to say gentle, not fierce, beginning where Nature left off.

You must not forget that Nature put your prime matter into the mineral kingdom; and, although we have been taking examples from plants and animals, it will still be necessary for you to find a suitable analogy from its own sphere. If, for example, I make the comparison between the generation of a man and the fertilisation of a plant, do not imagine that I suppose the heat required for the one will be the same for the other; we are sure that in the soil in which vegetation grows there is a degree of heat that plants feel, especially at the beginning of Spring; but an egg could not be hatched at that temperature, and a man, instead of getting any sensation of warmth, would feel only a numbing cold. Knowing very surely that your prime matter lies wholly in the mineral kingdom, you must provide the warmth it needs, distinguishing carefully between high and low.

Remember now that not only has Nature left you to work in the mineral kingdom, but also that you are dealing with Gold and Mercury, both of which are incombustible; that Mercury is delicate, but that it may break the vessel containing it if the fire is too fierce; that it is incombustible, so that fire cannot injure it; but that it must none the less be kept in the same glass vessel with the male sperm, which could not be done if the fire were too hot; and that then you would be unable to complete the Work.

Hence, the degree of heat that would keep lead and tin in fusion, or possibly slightly higher—though not so high that the vessel could not sustain it without being fractured—must be considered to be the proper degree, in other words a temperate heat. It is clear from what has been said, that the temperature must be started at a degree suitable to the kingdom in which Nature has placed your substance.

14. The whole of this operation—which is like a distillation by the Moon over the Earth—causes matter to rise as mist and to fall back as rain; this is the reason why I counsel you to keep sublimation continually steaming, in order that the Stone may have air and live.

15. But to obtain the enduring tincture, this is still not sufficient; the water from our lake must be boiled over logs from the tree of Hermes. I advise you to keep it continuously at boiling point by day and by night, so that the tumultuous force of our stormy sea may cause spiritual elements to rise and terrestrial elements

to fall. Unless this operation is carried out meticulously, our operation can never be called cooking but only digestion, because when the liquids—that is, the spirits—move only gently, and the solid ingredients below are not stirred by ebullition, the process is more properly called digestion.

16. Do not hurry anything in the hope of gathering your harvest —that is, the result of the Work—prematurely; but proceed with confidence for the space of at most fifty days, and you will see the beak of the raven of good omen.

Many people, says the Philosopher, believe that our solution is easy of achievement, but those who have made the essay, or who have experimented with it, know how great are the difficulties. For example, if you plant a grain of wheat, you will find three days later that it has swelled; but if you pull it up from the earth it will dry out and return to its former state. Yet it had been put into a suitable matrix, earth is its proper element; but the time necessary for its germination was lacking. Tougher seeds, such as nuts or the stones of plums and other fruit, need a longer time before they will sprout. There is a season for everything; and to wait for the prescribed time, avoiding premature haste, proves that an operation has been carried out naturally and fruitfully.

Can you suppose that Gold, which is the densest body in the world, could change its form in any brief space of time? You must be content to live in hope until the approach of the fortieth day, when it will begin to turn black. When you see this, you can be sure that the body has been destroyed, which is to say that it has been transformed into a living soul; and the spirit is dead, that is, it has fused with the body; but until it turns black, Gold and Mercury each retain their own form and their own nature.

17. Be careful that your fire does not go out for so much as a moment; for if once the matter grows cold, the Work is certain to fail.

From what has been said, it is clear that the whole of our Work consists in causing our compost to boil at the lowest possible degree of heat that will liquefy anything in the mineral kingdom, so that the internal fumes circulate around the substance, and in this vapour both the one and the other will die and be resuscitated.

18. Keep up your fire until the colours appear, and in the end you will find that it is white hot. When this stage is reached (which will be towards the end of the fifth month) the white Stone is nearing completion. Rejoice; for the King, who has overcome death, appears in the East, surrounded by a glory, heralded by a citrine halo, his fore-runner or ambassador.

19. Keep up your fire with a good will until the colours appear once again, and you will see a splendid vermilion and the scarlet of the field-poppy. Glorify God, and be thankful.

20. Finally, although your Stone has now been made perfect, it must be boiled—or, rather, ripened—anew, in the same water, in the same proportions, and in the same manner; let your fire be only slightly lower; and by this means you will increase the volume of the Stone and its potency to whatever extent you wish, and you may repeat this as often as seems good to you.

May God, the Father of light, Sovereign Lord, Author of all life and all good, of His Grace grant that you may see the regeneration of light, so that you may enter into the realm of life, the kingdom promised to the Faithful, and that you may one day share in life eternal. Amen.

End of the treatise.

*

The *Principles* may be regarded as an abstract of his best-known work. It has been reproduced here in its entirety—as was the *Emerald Table* above—so that some idea may be given of the main difficulties confronting a student of the Art.

The major obstacle to understanding Hermes Trismegistus' text lies in its ambiguities; the *Table* is almost impossible to grasp, and commentaries that have been written about it are scarcely less so. In Philalethes' treatise, on the other hand, everything appears to be straightforward. He tells us that the prime substance is gold (specifying particularly that he means natural gold), and he suggests that philosophic mercury might well be ordinary commercial quicksilver, prepared in a particular way. His explanations altogether seem quite convincing. Unfortunately it is one of the most delusive texts!

Before examining it in detail, it will be well to bear in mind

Schroeder's words: "When philosophers talk in plain language, I mistrust what they say. When they speak in riddles, I think about it!" Artephius, too:

"Poor fool! Are you simple enough to believe we would tell you clearly and openly the greatest and most important of our secrets —that our words can be taken literally? I assure you that anyone who tried to interpret in plain words what philosophers have written would find himself involved in the mazes of a labyrinth from which he would never escape, lacking Ariadne's thread to guide him. And no matter what he had spent on the work, it would all be wasted."

Finally and most importantly, the words of Philalethes with which he ends *The Open Door*: "I admit that I have so twisted the subtleties of philosophy, that unless many things that I have written in the preceding chapters are taken metaphorically, nothing will be gained, and money will have been spent uselessly."

This being established, I can assure my readers that the identification of prime matter with ordinary gold is to be "taken metaphorically", as will be seen in a later part of this book. Neither is it in any way doubtful that philosophic mercury has not the slightest connection with the commercial article. This fact in no sense implies that, in other ways, Philalethes' text is uninteresting. Far from it. It is most valuable on certain practical points of technique.

Actually, it is only by collating the innumerable existent treatises that it is possible to come to grips with the question. One writer will tell you what the prime substance looks like, another what colour it is, a third mentions its weight, yet another suggests what might be one of the components of the secret fire, and one more indicates the temperature required in the athanor or furnace. The Work is not intended for people who are in a hurry, but only for enthusiasts.

*

By way of comparison, I propose to describe how M. Roger Caro, a contemporary alchemist, attacks the Work. It was at my request that he wrote the following, and I have his permission to publish it. He is, of course, as reserved as his predecessors about prime matter, the secret fire, and philosophic mercury.

"To begin with, he says, *prime matter* and *primordial matter* must not be confounded. *Prime matter* refers to the lode that embosoms the *Philosophers'* sulphur, mercury, and salt (the latter being used only in minimal quantities). *Primordial matter* designates the secret merger, or secret fire, or philosophic mercury, or white tincture, or vitriol, to give only a few of its aliases. *Salt* in itself represents all four elements: it is *Earth* in its solid state, *Water* when it melts, *Fire* in its pungency, and *Air* when it evaporates. It is by means of this substance alone that everything is achieved.

"The principle of alchemy is contained in two main processes: SOLVE and COAGULA.

"SOLVE is in some sense an *analysis* that breaks down and separates the three constituents. COAGULA is a *synthesis*, that is to say an operation which reconstitutes the substance, after the components have been purified.

"There are four primary operations:

"(a) PREPARATION, that is, the art of separating Philosophers' sulphur and mercury (*not* philosophic sulphur and mercury), by means of *philosophic salt*. The separation is carried out over what is called an *athanor*, in what is typically a flask with a long bent-back neck.

"(b) SOLVE, the purpose of which is to purify the two substances (Philosophers' sulphur and mercury) after separation; this process is carried out in a closely sealed vessel.

"(c) COAGULA, by which the two substances are dried and reconstituted after purification by the secret fire, or salt. This is carried out in an open vessel.

"(d) Finally, MULTIPLICATION, the aim of which is to purify still further the finished Stone, by beginning all over again with SOLVE."

M. Caro was kind enough to complete his explanation by giving the following particulars about *salt*.

"*Salt* appears in three aspects:

"(1) *Shining*, when it is extracted, in minute quantities, from its source.

"(2) *White*, when it is heated over oaken embers;

"(3) *Red*, when it becomes the quintessence or dragon's blood, which may be otherwise expressed as the *white* aspect after being tinged with Philosophers' sulphur during *Solve*."

*

Needless to say, I cannot guarantee that some of these expressions are not to be understood "metaphorically". The point will be taken up again in a later chapter; but I thought it better to raise the question at this stage, in order to give readers some idea of the technique of producing the Philosopher's Stone. It will make it easier to follow the descriptions of transmutation later in this book, when we come to the life-stories of the principal Adepts.

Before we reach that stage, however, we must stop to examine the position of the Hermetic Art as compared with Science in this second half of the twentieth century.

5. Alchemy and Modern Science

Unlike astrology, which has at times been taught in the universities side by side with more classic disciplines, alchemy has always been looked upon with suspicion in scientific circles. No doubt this is because alchemy cannot be taught from the height of a Chair, but has always been an essentially secret, traditional subject that is to be learnt only by initiation.

Secret, because—in obedience to ancient prohibitions—the true nature of the substances called prime matter, the secret fire and philosophic mercury is never divulged, which precludes any form of public instruction.

Traditional, because alchemy is founded, not upon scientific theories that are continually liable to be called in question, but upon certain basic principles that have never varied and that never can be varied.

Initiatory because—excepting only for the very few elect—academic study of the Mystery is not enough; direct initiation from Master to pupil is essential, and is the only way in which the real *modus operandi* can be taught.

This makes it obvious why alchemy has never been smiled upon by official science, more especially since, up to the last few years, the very idea of transmutation was considered absurd. Nowadays people think differently. The scientist Jacques Bergier wrote in a recent article:

"Once again, things have changed; science reverted to alchemy on the day it was decided that the atom was not the smallest possible part of matter. With the discovery of elementary particles, transmutation became a possibility. Today it is practically a commonplace—witness only the hundreds of tons of plutonium that are

51

manufactured every year, an element that does not normally exist in nature."

Other scientists also mention transmutation. Thus Sherr, Bainbridge and Anderson in 1941 obtained isotopes of radio-active gold by bombarding mercury with rapid neutrons. Mercury may also be transmuted to platinum by reaction, and to thallium by protonic or deutonic bombardment.

One fact is particularly striking: that mercury—so closely connected with alchemy—can be turned into gold; and later it will be seen that the same is true for lead. Does it not seem very strange that among the seven metals known at the time, and all the other chemical substances at their disposal, Hermetic Philosophers should have hit on mercury and lead as being easily transmutable to gold, which happens to be true? Pure chance, no doubt any Faculty of Science would say, since actually it concerns the transmutation of radio-active isotopes. *Chance* is, of course, one possibility, but a highly improbable one. *Knowledge* would appear to be a much more reasonable answer—knowledge of a method by which one set of stable isotopes can be transmuted into different stable isotopes, without the necessity of releasing terrific energies.

We shall return to this point. Meanwhile, since the fact of transmutation has now been proved, the question arises: have views on alchemy changed? Not in the least! Once more Jacques Bergier has something to say on the subject: "The arguments against alchemists are different now. Everyone agrees that by some chance they foresaw the possibility of transmutation; but their mistake lay in trying to do it by chemical means. It can only be done by using complicated apparatus about which they could not possibly have known."

In fact today, as in the last century, the position of official science remains unchanged. The Hermetic Art is denied all validity; only the discoveries made by Adepts about mineral or organic chemistry are considered to be worth taking seriously. This, to say the least, is a surprising view; it comes back to saying that, in one and the same treatise, an alchemist could describe a new substance, state its composition and its properties, in short do a piece of genuine scientific work, and then go on to tell lies like any common charlatan by claiming to have produced the Philosopher's Stone. Such an attitude can hardly be regarded as anything but absurd, if not actually dishonest. Either Basil Valentine, Paracelsus, and numbers of their co-workers, who added the knowledge of many substances to science, were swindlers who could never have made those discoveries; or else they were indisputably scientists, in which case all their work merits equal consideration.

While the discoveries we owe to them were far from being minor ones, they were nevertheless a bye-product of their real work. Albertus Magnus was the first to make caustic potash, and he knew the chemical composition of cinnabar (sulphide of mercury), of ceruse (white lead), and of minium (red lead). In addition to antimony, Basil Valentine discovered hydrochloric acid and sulphuric acid, Paracelsus recognised the existence of zinc, Glauber of sulphate of soda, and Brandt of phosphorus. These are only a few examples out of many, but it is hardly necessary to extend the list—its importance will be obvious to every reader. The men who identified, recognised, discovered, or evolved these substances can in no sense be regarded as charlatans.

It should also be noted that Hermetic Philosophers did not write two sorts of treatise—one in which they set out their purely chemical discoveries and another that referred to the Philosopher's Stone. No—their publications were concerned solely with the Great Work; but in the course of these they mentioned, in passing, any additional chemical discoveries they came upon. Such a procedure is not that of a braggart or a crank. It is the way in which a man of science behaves, who does not wish to hide any discovery, however small, from his contemporaries, and whose work as a whole must be regarded as meticulously honest.

Actually, the objection which insists that transmutation is possible only by the use of tremendous nuclear energy has to all intents and purposes been demolished. Discoveries by the biologist Kervran have shown that spontaneous transmutation is a normal occurrence in organic matter. Moreover, it is now certain that the relation between a nucleus and its electrons is quite different in organic substances from what it is in mineral substances. An interesting experiment was carried out with hens. Fowls need calcium to form the shells of their

53

eggs, and in this experiment a number of hens were fed on a diet containing no calcium whatever. Instead, their feed was mixed with mica, which is a silicate of aluminium and potash. It was found that the hens produced the necessary calcium for themselves, which shows that potassium (K=19) together with an ion of hydrogen (H=1) was transmuted to give calcium (Ca=20).

One conclusion is inescapable—there are evidently different methods of transmutation. Alchemists may well have been able to achieve them at the level of the atom and peripheral electrons without being obliged to bombard the nuclei with colossal energies.

A new theory, called the Theory of Magic Numbers, now current in the Soviet Union, shows that beyond uranium there must be super-heavy elements—which yet are stable—although up to the present it was thought that all elements beyond uranium were radio-active and had only a brief life-span. So now there is talk of an element with weight 310 and the atomic number 135, that is known as eka-lead or super-lead. Infinitesimal traces of eka-lead are said to be naturally present in ordinary lead. A study of its properties, theoretical at present, shows that if transmutation were induced, it would be likely to result in the stable isotope of gold.

So for the second time we should be faced—just as happened in the case of mercury—with the astonishing prescience of alchemists that lead was one of the most suitable metals to transmute to gold. Chance again? Surely not. Once more the right answer *must* be: knowledge.

*

This ends our brief review of alchemical theories which, it is hoped, may encourage readers to go into the subject more deeply. It is a necessary preliminary to the clear understanding of the story which follows of the principal, historically based, metallic transmutations.

Is it really possible to draw any conclusion from this introductory study? Probably not. In 1856 Louis Figuier said: "The present state of chemistry prevents our thinking that the transmutation of metals is impossible. Recent scientific discoveries and the opinions that chemists have about them make it probable that the transformation of one metal into another can be achieved. On the other hand, how-

Pl XVII.

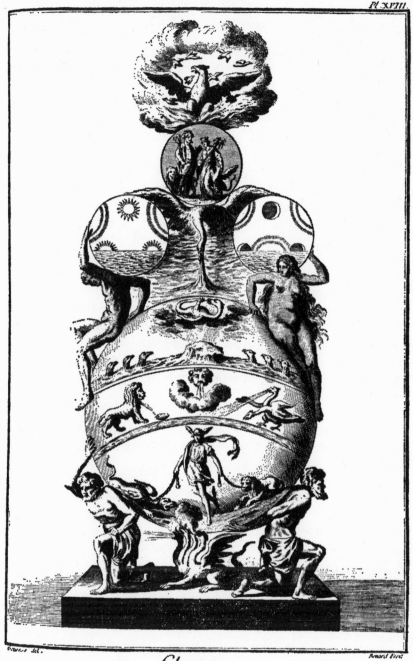

Chymie:

Chymia: An illustration of the Great Work by Libavius (1660)

ever, history has shown that up to the present time no one has succeeded in transmuting metals." Nowadays we know for certain that
transmutation is possible, and only one question remains: did alchemists carry it out by some means other than those we know of
at present?

On the answer to this question depends our verdict on the Hermetic
Art. Either we shall be convinced that mercury and lead were transformed into gold by the Adepts, in which case alchemy is fully
validated and scientific concepts will have to be reconsidered; or
else no such assurance is possible and Hermetic theories remain as
an example of the superstitions of the past.

But how is conclusive proof to be obtained, since in these days
Adepts keep themselves to themselves and no longer give public
demonstrations as they used to do in past centuries?

It was in order to find an answer to this question that I studied
all the documents and writings I could come across that dealt particularly with the transmutation of metals, hoping to discover whether
any positive assessment could be made, whether there had been
enough trustworthy witnesses—such as contemporary scientists—to
the experiments, for one to be able to consider the results as convincing.

It is therefore proposed to take a close look at the lives of some
of the great Adepts. It will be an essentially "materialistic" enquiry
because this time we shall be confining our interests entirely to *Gold*.

BOOK II

The Alchemists

1. Three Thirteenth-century Graduates of Montpellier University

Transmutation of metals is credited to Adepts of ancient times and to those in the early centuries of the Christian era. But the interval of time is too great to permit of any sort of verification, nor is there much chance of disentangling legend from history. I therefore decided to begin my study with three of the greatest alchemists, who succeeded one another at the University of Montpellier, which was founded in 1181 and became the nursery of exceptional talents thanks to the enormous independence of spirit cultivated there.

Among pupils of this University were such eminent men as Albertus Magnus, Thomas Aquinas (both now sanctified by the Church), Roger Bacon, Arnold of Villanova, Raymond Lully, in the thirteenth century, and later Michel de Nostredame (better known by his pseudonym Nostradamus), Rabelais and Erasmus. True, Alchemy did not figure among the official disciplines at the University, but all instruction was strongly influenced by Arab and Jewish Doctors —all of whom were steeped in Hermetic Philosophy—which leads one to assume that Alchemy cannot have been neglected. In any case, Albertus Magnus, Thomas Aquinas, Roger Bacon, Lully and Arnold of Villanova all came to be among the greatest of Hermetic philosophers. Less well known is the fact that the same is true of François Rabelais. Some chapters in his *Pantagruel* are allegorical paraphrases of the Great Work of Alchemy. Nostradamus, perhaps the best-known seer of all time, never concealed his interest in the Hermetic Art. All this shows that there was a leaven of alchemy in this University, and it will be interesting to review the lives of three great Adepts who studied there.

Albertus Magnus

Albert was born into a wealthy family at Lauingen in 1193. His early attainments were extremely mediocre, and gave no indication that he was to become the greatest scientist of his day. Legend has it that the enigma is to be explained by a miracle. It is said that the Virgin Mary appeared to the youthful Albert and asked what science he would wish to be eminent in. The boy chose Philosophy, and the Virgin promised that his wish should be granted, though she added that she was disappointed that he had not decided upon Theology, and that he would be punished for his lack of piety by returning to his original obtuseness in old age.

At all events, Albert proceeded to lead the life of an opulent student in Pavia up to the time when he met an itinerant friar, who persuaded him to join the Order of Saint Dominic—a very powerful fraternity at that date—since this would enable him to devote himself to his studies in complete tranquillity. In the midst of the incessant wars of the Middle Ages the Abbeys were indeed the only places where learning could be cultivated in peace. Albert therefore became a Dominican; and an important and quite exceptional concession was made to him by the Order in that he was permitted to keep and live on his own resources until his death.

He then went to Cologne and, after spending some time there, moved to Paris in 1245, in order to qualify for the coveted degree of *Magister* (Master) conferred by that University. To accomplish this it was necessary to be a successful teacher at the Sorbonne for three years. The first public lectures Albert gave were a triumph. The lecture room was thronged, and attempts were made to provide some larger hall for him. But nothing could be found big enough to accommodate his audience, and Albert was driven to holding the lectures out of doors in a public square that has ever since been known by his name—the Place Maubert (M=Master; Aubert= Albert).

Albert was not interested only in philosophy but was an all-round scholar. Among other things, he has left works on chemical mineralogy far in advance of anything else of that date. And, of course, he became a votary of Alchemy. Five treatises on alchemy, signed by him, are still extant, the best known of them being the *De Alchimia*. In addition are two small manuals on magic: *The Excellent Secrets of Albert the Great* and of *Albert the Less*. His scientific authority was such, that for a long time no doubt was ever cast on the lineage of the various works. It was only later that the two manuals on the practice of magic were adjudged apocryphal, when a more observant critic remarked that Paracelsus and Basil Valentine, for example, were quoted in *Albert the Less*, although they lived nearly two centuries after the supposed author. Finally, at the beginning of the twentieth century, when Albert was canonised, the Church denied that he had ever been interested in alchemy, and that therefore the Hermetic treatises attributed to him were forgeries. That Albert was an alchemist is nowadays in no doubt, for several great libraries possess manuscripts written in his own hand (his writing is perfectly well known), recording his hermetic researches. As regards the authorship of the published treatises, the question is more difficult. It would seem that Albert was the author of the *De Alchimia*, or at any rate that the work was produced under his direction. It is practically certain that he did not write any of the other treatises attributed to him; but—and this is not the least astonishing part—some research carried out at a large American University has proved irrefutably that a part at least of the *Secrets of Albert the Great* really was by him. Actually, this plunged the transatlantic university authorities into great confusion. They decided that either Albert had gone mad or else that he was intentionally fooling the world. Their bewilderment was still further increased when later research showed that the greater part of Albert's unpublished works consisted of texts quite comparable to those on popular magic. No doubt, they supposed, Albert had not wished them to be published because he thought them too important to be made available to all and sundry! The truth is quite fantastic and at the same time very simple: the books on magic are alchemical treatises but written in a code even more complicated than other works of the same kind.

Here is an extract from the first chapter of the second book of *Albert the Great*:

"The first herb comes under Saturn and is called offodilius. Its extract is excellent for alleviating and curing diseases of the kidneys and of the legs. It may also be given to those with bladder trouble. A small quantity of the root, boiled and carried wrapped in a white cloth will relieve persons possessed by devils or who suffer from melancholy madness. Moreover, this same root will exorcise evil spirits from a house."

This apparently nonsensical text becomes significant as soon as it is realised that it is an alchemical recipe referring to Saturn, that is to say to *lead*. To boil the root, in other words to extract the metallicity of the metal by fire, is to bring it to the *white* stage of the Work, symbolised here by a cloth of the same colour. In fact this supposedly magic formula simply describes one stage of the Master Work.

From 1244, Thomas Aquinas—also a future Saint of the Catholic Church—became the pupil of Albertus Magnus, who not only taught him the science which he professed publicly, but also initiated him into alchemy; several Hermetic manuscripts in the handwriting of Thomas Aquinas are extant. In one of these, the *Summa Theologica*, he queries whether the use of Hermetic gold is lawful, and comes to the conclusion that natural gold is in no way preferable to it; and that, so far as he is concerned, he has always used either indifferently—which seems to show that he assisted in transmutations effected by Albert. Both, too, were interested in mechanical contrivances, much in favour at the time. It is said that they created a head that could talk and answer questions (though this story has also been told of the alchemist Gerbert who later became Pope Sylvester II). But the head got out of control on one occasion, and irritated Thomas so much by its incessant chatter that he picked up a stick and smashed it. Needless to say, there is no foundation for the story. It was not published until the eighteenth century, and it may have been either pure invention or a misunderstanding of one of Albert's alchemical texts, in which mention is made of a "head" (*caput mortuum*), which refers actually to one of the phases of prime matter in the Master Work, that is, the residue left after distillation.

On the other hand, another strange story in the life of Albertus Magnus, which is generally taken to be legend, is quite possibly authentic. Recent research in some archives near Cologne where the affair took place shows that a number of witnesses were present on the occasion of the alleged "miracle", and left records that all tally with one another. The story goes that Albertus Magnus, having been granted a Master's degree in Paris, retired to somewhere near Cologne, where he was anxious to acquire a piece of land belonging to William, Count of Holland, in order to build an Abbey on it. As the Count refused to sell, Albert had recourse to a very peculiar stratagem. While the Count happened to be on a visit to Cologne, Albert invited him to a banquet he proposed holding in the Count's honour. The Count accepted, and came to the house of the celebrated scientist accompanied by a large suite. It was in the depths of winter and the weather was so cold that the Rhine was frozen over. The Count and his suite were therefore startled to find that Albert had prepared the collation in the open air, the tables being spread in a field covered deep in snow. The Count, greatly displeased, was about to leave, when Albert begged him to come and sit beside him. The reputation of Albertus Magnus was such that after some hesitation the Count consented. No sooner was he seated than the sky cleared, the sun shone warmly, and the north wind, which had been blowing great guns, dropped suddenly. The snow melted and some witnesses even reported that flowers came up and the first buds appeared on the trees. The Count was so staggered by these marvels that he agreed to the sale of the land that his host wanted. After the end of the feast, at a word from Albert, the sky grew overcast again, snow fell, and the untimely buds were frozen.

Did Master Albert apply collective hypnosis or use some other method? Who can say? One thing is sure: numerous members of the Count's suite, some citizens of Cologne, and peasants on Albert's estate, all told the story in identical terms, that allow no doubt of their sincerity.

In 1259 Albert was appointed Bishop of Ratisbon, an office he did not hold for long, because he detested functional duties. After making a brilliant appearance at Lyons, he went back to teaching, until he suffered an apoplectic stroke while giving a lecture. So the prophecy of the Virgin Mary was fulfilled, and he relapsed into his former dull-wittedness, living for another three years with greatly diminished intellectual powers, before dying in 1280 at the age of eighty-seven. His friend Thomas Aquinas had predeceased him, and the old man became the butt of all his enemies, who took advantage of his inability to defend himself to accuse him of sorcery and of being in league with the devil. One of them went so far as to write: "Master Albert, who was once changed from an ass into a philosopher, was later changed from a philosopher into an ass."

Apart from the testimony of Thomas Aquinas there is no evidence that Albertus Magnus really transmuted metals, so that the first part of this enquiry must be considered to have come to a negative conclusion. It is worth noting, nevertheless, that in his treatise, *Aurora Consurgens*, Thomas Aquinas indicates that he felt he had chosen the wrong path by becoming a theologian, and that the real way to glorifying God lay through alchemy.

Before proceeding to study the life of Arnold of Villanova, it will be convenient to cite the advice given by Albertus Magnus to alchemists in his *De Alchimia*, advice which is today as valuable to Hermetic philosophers as ever it was:

"1. An alchemist should be discreet and reserved; he should not let anyone know the results of his Work.

"2. He should live alone, in a private house, in which two or three rooms are set apart exclusively for his Work.

"3. He should choose carefully the time and the duration of his Work.

"4. He must be patient, persistent, and unwearying.

"5. He must faithfully observe the precepts of the art in trituration, sublimation, fixation, combination, solution, distillation, and coagulation.

"6. He should use only vessels made of glass or glazed pottery, so as to avoid contamination by acids.

"7. He should be in possession of funds sufficient to defray the necessary expenses of the Work.

"8. Above all, he should avoid involvement with princes and lords. To begin with, they will urge him to accelerate the Work unduly, and in case of non-success he will be subjected to the worst torments; while if he does succeed, prison will be his reward."

Arnold of Villanova

"Here begins the *Way to the Path*, a short, concise, succinct treatise that will be useful to him who is able to understand it. Competent workers will find in it a part of the Vegetal Stone that other philosophers have taken care to conceal." Thus Arnold of Villanova, in a brief treatise he sent to Pope Benedict XI in the year of Grace 1303.

This is only one of a number of alchemical works that have come down to us from him, among which the *Grand Rosaire* (Great Rosary) is accounted the brightest jewel. Arnold of Villanova was born at some time between 1235 and 1245, the year 1240 being the most likely date. He first studied the classics in the faculty of Aix-en-Provence, then went on to become a medical student at Montpellier, before finishing his studies at the Sorbonne in Paris. He is supposed to have attended the lectures of Albertus Magnus, but this is doubtful considering the dates. He probably knew Roger Bacon, author of the *Mirror of Alquimy*, for their writings have a number of points in common. Possibly it was through Bacon that he came to know Albertus Magnus, because the English alchemist was in touch with him—and, it is said, envied him because his own researches, unlike Master Albert's, were financially hampered by his Order.

Having completed his student years, Arnold of Villanova began to travel, practising medicine all over Europe, and soon became a fashionable and much sought-after consultant. His unorthodox treatments and his freedom of speech often got him into trouble with local religious authorities. As René Marcard says:

"It is certain that the accusation of habitually trafficking with the devil rested, not without some justification, on his peculiar prescriptions, the wearing of amulets, and his use of hypnotism and magic. The Master's reply to this was that the influence of a doctor over his patient was by tradition an essential part of the treatment, that it was one of the main factors in effecting cures, and that no means should be neglected to make it irresistible."

He was certainly a much more colourful figure than Albertus Magnus, Roger Bacon, or Thomas Aquinas, whose lives were closely regulated by the rules of science and religion. Master Arnold was an early forerunner of such men as Paracelsus and the charlatan Cagliostro.

Returning to Paris to become a lecturer, Arnold of Villanova soon became notorious through a flood of statements that stirred up the tribunal of the Holy Inquisition. He declared publicly that greater merit was acquired by charity than by prayer, and that papal bulls were only human pronouncements and in no sense infallible—or, at least, "that their infallibility was about as certain as his own diagnoses". The question of papal infallibility has to this day never ceased to agitate the Catholic Church, and it is easy to imagine the fury of the thirteenth-century prelates on hearing such a proposition. . . . Arnold was therefore obliged to leave France at speed and to continue his travels about Europe. He appears to have been on the point of being reconciled with the pontifical authorities—Pope Clement V, who suffered from gravel, had sent for him—when he died suddenly at sea, within sight of Genoa.

His death did not pacify the tribunal of the Inquisition, which decided to impeach him posthumously and in 1317, some four years after his death, he was found guilty and the greater part of his writings was seized and destroyed in an auto-da-fé. This explains why, in addition to longer works, a certain number of small and rather obscure treatises exist, signed with his name, though it is very doubtful that they are really his. Some of the Puffers probably made the most of the fact that there was a good deal of uncertainty about the number of Master Arnold's works that had survived, to sign his name to their own wafflings. Opponents of alchemy will of course have decided from this that all his treatises are apocryphal.

Amid the doubtfully genuine minor works there is, however, one which is not lacking in zest. This is a manuscript discovered by a M. Poirier in the sixteenth century, and the handwriting seems to justify its attribution to Arnold of Villanova. It deals with the problems of rejuvenation confronting persons who live for several centuries. Here is a recipe given by the philosopher:

"Anyone wishing to prolong his life should anoint himself two or three times a week with the pith of the cinnamon tree. Every night before retiring he should apply to his head a poultice compounded of oriental saffron, the petals of red roses, essence of sandal wood, aloes and amber, all liquefied in oil of roses to which a little wax has been added. In the morning the poultice should be removed and placed carefully in a lidded leaden box until the following evening, when it should again be applied."

From the strictly alchemical point of view, Arnold of Villanova is regarded as an Adept who obtained the Philosopher's Stone. Study of his *Grand Rosaire* allows the assumption, but there are no historical facts to bear it out. Once again, there is nothing but his own affirmation that he had resolved the Mystery and had changed lead into gold—an affirmation that would hardly stand up to an impartial and searching enquiry. For the second time, therefore, it would seem necessary to put a minus sign to the result, and to hope for greater success with the story of Raymond Lully, the celebrated "Enlightened Doctor" from the island of Majorca.

Raymond Lully

Alchemical tradition—not written tradition but the much more reliable tradition that is passed direct from Adept to enthusiastic seeker (or "lover of the science")—regards Raymond Lully as one of the greatest alchemists of all time, comparable only with Basil Valentine and Eirenaeus Philalethes. The tradition does not rely upon more or less apocryphal documents nor upon possibly suspect historical data, but upon assured knowledge, passed on from age to age. It is therefore tedious to hear and to read in modern works on the subject that Lully never wrote a line on alchemy and, what is more, that he knew nothing at all about the science. Before studying his life this point must be cleared up.

The reasons advanced by contemporary writers for denying to Raymond Lully the paternity of his alchemical works are the following:

First, in 1311, he issued a sort of autobiography containing a full list of his published works. Nothing relating to alchemy appears in it. This is not conclusive because, as has been said above, Lully seems to have preferred, probably on religious grounds, that his Hermetic works should not be published until after his death. The manuscripts are all dated within Lully's life-time, and several of them contain historical allusions or dedications to contemporary princes. Oddly enough, this seems only to have strengthened the conviction of some people that the works are apocryphal. These cavillers claim that historical allusions were introduced, and that Lully's style was imitated, simply in order to justify the attribution of the treatises to him.

One might, in fact, sum up the situation by saying that dissentients think that the works are so obviously like Lully's that someone else *must* have forged them. Nevertheless, unless further information comes to light, the authorship of the works that bear his name will in this book continue to be regarded as his.

Raymond Lully was born either in 1233 or 1235, the son of a moneyed and aristocratic family at Palma in Majorca. His father destined him for a military career, and the sole occupation of his youth seems to have been the pursuit of pretty girls. Even after he was married and the father of a family he did not give up the chase; but when he was getting on for thirty years of age he fell seriously in love with a Genoese lady living in Palma, the Señora Ambrosia de Castello. Paradoxically, it was this love affair which brought about one of the most dramatic conversions known to history, comparable perhaps only with that of Saint Augustine.

Ambrosia was a married woman, steady and discreet, who was greatly embarrassed by the handsome young man's continual importunities and the extravagant demonstrations of his passion. One day, for instance, he rode into the cathedral on horseback to lay a madrigal at her feet and was thrown out by indignant worshippers. It was after this episode that she agreed to an interview and invited him to visit her in her own room. Lully felt convinced that he had at last worn down her resistance and went to the meeting with the air of a happy conqueror. Ambrosia received him coolly, and asked if he would like to see her breast, which he had hymned in several of his verses. Lully, though surprised at the question, vowed that there was nothing he longed for more ardently. She undid her dress and showed him her breast, partly eaten away by cancer, saying: "Look, Raymond, see the unloveliness of the body on which you have centred your desires. Would you not have done better to offer your love to Jesus Christ of whom you will have joy everlasting?"

Lully was shocked to the core and for some days he shut himself away from everyone, trying to write lyrical love-poems, when he suddenly saw a vision of the crucified Christ. At first he refused to believe what he was seeing, and went back to his writing, but the same vision reappeared four times. After a sleepless night, struggling with shame and remorse, he rushed to the confessional and swore to the priest that he would thenceforward consecrate his life to the glory of God and the conversion of infidels.

Raymond Lully tells that he thereupon made the pilgrimage to Saint James of Campostella, to pray for confirmation in his new vocation. Was this an actual journey, one wonders, or was it initiatory? For the moment the question may be left in suspense; there will be an opportunity to examine it in greater detail when we come to Nicholas Flamel in the next chapter. The fact remains that on his return to Majorca, Raymond Lully retired to live on Mount Randa, one of the highest mountains on the island. After a long period of fasting and meditation, he received sudden enlightenment from God, which revealed to him that the Great Art would help him to overcome the heathen and proclaim the truths of the Christian faith. Legend says that some lentisk shrubs thereupon sprouted into what looked like multitudes of alphabetical letters of all the languages in which he would be teaching the Great Art. Lully began immediately to study the various tongues, Arabic in particular, since he hoped to evangelise the peoples of northern Africa. He also learnt enough French within a brief space of time, to be able to follow lectures at the Sorbonne.

And it was in this venerable faculty that he picked a public quarrel with Duns Scotus, who was giving a series of lectures there following his triumphal career at Oxford. While Duns Scotus discoursed Raymond Lully showed signs of disapproval or disagreement with everything he said; all very disturbing to the speaker. At length Duns Scotus interrupted himself to put a purely routine question to his opponent: "On which side is God in this inquiry?" To which Lully replied: "God is on no side—He is All." This was not the end of it and, finally silencing the unfortunate Duns Scotus, he made an interminable, vituperative speech, extolling the perfection of God. The upshot of it all was that he achieved the signal honour of becoming a teacher at the Sorbonne, although he had no university qualifications, and his relations with Duns Scotus improved to such an extent that they parted the best of friends.

From Paris Raymond Lully went on to Montpellier, where he attended the lectures of Arnold of Villanova who, about the year 1289, initiated him into alchemy. He did not, however, forget his missionary vow, and soon took ship for Tunis, hoping to put it into practice there. As a result, he was condemned to death by the Bey. Fortunately for him, a friend of the Bey was able to have the sentence annulled after having had a long talk with the prisoner, which made him realise that Lully was a man of exceptional attainments. Lully was banished and left the country, pursued by a furious mob threatening to stone him. He returned to Naples, where he rejoined Arnold of Villanova and took up the practice of alchemy again. Later he resumed his travels, and his tracks may be found in Spain, Palestine, Algiers and Vienna, and even in England.

Numerous reports indicate that during his stay in England he accomplished a remarkable transmutation. He made six million pounds of gold for King Edward III in the Tower of London. This last statement is inaccurate, because Edward III's reign began in 1327 and Lully died in 1315. But the two preceding Kings of England were Edward I and Edward II, and it is quite possible that Lully might have carried out some alchemical experiments before one or other of these two. The episode is recorded by Lully himself in *De Transmutione Animae Metallorum*, where he states expressly that he went to England at the request of the King. The most probable date for the journey was 1312, which was during the reign of Edward II, who needed money for the Crusades at that time; but recent researches into historical documents have shown that Raymond Lully did not provide it by alchemical means, but quite simply by suggesting that a new tax should be imposed on wool.

This does not, indeed, prove that Lully was incapable of transmuting base metals into gold, but it should be remembered that no true alchemist would *ever* prostitute his Art by using it for the enrichment of princes. The story that the money derived from a new tax, therefore, seems a good deal more probable, if less impressive! After his visit to London, Lully returned to Africa; but he was stoned at

Bougie, and died at the age of eighty on board a Genoese ship whose crew had rescued him.

To end this section, and to give readers some idea of Lully's style, here is a quotation from the beginning of his *Clavicula*:

"This work has been entitled *Clavicula* (Little Key), because without it our other books will be incomprehensible. These books embody the whole of the Art, but the words we use cannot be understood by the unlearned. I have written many treatises, long and detailed, but split into sections and obscure as to language, as may be seen in the *Testament*, in which I refer to the principles of Nature and to all that concerns the Art, although the text has come under the hammer of philosophy."

Incidentally, it is in this very book that Lully refers to having transmuted fifty pounds of mercury and lead into gold. But again there is no witness to sustain the truth of the assertion. The only proof that Raymond Lully had really effected transmutations would have been gold produced in the Tower of London—and we have seen that the money obtained by the King owed nothing to the Hermetic Art, but was raised by a system that, regrettably, is very much more usual at all periods. So, once more, it is impossible to record anything positive in favour of the Philosopher's Stone. However, all hope is not lost—for we come now to Nicholas Flamel, a man famous for being a great producer of gold.

2. Nicholas Flamel, Public Scrivener

Alchemists have at all times flourished in France, as indeed they still do. But none, not even the contemporary Adept Fulcanelli, has had a reputation equal to that of Nicholas Flamel. The parish of Saint Jacques-la-Boucherie, in a crowded part of Paris, had, as lately as the beginning of the nineteenth century, lively memories of the man and his wife Perrenelle, of his lavish charities and of his immense riches.

Flamel was probably born about the year 1330 near Pontoise into a family that, though not well off, managed to procure him a literate education. While he was still very young, it is believed, his parents died and he went to Paris to establish himself as a Public Scrivener. He set up near the cemetery of the Holy Innocents, and then a few years later moved, with others of his craft, to a place under the portico of Saint Jacques-la-Boucherie. Meanwhile, he had married a woman of mature years who had already been twice widowed and who brought him a modest competence, so that he was able to rent two booths, one for himself and one for his copyists and apprentices. Not that he could be regarded as a rich man. The place he worked in all his life was smaller than anything that would be found nowadays except possibly in some derelict back street—a lean-to rather than a shop. A few years later, thanks to the money brought by Madame Perrenelle and his own careful economy, Flamel managed to build himself a little house opposite the booths. Though his circumstances had now improved, this is not to say that he was affluent; a deed still exists, signed a few years after his marriage, according to which the couple bestowed all their worldly goods upon one another, and this parchment shows that their possessions were still very exiguous.

However, having made a prudent marriage, Flamel was now on the way to becoming a member of the minor propertied classes. He was not at the time concerned with Hermetic philosophy, but rather with extending his trade to include books, and this came subsequently to occupy his whole interest. The new business introduced him to alchemical works, which he obtained for either copying or resale, and these were clearly the proximate cause of the dream that was the starting point of his career as an alchemist. Later on he told the story of this dream: An angel appeared to him, holding in his hand a large volume bound in copper. He opened it so as to show the title page, saying: "Flamel, take careful note of this book. You will not understand any of it at present, nor will many another; but one day you will discover from it what no one else will be able to do." Then the vision faded; but the memory of it never left him.

The dream suddenly came true many years later, when that very book came into his hands. This is how he tells the story, in his own work, the *Interpretation of Hieroglyphic Imagery*:

"Then I, Nicholas Flamel, Scrivener, after the death of my parents made my livelihood by the art of writing, taking inventories, making up accounts, checking the expenditure of guardians of minors. —It chanced that, for the sum of two florins, a very large and ancient gold-embossed book came into my possession. It was not made of paper or parchment like most books but, so it seemed to me, of loose pieces of the bark of young trees. Its cover was of copper, finely chased, depicting curious letters and figures. As far as I could judge they might have been Greek or some such ancient language. All I knew was that I could not read them and that they certainly were neither Latin nor Gallic, with which I was reasonably familiar. As regards the contents, the pages were written with very great skill, with an iron stylus, in clear and beautifully illuminated Latin characters. The book contained three times seven pages (they were numbered in this way at the head of each page), the seventh always being blank, except that round the margins were painted intertwined serpents. On the second seventh page was a cross on which a serpent was crucified. On the last seventh page was the painting of a desert with several beautiful springs of running water, from which issued serpents ranging in all directions. On the front page was written in large gilded capitals: ABRAHAM THE JEW, PRINCE, PRIEST, LEVITE,

ASTROLOGER AND PHILOSOPHER, TO THAT TRIBE OF JEWS WHO BY THE WRATH OF GOD WERE DISPERSED AMONG THE GAULS, SALUTATION D.I. Then followed the most fearful denunciations and curses (the word MARANATHA being frequently repeated) directed at anyone who should dare to look upon this unless he were a Priest or a Scribe."

According to his own admission, Nicholas Flamel did not understand much of it. The first page contained only the title quoted above, the second an invocation to the Israelites, while the third referred to the transmutation of metals as a means of paying tribute exacted by the Roman emperors. The text relating to the production of the Philosopher's Stone was comparatively clear but—as is traditional in all Hermetic works—made no mention of the nature of the prime matter required. What the prime matter is was to be deduced by interpreting the fourth and fifth pages which contained no written text but only some very beautifully illuminated drawings. Flamel states that, though these pictures certainly indicated the substance to be used, it was necessary to be an expert in the Art in order to be able to interpret them, and he realised that at the time he was totally incapable of extracting any meaning whatsoever from them.

I have myself carefully examined these hieroglyphic symbols and, just as in the case of other purely allegorical works, I never really understood what the author meant by them. Even when I *know* what is symbolised, I feel that other emblems might have been used, and that all kinds of other meanings might be read into the same figures.

Like the illustrations, the text in this book leaves our hope unfulfilled, for Flamel is most circumspect and says only: "I may not explain what is written on the other pages in good and perfectly intelligible Latin, for God would punish me. I should be committing a greater sin than the man in the story who said he wished that all the people in the world had only one head, so that he might cut it off with a single stroke." (It is quite likely that he left more precise information in his *Chemical Psalter*, a short treatise that he bequeathed to his nephew Perrier. But the text, which he wrote in the margin of his own missal, is in code.)

Having now acquired the book and being convinced, because of his dream, that it was predestined to him, Flamel set about studying the text and the illustrations. He spent months and years on it, but without making any progress. There was one new factor, however. Perrenelle, who had realised that her husband was working on a secret of some sort, had been associated with him in the research and had greatly encouraged him, while keeping it completely dark from the neighbours. So, helped by his wife and, as he believed, inspired by God, Flamel continued to work. But in vain.

One might wonder why he, who as a Public Scrivener must have known plenty of learned men, did not tell some of them about his discovery and ask for their help. There was at least one excellent reason for it, which was that alchemy was not approved by the religious authorities. In 1317, Pope John XXII fulminated in a Bull:

"Alchemists deceive us and promise what they cannot perform. Although they believe themselves to be learned, they will themselves fall into the pit they have dug for others. They give themselves out, absurdly, to be Masters of Alchemy, but prove their ignorance by always quoting older writers; and, although they are unable to accomplish what these latter never discovered either, they still think that the mystery will be resolved in the future. When they pass off base metals as real gold and silver, they do so with a great many meaningless words. Their impudence has no bounds —for in this way they may issue counterfeit money and thereby cheat everyone. We command that such men shall be permanently banished from the country, as well as those who employ them to make gold or silver, and any who conspire with them to produce it. And we ordain that, to punish them, any real gold they possess shall be distributed to the poor. Those who circulate false gold and silver are men without honour. If the means of those who infringe the law are not sufficient to pay the fine, some other punishment may be inflicted. If any members of the clergy are found among alchemists, they will receive no mercy and will be deprived of their ecclesiastical office."

It is worth noting, by the way, that it was a matter of public notoriety that Pope John XXII himself practised alchemy, and at his death left such an enormous fortune that everyone without hesitation attributed a Hermetic origin to it. He is also credited with writing a treatise on the subject, entitled *Ars Transmutatoria*—but it is not definitely known that he really was the author.

To return to Flamel who, by diligent study of the book of Abraham the Jew, had discovered everything about the Great Work except the one essential that always eluded him—the nature of prime matter. And the angel never appeared again, so Flamel, rightly feeling that it would be better to appeal to God rather than to His Saints, made his prayer as follows (it is quoted by Manget in the *Bibliotheca Chemica Curiosa*):

"Oh Almighty and Eternal God, Father of light, Author of all good things and Giver of all perfect gifts, I implore Thy infinite mercy; make me to understand Thy eternal Wisdom; it is that which encompasses Thy throne, which creates and makes, which guides and preserves all things. Deign to bestow it on me from Thy sanctuary in heaven, and from the throne of Thy glory. May it be with me in all my works, that through it I may receive true knowledge, and that I may continue unerringly in the noble Art to which I have dedicated myself, in my quest for the miraculous Stone of the Philosophers that Thou hast hidden from the world, but that Thou hast in some measure revealed to Thine elect. May the Great Work that I have to do here below be begun, continued and brought to a right conclusion; may it be mine to enjoy in eternal bliss. I ask this in the name of Jesus Christ, who is the celestial Stone, the glorious Cornerstone existent from all eternity, who liveth and reigneth with Thee."

Divine inspiration was not granted, at least not in any direct form So at length, worn and weary, Nicholas Flamel showed copies he had made of some of the illustrations to a medical friend, Master Anseaulme (Anselm). This man was greatly interested in alchemy, and immediately asked to see the book from which the drawings had been taken; but Flamel felt obliged to tell something less than the truth to persuade Master Anselm that he had no more than the pictures. Master Anselm did not understand the symbolism of Abraham the Jew any better than did Flamel—but he explained them none the less. And the explanations only confused the unhappy Flamel still further, as he tells us: "It was the reason why, for twenty long years, I carried out thousands of experiments, though not with the blood of living creatures, which is sinful and evil; for my book informed me that philosophers refer to the metallic spirit that is in metals as 'blood', especially that which is in the Sun, the Moon and Mercury." The allusion to blood is due to the fact that Master Anselm, like many another puffer, had confused alchemy with magic, and had therefore suggested mixing quicksilver with the pure blood of young children. Fortunately Flamel was wise and rejected the idea.

At long last inspiration, possibly divine in origin, came to him. Realising that he would never get anywhere without help, Flamel decided to take with him a copy of the book and visit some country where he might meet learned members of Abraham's race. There were at that time several famous synagogues in Spain, especially round about Saint James of Campostella. So, quite naturally, Flamel announced that he was going there on a pilgrimage.

This reminds us of the pilgrimage already made by Raymond Lully, and which Basil Valentine later also claimed to have undertaken. It is interesting to see what a Master such as Fulcanelli has to say about it in his book *Demeures Philosophales*:

"These suggestions help us to understand the mistakes which many occultists have made by taking literally various purely allegorical writings that were intended for the information of some but had to be kept secret from others. Albert Poisson himself was taken in. He believed that Nicholas Flamel, leaving his wife, his business and his illuminations, had actually fulfilled the vow made before the altar of his parish church to go on foot by the long road to Iberia. But we are prepared to certify—if our sincerity is to be trusted—that Flamel never quitted the cellar where his furnaces roared. Anyone who knows the significance of the pilgrim's staff, the begging bowl and the cockle-shell in St. James' hat, will also know that we are speaking the truth. By substituting himself for the material and modelling himself upon other secret workers, the great Adept was obeying the rules of philosophic discipline and following the example of his predecessors."

Fulcanelli is saying that in his writings Flamel used himself as symbol for the prime matter, and that all the incidents of the journey are really allegories of the various operations performed upon that substance at different stages of the Master Work. One episode is particularly illuminating. While Nicholas Flamel was on his way back from the supposed journey to Spain, he was taken ill and halted at the town of León. On the advice of a Bolognese merchant there, he consulted a Jewish physician named Canches. In the course of a conversation, the doctor displayed so extensive a knowledge of the Jewish Cabbala, that Flamel showed him the illustrations from his book. The doctor exclaimed excitedly that they were from the lost work of the Rabbi Abraham, the *Asch Mezareph*, which had been thought to have been destroyed, and he proposed accompanying Flamel back to Paris. But, when they reached Orleans on that journey, he died without having opened the gates of wisdom to Flamel. This allegory is the barely disguised story of the dissolution of the prime substance, which is the essential point of departure for the philosophic Master Work.

I would not personally be quite as definite as Fulcanelli in saying that Flamel never left his furnaces. I think that one may equally well regard the journey in an initiatory sense: Flamel had for many years been hampered by lacking knowledge of the prime substance, so it would seem probable that he was set on the right path by another Adept, whose name is no longer known and who is symbolised by Dr. Canches. The so-called journey, therefore, is to be taken as a reminder of the necessity for initiation and as an allegorical representation of the *modus operandi* (method of work).

So at long last Nicholas Flamel was in possession of the knowledge he needed, and especially of the true nature of the prime substance. He therefore resumed his work, but another three years were to pass before he was able to bring it to a successful conclusion. As will be shown in the last part of this book, three years is the normal time required for the Master Work, when proceeding by the White path, so the delay mentioned by Flamel after his return from the "pilgrimage" would seem to be a definite indication of his good faith. But let us have his own description of the circumstances in which he obtained the Philosopher's Stone:

"At length I found what I had sought, and I recognised it by the pungent smell. Having that, I easily completed the Work; and once I had discovered how to prepare the primary substances, following to the letter the instructions in my book, I could not have failed even if I had wished to do so.

"The first time I performed the Work, I used mercury, about half a pound of which I converted into pure silver, better than that which comes from the mint, as was proved by repeated tests carried out by myself and others. It was at about noon on 17th January, on a Monday, at my own house, with only Perrenelle present, in the year of Grace 1382. And then, still obeying the instructions in my book word for word, I used the red Stone on roughly the same quantity of mercury, in the same conditions, with no one present but Perrenelle and in my own house, on 25th April of the same year at about five o'clock in the afternoon. I transmuted this mercury into an approximately equal quantity of pure gold, very definitely superior to ordinary gold, softer and more malleable. I can say truthfully that I achieved it three times, with the help of Perrenelle who understood the process as well as I did, having helped me in all the operations, and who undoubtedly could have carried it out successfully by herself if she had wished to do so."

That same year 1382 saw the beginning of Flamel's material prosperity. Within the space of a few months he became the owner of over thirty houses and lands in Paris alone. Then he paid for the building of a number of chapels and hospitals. In addition, he had the West door of the church of Sainte-Geneviève-des-Ardents restored, and gave a large donation to the Quinze-Vingts, a hospital for blind men, who until 1789 used to organise a procession to Saint-Jacques-la-Boucherie every year, to pray for the soul of Nicholas Flamel. In this, his own parish, some forty deeds have been found, legally drawn up, showing evidence of the considerable gifts made by the one-time humble Public Scrivener. Finally, he repaired various buildings in the Cemetery of the Holy Innocents—a fashionable cemetery, which was also a place much favoured for lovers' meetings, the huge statue of Death that dominated the place being no longer an object of terror to anyone. At his orders copies of hieroglyphic pictures taken from the book of Abraham the Jew were painted on one of the archways of this cemetery. Several of the buildings he had paid for carried his portrait carved in the stone-work, holding a scroll in his hand. Some of these sculptures survived until the nineteenth century.

Needless to say, Flamel's sudden accession to riches did not pass unobserved, careful though he had been to conceal his work from the neighbours. Although he was an obscure craftsman with no con-nections in high society, information of his rapid rise to fortune reached the ears of King Charles VI, which shows that it must have appeared fabulous to his contemporaries. A first enquiry by the royal servants having shown that there really was something unusual about it, the King sent his Chief Tax Inspector, the Sire de Cramoisy, to visit Flamel. In 1655, Pierre Borel, Councillor and Physician-in-Ordinary to the King, wrote in his *Treasury of Gallic and French Discoveries and Antiquities*:

"News of Flamel's wealth reached the King, who sent M. de Cramoisy, his Chief Inspector of Taxes, to find out if there was any truth in what he had heard; but this gentleman found him living in humble circumstances, even to using only earthenware crockery. Tradition says, however, that Flamel, finding him to be a decent sort of man, told him the truth and gave him a flask full of his powder, which is said to have been preserved in that family for many years. This saved Flamel from further royal attentions."

The Sire de Cramoisy having been bribed—as one is bound to call it—Flamel was able to carry on his work tranquilly. Yet he hardly changed his way of life. He continued to live in peaceful obscurity with Perrenelle until, in either 1397 or 1404, she died and was buried in the cemetery of the Holy Innocents. He himself pursued his quiet existence until his own death at the age of eighty. Vallet de Viriville, an excellent nineteenth-century historian, well known for his works on Joan of Arc, was also interested in Flamel, and has this to say about him:

"His house, *Great Gables*, has lost its gables, as well as most of its sculptures and ancient ornaments. But it still stands at No. 51 rue Montmorency, and presents to public view the following original inscription: 'We working men and women, living at the gates of this house, which was built in the year of Grace 1407, are bound, one and all, to say the Lord's Prayer and a Hail Mary every day, praying that God may in His mercy pardon poor sinners. Amen.'

"Nicholas Flamel died in 1418, his riches and his renown having continually increased. He bought a burial place for himself inside the church of Saint-Jacques-la-Boucherie, as we are told in one of the clauses of his remarkable Will, according to which—as he had no children—he bequeathed most of his belongings to this church. In addition, the Will contains many noble examples of his generosity."

A number of writers who find it impossible to swallow the idea of alchemy, have tried to show that Flamel's wealth was only a legend. Unfortunately for them, the deeds referring to his possessions exist and give proof of his colossal riches. Others have suggested that his craft, in which he excelled, sufficed to bring him the money required to pay for everything. This last is an obvious absurdity to anyone who knows anything about the standard of life of a craftsman in the Middle Ages. Others again refer to him as a usurer or allege that he falsely claimed to have deposits of Jewish gold. Louis Figuier has the perfect answer to this: "Not only are such accusations entirely unfounded," he says, "but all known historical facts about the life and character of Flamel combine to clear his memory of the imputations."

He was a man who, according to his own account, dedicated his life to alchemy and achieved great riches thereby. Does this correspond with the accepted image of an alchemist to whom the transmutation

of metal is only one stage in the achievement of semi-immortality?
The answer would be in the negative if the story of Flamel ended
there, that is to say with his death. But actually, as in the case of
Saint-Germain and some other great Adepts, Flamel's story goes on.

Paul Lucas, a seventeenth-century traveller, tells the story of an
episode which occurred when he was in Asia Minor:

"At Bournous-Bachi, having discussed Hermetic Philosophy with
a religious leader of the Uzbeks, I was told by this man that true
philosophers had the secret of prolonging life for anything up to
a thousand years. I mentioned the renowned Flamel and remarked
that, despite the Philosopher's Stone, he was undoubtedly dead.
When he heard the name, he began to laugh at my simplicity.
As I had almost begun to believe the rest of what he said, I was
considerably surprised to find that he questioned what I told him.
Noting my astonishment, he asked me in the same tone whether
I was innocent enough to believe that Flamel was really dead.
'No, no,' he said, 'you are wrong. Flamel is alive; neither he
nor his wife has yet tasted death. It is barely three years since I
saw them both in India—he is one of my closest friends.' "

Later the dervish gave Paul Lucas some further information:

"Fame can sometimes be very inconvenient, but a wise man may
avoid it by taking precautions. Flamel realised that he was sure
to be arrested as soon as he was suspected of having the Philosopher's Stone, and there was little doubt that it could not be
long before he was accused of being an alchemist once the stories
of his munificence were noised abroad. He avoided persecution
by having the deaths of himself and his wife published. On his
advice, she feigned an illness and when it had seemingly run its
course she was reported to be dead, although in fact she was in
Switzerland, awaiting his joining her. Instead of herself, a log of
wood was buried, dressed in her clothes; and, so that everything
might be done with due ceremony, the interment took place in
one of the chapels she had been instrumental in having built. Later
on he adopted the same stratagem and, since money can make

most things possible, little difficulty was experienced in winning over medical and clerical agreement to the deception. He left a Will in which he requested that he should be buried in the same grave as his wife and that a pyramid should be erected over the sepulchre. So, while the living Adept was on his way to join his wife in Switzerland, a second log of wood was buried in his stead. Since then both have lived their lives as philosophers, sometimes in one country, sometimes in another. This is the true story of Nicholas Flamel, and not what you believe or what is foolishly believed in Paris, where there are very few people who have any true knowledge. . . ."

Many other stories are told of the survival of Flamel. Oddly enough, they all agree on one point—that he and his wife retired to India as soon as he had rejoined her in Switzerland.

Obviously, it is impossible for me to decide one way or the other about their survival. On the other hand, as regards transmutation I feel that this story has provided us with the first definite proof. There was nothing to support the claims of Albertus Magnus, Arnold of Villanova or Raymond Lully to have made gold. The situation is otherwise as regards Flamel, for his sudden rise to wealth can have been due to nothing but the Hermetic Art.

My verdict will therefore be: yes, very probably Nicholas Flamel did find the Philosopher's Stone.

Yet "very probably" does not satisfy me fully. What I require, before I am convinced, is absolute certainty. So I invite my readers to continue the pilgrimage through the years with me, our first stop being in the fifteenth century with Basil Valentine, the German Benedictine monk.

Top, The First Key of Basil Valentine
Below, The title-page of the last Will and Testament of Basil Valentine

THE LAST

VVILL

AND

TESTAMENT

OF

Basil Valentine,

Monke of the Order of
St. BENNET,

which being alone,
He hid under a Table of Marble, behind the
High-Altar of the Cathedral Church, in the Imperial City of Erford : leaving it there to be
found by him, whom Gods Providence
should make worthy of it.

To which is added
TWO TREATISES
The First declaring his Manual Operations.
The Second shewing things Natural and Superna-
tural.
Never before Published in English.

LONDON,
Printed by S. G. and B. G. for Edward Brewster,
and are to be sold at the sign of the Crane
in St. Pauls Church-yard, 1671.

3. Basil Valentine, the Monk of Erfurt, and Bernard, the Good Man of Treviso

Basil Valentine, a monk at the Benedictine monastery of Erfurt in Germany, is undoubtedly one of the best-known alchemists; even today his writings are often translated and republished. Moreover, the name Basil Valentine is frequently quoted in scientific works and reference books on account of the many chemical discoveries he made.

Nevertheless, he is one of the most mysterious of all Adepts of whom any historical memories remain. His works were not published during his life-time and were not even known then, that is to say about 1413. A legend says that some decades after his death one of the pillars in the cathedral at Erfurt suddenly split open, revealing a collection of the monk's alchemical treatises, which had until then been known only through a vague oral tradition.

In his introduction to the new edition of the *Twelve Keys to Philosophy*, Eugène Canseliet says:

"After so much research by people far better equipped, we do not hope to be able to explain this historical enigma, which has not been and probably never will be solved. . . . It does not appear to us to be indispensable to know precisely that the author of the *Twelve Keys* was this or that particular individual, or whether the anonymity imposed by tradition covers one man or several, since it is only the work itself that matters. The desire of far too many people to insist upon pinning a label onto some philosopher who has voluntarily renounced the vanities of this world, seems simply childish and ill-mannered."

Even the existence of the monastery at Erfurt has been questioned, although there is a letter written by the celebrated philosopher Leibnitz in which he refers to Basil Valentine and says definitely:

"I know this—that Johann-Philip, Elector of Mainz, ordered research to be carried out among the Benedictines at Erfurt, but with no result." In addition, Eugène Canseliet consulted the *Historia Erfurtensis* compiled by Johann-Maria Guden, Count Palatine, in which a Professor of Law, who was burgomaster of the city and Rector of its University, wrote in 1675:

"Basil Valentine (in the year 1413) lived in the Monastery of St. Peter, and was highly commended for his profound studies in the arts of medicine and the natural sciences. In addition, he is said to have had the superstitious hope of making gold, an ill-advised folly for which he was perhaps the less to blame, since it has not merely deluded its students for many centuries, but finally deprives them of their intellectual faculties."

It is, therefore, permissible to believe that there really was a Benedictine monk who adopted the pseudonym Basil Valentine, and wrote treatises in the fourteenth and fifteenth centuries that are known to this day. A few biographical details have been extracted from his work, among them that he travelled to Belgium and to England in his youth. On the other hand, his "journey" to Saint James of Campostella, to which he refers in *The Triumphal Chariot of Antimony* can certainly not be considered factual:

"After I had undertaken the arduous pilgrimage to Campostella in consequence of a vow, I returned to my monastery (for which I always thank God). I thought that many would be filled with joy, as I was by the Grace of God, for the holy relics that I brought back to give help and solace to our own monastery and to all poor sinners. But far from it. Few amended their lives, few showed appreciation of the goodness of God. On the contrary, mockery, insults, blasphemies, all increased. But at the Last Judgment the Just Judge will punish them as they deserve."

From the point of view of alchemical philosophy, Basil Valentine's great achievement is to have directed attention to the third principle —salt. On this point Eugène Canseliet quotes an extract from *The*

Garden of Medicine by Jean-Baptiste van Helmont, physician to the Prince of Orange in 1652, who wrote: "Basil Valentine, a Benedictine monk, later gave a more definite description of the essence or soul of metal, which he named sulphur or tincture; of the body, that is, salt; and the spirit, which he called mercury. These principles, as applied by Basil, were admirably extended by Theophrastus Paracelsus a century later to cover all substances."

To round off the hopeless quest into the well-concealed life of this unknown Adept, his celebrated maxim may be quoted: "Search in the bowels of the earth; and as you progress you will find the hidden Stone, the true panacea", which in Latin reads

VISITETIS INTERIORA TERRAE RECTIFICANDO
INVENIETIS OCCULTUM LAPIDEM VERAM
MEDICINAM

and the initial letters of all the words in the formula spell V.I.T.R.I.O.L.U.M.—vitriol—the name which Basil Valentine gave to the secret diluent salt in the Master Work.

Bernard of Treviso

Bernard was Count of the Mark of Treviso, a small subdivision of the State of Venice. The people of the neighbourhood still remember him as the "good man of Treviso", and he certainly deserves special mention among Adepts, if only for his perseverance. Bernard began his work when he was fourteen years old and is believed to have found the Philosopher's Stone when he was over eighty-two, after a life of repeated frustrations. One might almost apply to him the maxim that Jules Verne put into the mouth of the engineer Cyrus Smith at the beginning of *The Mysterious Island*: "A man need not be hopeful before starting on anything, nor be successful in order to persevere"—a saying of which William of Orange was probably the original author.

Count Bernard was born in 1406 in the city of Padua. From the time he was fourteen his father began initiating him into the study of the early Masters of alchemy, in particular the two Arabs Jabir and Rhases. For the first four years he faithfully pursued the methods of Rhases, but all in vain; the only result of his concentrated efforts was the loss of three thousand crowns. So, abandoning his confidence in this philosopher, he switched over to Jabir and began work afresh. Two more years passed, ending in nothing but the loss of another six thousand crowns. All the Puffers and self-styled alchemists in the town had, of course, come to help him spend his money!

One of his friends, a monk, produced some treatises written by a couple of Puffers named Archilaus and Rubicesca, and so Bernard began working along their lines, but with no greater success. Another of his coadjutors told him that he ought to try a base of rectified alcohol, repeating the experiment over and over and over again—which he did. All this early work consumed fifteen years of his life and a large part of his fortune without getting him one step nearer to the Great Work. A local Government official visited him one day and informed him that the prime substance was sea salt. Procedure along these lines having also failed, the same gentleman told him of another recipe, which consisted in dissolving silver and mercury in cold water. The solutions were to be made separately and then left to stand for a year, after which they were to be combined and condensed over hot embers. The residue, poured into a retort, was to be exposed to the rays of the sun which would induce crystallisation—the resultant crystals would definitely be the Philosopher's Stone. For five years Bernard waited patiently for the crystals to form—but nothing happened.

He went on experimenting with other methods, other puffers, other treatises—getting no results except that he reached the age of forty-six and was practically ruined. He spent the next eight years in the company of a monk named Geofroi de Leuvrier, who told him about a new process involving hens' eggs. First the eggs must be hard boiled; then the yolks and the whites separated and left to rot in separate vessels surrounded by manure. The results must be distilled many times over, until one turned into a white liquid and the other red. The whole operation was then to be repeated until such time as the prime matter emerged. And Bernard spent yet another eight years over this. Thereafter, in company with a new theological friend, he tried to extract the Stone from sulphate of iron. The sulphate was put into vinegar eight times distilled, then the mixture was poured into an alembic and fifteen further distillations were carried out daily. This went on for a year. Bernard did not find the Stone, but the exhausting work brought on a quartan fever from which he suffered for over a year and nearly died.

Still undeterred, Bernard went to Germany, where the Emperor's confessor was said to possess the secret. This man averred that he knew an infallible method based on mercury, silver, sulphur and olive oil. All the ingredients were to be melted in a double boiler, while being stirred continually; then they were to be dried in a glass vessel and this placed over a hot fire for one whole month. Some lead was then to be added to the mixture and the lot melted down in a crucible. According to Master Henry, the Emperor's confessor, the silver—ten marks provided by Bernard—should show a considerable increase. In fact it was found to have been reduced to four marks.

After that, Count Bernard admitted to being somewhat discouraged —as who could fail to be? For two months he discontinued his alchemical researches, to the great relief of his family; but soon the insatiable thirst for knowledge that had possessed him since early youth overcame him again, and he began to scour Europe for an Adept who would initiate him. He went to England and Scotland, Holland and Germany, France and Spain. From there he went to the East, and spent some years travelling in Persia, Palestine and Egypt. On the return journey he stayed for a long time in Greece, hoping to discover the Hermetic secret in the library of one of the many monasteries there. All his efforts were in vain, and at the age of sixty-two he found himself in Rhodes, penniless, his whole fortune having been dissipated in the frenzied search; friendless, but still persuaded that he would one day find the clue to the great secret.

He soon learnt that there was a monk in Rhodes itself, who was generally reported to have made the Stone. One could not expect to come in contact with so eminent a man empty-handed, but Count Bernard was lucky enough to meet a rich merchant, a friend of his family, who lent him eight thousand florins. Armed with this, he obtained an introduction to the scientist, who instructed him in the method he had himself used, and allowed Bernard to work under his direction for three years. His process was based on a mixture of gold and silver combined with mercury—but again this was totally unproductive. So Bernard returned to Treviso, utterly ruined and ignored by all his family who thought he was mad and refused even to see him. At last, at the age of eighty, he decided to start again at the very beginning and to study Jabir's method once more, thinking that he might previously have misunderstood him. He therefore returned to Rhodes for the last time, and remained there until his death in 1490. According to alchemical tradition it was there, at the age of 82, that he at long last succeeded in the Great Work. So he spent the last three years of his life in possession of the coveted secret. Moreover, he had acquired serenity, a serenity which he shares with us in his writings: his conclusion is that a man should learn to be satisfied with what he has.

The best known of the alchemical books he wrote are the *Treatise on the Natural Philosophy of Metals* and *The Lost Language*. The latter is fairly easy of access, because Claude d'Ygé has reproduced it in his *New Assembly of Chymical Philosophers*. Part of the *Natural Philosophy of Metals* is a piece known as the *Allegory of the Fountain*, in which Bernard explains symbolically the operations performed in one of the three parts of the Master Work. It is worth quoting:

"I was walking through the fields, deep in thought.

"It was an evening when I had to study for an examination on the following day. I found a little spring of beautiful clear water, enclosed in a fine stone basin; above the basin stood an ancient hollow oak, and the whole was surrounded by walls, lest cattle or wild animals or winged creatures should come and bathe in it. I longed greatly for sleep. I sat down beside the fountain, and saw that there was a cover over it, and that it was all shut in.

"Then an old priest came by. I asked him why the fountain was enclosed above, below, and on all sides. He replied in a friendly, gracious manner, saying: Sir, the fact is that this spring has a fearful power, more than any other in the whole world. It is intended to be used only by the King of the land; each is well acquainted with the other, for the King never approaches without entering; and he remains bathing in the fountain for two hundred and eighty-two days, which rejuvenates him so marvellously that there is no one whom he could not overcome.

"Then I asked him if he had seen the King, and he replied that he had seen him enter; but that once he had gone in and his guard had closed the door, he was not seen again for one hundred and thirty days; after that, he would show himself in his splendour. The door-keeper who guards him keeps the water continually at the required natural temperature.

"Then I asked in what colour the King was seen. And he replied that he was clothed first in a vestment of cloth of gold, then in a doublet of black velvet, with a shift as white as snow, and that his skin was red as blood.

"After this, I asked whether, when he came to the fountain, the King brought with him a great company of outsiders or of the populace? He replied pleasantly, smiling to himself: The King brings no one but himself, leaving everyone else behind; none but he approaches the fountain, and his guard, who is a simple man. . . . And whenever the King enters, he first removes his robe of cloth of gold, made of gold-leaf beaten very thin, and hands it to his first attendant, who is Saturn. Saturn takes it and keeps it after he has received it, for forty days, or forty-two or longer. Then the King takes off his black velvet doublet and hands it to the second attendant, who is Jupiter and who keeps it for a good twenty days. Thereafter Jupiter, at the order of the King, passes it on to the Moon, who is the third attendant, beautiful and lustrous, who keeps it for twenty days. So the King is now in his pure white shift, strewn with delicately scented flowers. Then he divests himself of this white shift and hands it to Mars who in the same way keeps it for forty or sometimes for forty-two days. And after that, if God wills, Mars passes it to the Sun, who is yellow and shrouded in mist, and he keeps it for forty days, after which the Sun shines in full glory, and he retains it. . . .

"And I asked him: Does no Doctor or anyone ever come to this fountain? No, he replied, no one ever comes here except the guard down below, who ensures that the heat remains at the right temperature throughout and is not too dry.

"Does this give the guard much trouble?—He has more difficulty at the end than at the beginning, because the fountain bursts into flames.

"And I said to him: Have many people seen this? Everyone in the world has it before his eyes, but no-one recognises it, he replied.

"Then I said to him: What do they do afterwards? If they wish, they may purify the King in the fountain, surrounding it and keeping him within its confines, restoring his doublet to the King on the first day, his shift on the next, and his blood-red flesh on the next, was the answer.

"So I said to him: What does all this mean? And he replied: God may require one, ten, a hundred, a thousand or a hundred thousand, and then multiply the number by eleven.

"I said to him: I understand nothing of what you have said. To which he replied: I shall tell you no more, for I am weary. And I saw that he was weary, and I too was weary, and longed to sleep, for I had been studying all the previous day."

If, reader, you had perused the story without having gone through the preceding pages in this book, you would very surely have decided that it was simply nonsense. Yet to a student such as I try to be it offers certain points of understanding. At a first glance one sees that it is an allegorical description of one part of the Master Work— in fact of the third part, when the substance reaches the *rebis* stage and is fired in the philosophic egg. The water in the little fountain symbolises the philosophic mercury and the water of the magi, or *Virgin's Milk*, which will be absorbed into the substance in the course of the third phase. The walls surrounding the spring represent the prohibitions that prevent the secrets of alchemy from being divulged. The different garments that clothe the King—that is, the *rebis*— correspond to the seven stages of preparation, generally referred to as the *System of Philalethes*. For instance, when Bernard says that the King hands his golden robe to Saturn it does not mean that lead plays any part in the affair, but that under the influence of Saturn the *rebis* loses its original colour and acquires the dense blackness correct for this part of the Work. The durations of time given mean exactly what they say—that, for example, Jupiter's influence lasts for twenty days.

The final dialogue is particularly important and illuminating, because it insists first, that no substance unconnected with the Work may be allowed to intrude, except the guardian who keeps the heat at the right temperature, that is to say the secret fire. Then follows an indication of the everyday nature of prime matter. Finally, the penultimate reply alludes to multiplication, that is to say the property that the Philosopher's Stone has of increasing its power almost to infinity if it undergoes further coction—in other words, if the whole Work is repeated with the finished Stone itself used as the prime substance. I shall not elaborate the point further here, because there will be an opportunity in a later section of this book to study in detail the system of Philalethes, of which *The Allegory of the Fountain* is an epitome.

It will be understandable from the above why scientists who studied alchemy only through books regarded texts such as Bernard of Treviso's as pure lunacy. Actually, the allegory, to anyone who can interpret it, is an extremely useful explanation of the system, designed to act as Ariadne's thread for non-practising initiates, or indeed for initiable readers who can use the alchemist's hints as a basis for further research.

Bernard of Treviso also quotes a second allegory entitled *The Green Dream*, of which he may himself be the author, and which describes another phase of the Work in the same picturesque fashion. It will not be reproduced here in full as it is very lengthy, but a few short extracts are given to show something of the symbolism used in certain alchemical writings.

Bernard was, it seems, sound asleep when a statue with golden lips suddenly appeared before him. This vision said that she was the genius of the magi, and asked him to follow her. In single file they passed through fantastic gardens, whose strange fauna the alchemist watched with delight. All at once Bernard complained that he had gone blind, and his eyes were immediately touched with a magical herb which gave him back his sight—an obvious symbol of an Adept's awakening to the understanding of things as they really are. He then saw before him a most extraordinary building, which he describes in the following terms:

"In the first suite was a large room hung with damask tapestries all covered with gold lace and edged with a fringe of the same. The basic colour of the material was iridescent green and gold, picked out with very delicate silver threads, the whole veiled in white gauze. Then there were several smaller rooms, decorated with jewels of different colours. After this came a great chamber furnished in fine black velvet, enriched with satin bands of the deepest and most lustrous black, the whole patterned with jet of coruscating brilliance."

Leaving aside a second apartment, we pass to the third: "The third apartment was furnished with a scintillating material, purple on a gold ground, incomparably richer and more beautiful than all the other materials I had yet seen."

Farther on, the philosopher refers to marriage customs in force in this strange country, by which is to be understood the marriage of sulphur with philosophers' mercury.

"The Hagacestaur unites a pure and beautiful maiden with a hale and vigorous old man. The maiden and the old man are cleansed and purified. Then the man offers his hand to the girl, who takes it in hers, and they are conducted to one of these apartments. The door is then sealed with the same material as that of which the whole edifice is built. They will remain enclosed there together for nine full months, during which time they make all the splendid furnishings I had been shown. At the end of that period they come out and are found to have been merged into a single body; and, having also a single soul, they are now one and indivisible, and their power upon earth is very great. The Hagacestaur then employs them to reform all the evil-doers in the seven kingdoms."

This again is easy enough to understand as an allegory of the Stone. The reference to the Hermetic closure of the room will be noted, and the indication that no foreign body must be allowed to contaminate the Work. The final sentence is, of course, an allusion to the transmutation of base metals and not to the reform of evil-doers.

94

These writings, it is hardly necessary to say, cannot be taken as proof that Bernard discovered the secret of the Philosopher's Stone, but only that he acquired complete knowledge of the Mystery from a theoretical point of view. But I hope, and like to believe, that his sixty years of effort were really rewarded by the discovery of the Hermetic secret.

If one may not reckon Bernard of Treviso as "positive" in this sense, at least so indomitable a Seeker deserves a special place in our esteem.

4. A Physician and a Gentleman

Paracelsus

In his *History of Hermetic Philosophy* the Abbé Lenglet du Fresnoy begins the article on Paracelsus with the following words:

"This famous man was born in 1493 at Einsiedeln near Zürich, in Switzerland. His name was Aureole-Philippe Theophrastus ab Hohenheim Paracelsus. Fortunately he is generally known simply as Paracelsus—for who could remember all that rigmarole! Never has there been a man so much abused; nor ever one who had so many admirers."

Paracelsus' father was a physician and also practised occultism. He taught his son to study the plants and herbs of the Swiss mountains at an early age, at the same time introducing him to the philosophy of Aristotle. A few years later, the family moved to Villach in Carinthia, where the doctor had obtained a teaching post at the School of Chemistry. It was here that young Paracelsus first heard about metalliferous minerals. He completed his education at the University of Bâle, but was not much interested in the scholastic instruction he received there. Instead, he attended the lectures of the Abbé Trithemius, a man as well known then as Roger Bacon. Among other subjects, Trithemius studied hypnotism and telepathy, sciences which to this day have remained mysterious.

After this, Paracelsus made the tour of the European universities —Padua, Montpellier, Bologna—and he very probably went on to the Low Countries and to England. Tradition has it that he also visited Turkey and the East, but there is no evidence of this. Having completed the journey—which may perhaps have been initiatory— the young man returned to Switzerland to establish himself as a physician. The Abbé Lenglet du Fresnoy continues:

Paracelsus

"After his travels, Paracelsus began practising medicine at Zürich. From there, his reputation obtained him a call to Bâle; but a curious and annoying adventure caused him to leave there again almost at once. One of the canons of the cathedral was ill and at the point of death. The whole medical faculty had given him up. Then Paracelsus saw him, and promised to restore him to health. A fee for his services was agreed. Paracelsus administered two doses only and effected the cure; but, as soon as he was well again, the canon began to dispute the charge. The argument between doctor and patient degenerated into a law suit, the canon complaining that he had been cured too quickly. The matter was brought before the city magistrates who, realising that the doctor had not taken the precaution to leave the canon to convalesce for a time, but had cured him practically instantaneously, allowed him only a very modest sum. Paracelsus complained publicly about this; but he had overlooked two important points—first, that to keep patients happy they should be restored to health gradually, a sudden cure will not please them; and second, that those in authority, however minor, may sometimes enjoy committing injustices when people have no chance to fight back."

So Paracelsus was obliged to leave the city hurriedly, lest the anger of the magistrates pursue him for the violence of his language. He went on to Strasbourg, and thence to Salzburg, where he died on 24th September 1541 at the age of forty-eight.

The real cause of his death is not known. His friends said he had been poisoned; his detractors, that his end was brought on by drink and debauchery.

It is undeniable that in addition to his work in medicine, occultism and magic, he studied alchemy; but it is equally undeniable that he never became an Adept. The different, often contradictory characteristics of his fiery temperament explain the very various opinions that were held of him at the time, and also the fact that nowadays both adversaries and partisans of alchemy claim him. Thus René Marcard says:

"There is no doubt that Paracelsus contributed enormously to the practice of reasoned and reasonable experiment in Medicine and other sciences, if only by proclaiming loud and clear that 'the patient must be the doctor's only lexicon', and by introducing systematic methods to the corporation of apothecaries who until then had been accustomed all too often to dispense medicines without knowing anything about the art."

In fact, although Paracelsus was the inventor of the word and practice of spagirism, he cannot be regarded as an alchemist in the full sense of the word. He certainly began work on the Philosopher's Stone, but he abandoned the Hermetic goal to devote himself to the practical medical application of particular processes in alchemical work.

Is he, therefore, to be considered as no more than one of the founders of modern medicine? That cannot be answered definitely. I used the word "initiatory" about his travels; and that is the conclusion to which Serge Hutin comes in his study of Paracelsus, which he ends with the following words:

"It is beyond question that Paracelsus was a Rosicrucian initiate, and undoubtedly we should regard him as one of those who are born to spread the divine light among men (many of whom are unfortunately slow to receive and understand it), as one of those whose mission it is to undergo the supreme test in this world of suffering, tribulation and misunderstanding, jealousy, hatred, meanness, wretchedness. Paracelsus faced all those, and possibly even martyrdom, when one remembers the mysterious, lonely death of this great physician, apparently abandoned by everyone."

One may therefore conclude that Theophrastus Paracelsus was probably an initiate of the Rose-Croix, assuredly a physician of genius, quite undoubtedly a drunkard, a boaster and something of a charlatan when he discussed occultism, but also a first-class scientist. He was the first to recognise the existence of zinc as a separate metal, to define the toxicity of arsenic, and finally to point out the therapeutic value of the red precipitate of mercury in the treatment of syphilis. But from the alchemical point of view, though it is evident that Paracelsus was not simply a puffer, it is nevertheless equally sure that he was never an Adept.

Denis Zachaire

As in the case of Basil Valentine, and later of Philalethes or Fulcanelli, the real name of the Adept known under the pseudonym Denis Zachaire remains a mystery. All that is known about him is that he was born in 1510 of a noble family living in Guienne. After receiving his early teaching at home, he was sent to Bordeaux to learn philosophy at the College of Arts. There he was put in charge of a tutor, who happened to be a student of the Hermetic Science.

So it came about that Denis immediately started on alchemical research. Instead of attending the course he was supposed to be following, he spent the whole of his year at Bordeaux in collecting recipes for transmutation. He filled an enormous folder with them, and carried it away with him when he left the university. Most of the recipes were attributed to celebrated people, and bore titles such as *The Work of the Queen of Navarre, The Work of the Cardinal of Tournon* and *The Work of the Cardinal of Lorraine*, names which encouraged him to believe that their descriptions of the processes must really be trustworthy.

After this, young Zachaire proceeded to Toulouse, still accompanied by his Bordeaux tutor, and this time with the idea of studying Law. But in reality neither the young man nor his tutor had any wish but to put into practice the recipes they had accumulated at Bordeaux. As soon as they arrived, they bought furnaces, glass vessels and tubes, retorts and everything needed for distillation, calcination and other alchemical processes. Of course all their operations turned out to be ineffectual, and the two hundred crowns that Denis's family had provided for a year's maintenance of himself and his tutor rapidly drifted away in the vapours of their crucibles.

Some excellent descriptions of the peregrinations that lay before the future Adept have been written, but it would seem to be more interesting to quote Denis Zachaire's own account, given in the autobiography that forms part of the book he called *A Short Treatise on the Natural Philosophy of Metals.*

"Before the end of the year my two hundred crowns had gone up in smoke, and my master died of a lingering fever that he contracted during the summer, largely because he rarely left his room, in which the atmosphere was terribly hot and unhealthy. I was the more troubled by his death since my parents would only send me the money for my keep instead of the amount I wanted to carry on my Work.

"To overcome these difficulties, I went home in 1535, so as to avoid being under a tutor, and aggregated three years' income, which came to four hundred crowns. I needed this amount of capital because I wanted to work out a recipe which had been

101

given me at Toulouse by an Italian who said he had actually been present at the experiment. I kept him with me so that he might see the end of his process. I calcinated gold and silver in *aqua fortis* (nitric acid), but this was no use because the gold and silver I used melted away to less than half the original quantity, and my four hundred crowns were soon reduced to two hundred and thirty. I gave twenty of these to my Italian to go and sort out the matter with the man who had given him the recipe and who lived, so he said, in Milan. I waited at Toulouse all through the winter expecting his return; but I might still be there if I had been prepared to go on waiting, for I never saw him again.

"Then came the summer, and with it an outbreak of plague, so I left the town. But I did not lose sight of my work. I went to Cahors where I made the acquaintance of an old man who was commonly known as the Philosopher—though this is a title easily bestowed in the provinces on anyone less ignorant than the rest. I told him what I had been doing and asked his opinion. All he did was to suggest ten or a dozen processes that he thought were better than most. The plague ran its course, and I returned to Toulouse. I resumed my work and did so well that my four hundred crowns were reduced to a hundred and seventy!

"Hoping to continue my operations with greater success, I made the acquaintance in 1537 of an Abbé who lived near the town. He was as enthusiastic about the Work as I was, and told me that one of his friends, a member of the Cardinal d'Armagnac's suite, had sent him a recipe from Rome, which he believed was really effective, but which was likely to cost some two hundred crowns. We provided half each of this sum, and set to work, using our capital as a common purse. As we needed some alcohol for the process, I bought a cask of excellent Gaillac wine. I rectified it several times to obtain the spirit we required; and we then put one gold mark that we had calcinated for a month into four times the quantity of spirit. This was poured into a retort as the Art requires, with another one to balance it, and deposited on a furnace to coagulate. We left it for a year; but, so as not to be idle, we amused ourselves by carrying out various less important experiments, which were just as profitable as our Great Work!

"The whole of 1537 passed without any change, and we might have waited for the rest of our lives for our brew to congeal, because spirits of wine are clearly not the diluent for gold. Still, we did recover all the gold, the only alteration it had undergone being that the metal powder was a shade finer than when we had put it in to soak. We scattered it over some hot quicksilver, but in vain. You may imagine how disappointed we were, especially the Abbé, who had already told his monks that all they need do was melt down a large leaden fountain that stood in their cloisters and it would be turned into gold as soon as our operations were completed. This failure did not prevent our continuing. Once more I aggregated my income, and drew another four hundred crowns. The Abbé added an equal amount, and I went to Paris, the best place in the world to meet practitioners of the Art. Having these eight hundred crowns, I was quite determined not to leave until either I had spent the lot or had discovered something worth while. My parents were not at all pleased about my undertaking this journey, and my friends expostulated with me for not buying a legal practice, as they thought I was a skilled lawyer. I made them believe that I was only taking this trip in order to do that very thing.

"I reached Paris on the 9th January 1539, after a fortnight's journey. For a month I hardly spoke to a soul, but as soon as I came in contact with other enthusiasts, some of whom even owned furnaces, I found that I was acquainted with over a hundred of them, each with his own particular system—some believed in precipitation, others in dissolution, others in using an essence of emery. Then there were those who first extracted mercury from their metals, in order to fix it afterwards. Not a day passed without our meeting at the lodging of one or another of us, to tell each other how we were getting on; we did so even on Sundays and feast days, when we foregathered at Notre Dame, the most popular church in Paris. Then some would say: if only we had the means to start over again we'd get somewhere! Others: if our vessels had been strong enough we'd have done it by now! Or: if I'd had a good, round copper pot with a lid, I could have fixed the mercury with silver. There was not a single one who had not got a plausible excuse; but I was deaf to them all, having learnt by experience how badly one can be let down by such expectations.

"A Greek turned up and I worked unsuccessfully with him on lumps of cinnabar. Almost at the same time I made the acquaintance of a foreign gentleman who had just arrived in Paris, and who used to sell the fruits of his operations to goldsmiths. I accompanied him, and got to know him quite well, although he would never tell me his secret. In the end he did tell me, but it proved to be simply another fraud, though rather more ingenious than most. I never failed to tell the Abbé in Toulouse all about everything, and even sent him a copy of this gentleman's process. He evidently thought that I was on the track of something at last, and exhorted me to stay another year in Paris, since I had made such a good beginning. Yet despite all my efforts, I made no more progress in the three years I spent there than I had done before.

"I had spent almost all my money, when the Abbé sent to ask me to come and see him immediately. I did so, and found that he had had letters from the King of Navarre, who was greatly interested in Philosophy, requesting him to send me to meet him at Pau in Béarn, so as to teach him the secret I had learnt from the foreign gentleman. He said he would pay me three or four thousand crowns for it. The sound of those four thousand crowns was so sweet in the Abbé's ears that he felt as if they were already in his purse, and he gave me no peace until I agreed to go and see the King. I got to Pau in May 1542, and successfully carried out the operation, as I had been shown it. When I had done all the King wished, I got the reward I expected—which was nothing. Although the King himself was willing enough to do the right thing by me, he was deterred by his courtiers, even by those who had encouraged him to send for me. So I was packed off with a big thank you, and told to try and find something in his realm that I would care to accept, something that might be confiscated, for example, which he would gladly give me. This offer, which still meant precisely nothing, gave me the impetus to go back to the Abbé at Toulouse.

"However, I had heard that there was a cleric who lived somewhere along the route I would be travelling, and who was well skilled in natural philosophy. So I called on him, and found him very sympathetic about my difficulties. He advised me most kindly and earnestly not to go on wasting my time over unsystematic experiments, none of which led anywhere, but to read the works of the older philosophers, both to discover what was the true substance and to find out exactly the right method of prosecuting the Work.

"I greatly appreciated his wise counsel, but before putting it into practice I went to see my Abbé at Toulouse, to account for the eight hundred crowns in our common purse and also to share with him what I had received from the King of Navarre!

"Although he was not very happy about what I had to tell, he seemed even less pleased with my determination not to continue our joint work, because he believed me to be a good Artist. Of our eight hundred crowns there now remained only ninety for each of us. I left him and went home, planning that I would go to Paris as soon as possible and stay there unless my reading of the Philosophers made me change my mind. I got there on the morning after All Saints' Day in the year 1546, with enough money to live on. I spent a year studying the works of the great writers, such as *The Assembly of Philosophers*, *The Good Trevisan*, works on Natural Philosophy, and other useful books. As I had no guiding lines to direct me, I did not know which to choose among the many.

"At last I emerged from my seclusion, not in order to meet my old friends the experimenters again, but to get to know some genuine philosophers. Unfortunately my confusion became even greater, because their works were so various and their methods so diverse. Nevertheless, I was stimulated, and I immersed myself in the books of Raymond Lully and in Arnold of Villanova's *Grand Rosaire*. My meditations and my researches continued for another year, and then I came to a decision; but in order to carry it out I had to make some arrangements about my property. I reached home at the beginning of Lent 1549, determined to put into practice all I had learnt. So, after some preliminaries, I bought everything I needed and began work on the day after Easter. All this did not go off without some discomforts and vexation. Every now and then someone would say: 'But what are you going to do? Haven't you wasted enough on this nonsense?' And someone else told me that if I went on buying such quantities of charcoal people would suspect me of being a coiner, of which he had in fact already heard rumours. As I had a degree in Law, they pressed me again to buy a legal practice. But the worst came from my parents, who reproached me bitterly for the life I was leading, and actually threatened to send the police to destroy my equipment.

"You can imagine how tiresome and harassing all this was. The only comfort I had was in my Work, in carrying out the operations which from day to day were becoming more successful, and to which I gave my whole mind. The interruption of all communications by another outbreak of the plague brought me into greater isolation and gave me the opportunity of concentrating wholly on my process and of realising the succession of the three colours that philosophers require before the Work is perfected. I saw them, one after the other, and I made the great attempt in the following year, on Easter Day 1550. Some ordinary quicksilver that I put in a crucible over a fire was in less than an hour turned into pure gold. You may imagine my joy. But I took care not to boast. I thanked God for His grace and I prayed that He would not allow me to use it except to His glory.

"On the following day I went to see my Abbé, faithful to the mutual promise we had made to tell each other of our discoveries. I also went to visit the religious philosopher who had given me such helpful advice. But to my regret I learnt that both of them had died about six months previously. I did not return home, but retired to another place to wait for one of my relatives whom I had put in charge of my affairs. I sent him a power of attorney to sell everything I possessed, whether in goods or buildings; I told him to use the money to pay my debts and to distribute what remained to any who had need of it, and especially to my family, so that they might have at least some share in the great gift that God had bestowed on me. Everyone gossiped about my precipitate departure. The 'clever' ones surmised that I was so overcome by my foolish extravagance that I was selling everything so as to be able to hide my shame in some place where I was not known. My cousin joined me on 1st July, and we went off to find somewhere where we could be untroubled. First we went to Switzerland, to Lausanne, and then decided that we would pass the remainder of our days in peace and quiet in one of the large German cities."

This ends Denis Zachaire's description of his quest in the Great Work. At Lausanne he fell in love with a local girl and married her before going to Germany, still accompanied by the cousin. It was at Cologne in 1556 that he came to a distressing end, murdered by the cousin whom he had trusted. This man strangled him while he was asleep and fled with the young wife, who may possibly have been an accomplice. The affair caused a great stir in Germany at the time, but the culprits were never traced.

Nothing in the life of Denis Zachaire encourages one to believe in the reality of the transmutation; but his claim, following on the recital of the many frustrations he suffered, has a ring of truth about it, and seems to me to carry some weight. Actually, the sale of his property might well have realised enough for him to live quietly, as he puts it, in Lausanne. As regards the murder, the motive may not necessarily have been his cousin's wish to steal the remainder of the Philosopher's Stone. It might equally well have been the result of a guilty passion for Denis's wife, who was probably half the age of her husband.

Apart from the case of Nicholas Flamel, which admits of little doubt, the results of my research would remain negative, were it not that there appears on the horizon, not an alchemist but a puffer, a most extraordinary individual, a criminal, who opens up unsuspected vistas.

5. The Life-Story of a Puffer

Edward Kelly, whose real name was Talbot, was born at Worcester in 1555. His parents wished him to enter the legal profession, and had him taught Law and Old English. As a result, he soon became expert in deciphering ancient scripts and old legal documents, and to his natural talents were added those of a copyist and then of a forger. He freely forged property deeds, which he sold to unscrupulous people at a good price. It was not long before he was found out and brought to justice; the magistrates sentenced him to banishment and ordered his ears to be cropped. The young man therefore left Worcester and changed his name to Kelly. He concealed the amputation of his ears by wearing at all times, day and night, a cap with a chinstrap which, so his contemporaries assured him, gave him a venerable, positively hieratic aspect.

After leaving Worcester, Kelly went to Wales, where a remarkable piece of good luck awaited him. He had stopped at a lonely inn quite by chance, and in the course of conversation had told the landlord that he was an expert in reading ancient languages, especially Gaelic. At this, the man went to fetch an old manuscript that no one in the neighbourhood had been able to decipher. Kelly saw that it had to do with gold and with the transmutation of metals. His interest was aroused and he asked casually where the manuscript had come from. The landlord told him that some years previously a Catholic bishop, who was reported to be very rich, had lived and died in the neighbourhood. He had been buried nearby, in the local churchyard. The landlord, who was a Protestant, had felt no sense of sin in violating the bishop's tomb, hoping to find gold or other treasure. His hope was not fulfilled and he found only the manuscript in question together with two little balls, one of which had unfortunately broken, spilling a small quantity of a very heavy red powder; the other contained a white powder. The landlord brought the white ball, the manuscript, and a pinch of the red powder that he had been able to save from the broken ball, in order to show them to his customer. It had never before occurred to him that his trove could be of interest to anyone.

Edward Kelly, supposing the powder to be an alchemical precipitate, at once offered one pound sterling for the manuscript, the white ball and the remainder of the red powder, earnestly assuring the landlord that these interested him purely as curiosities. The landlord accepted the offer, being only too pleased to be profitably rid of the things. Kelly set about studying the bishop's manuscript, but soon realised that, as his knowledge of chemistry and the Hermetic Art was practically nonexistent, he was incapable of understanding the terms used. He needed help. So he returned to London secretly and wrote to an old acquaintance, who happened to be John Dee, later to become famous as a seer and magician, who astonished the world in the sixteenth century and is to this day a familiar name to anyone interested in the occult sciences. In his letter, Kelly asked John Dee to visit him for the purpose of discussing a matter of great importance.

*

It is worth while digressing for a moment to give some idea of John Dee's life. He was born in London in 1527, and from earliest youth was passionately devoted to the acquisition of knowledge. While at the University of Cambridge at the (then normal) age of fifteen, he used regularly to work eighteen hours a day, sleeping only four hours and keeping the remaining two hours for recreation. An iron constitution helped him to survive this time-table, and he would certainly have been one of the most outstanding scientists of his day in traditional disciplines, if he had not chosen to turn to the study of astrology, alchemy and magic. Despite his youth, he acquired something of a reputation as a student of the occult, and when this reached the ears of the University authorities he was informed that his presence at that seat of learning was no longer required. He therefore retreated to the University of Louvain. There he met a number of people who had known the famous occultist Henry Cornelius Agrippa whose *Ritual of Higher Magic* finds a ready sale to this day. Besides magic, Cornelius Agrippa had also experimented with the Great Work of alchemy, and if he is not mentioned in this book it is because, by his own admission, he never achieved the Philosopher's Stone. He acknowledged this quite frankly in one of his books; on the other hand, he claimed to have raised spirits and to have carried out a number of magical operations successfully. Young John Dee was wildly excited by these stories, and applied himself with ever greater enthusiasm to the study of the Hermetic science and rituals of magic.

In 1551, at the age of twenty-four, he returned to England and was received at the court of Edward VI, to whom he rendered an important service, that was worth an annuity of one hundred crowns to him. It has never been known what this service was, though legends abound. It seems probable, however, that it was something to do with magic, because the reasons for granting the annuity were never made public. His good fortune came to an end with the accession to the throne of Queen Mary. He was accused of conspiring against the life of the Queen by casting spells and, since it was impossible to prove the truth of this, he was thrown into prison on a charge of heresy. He escaped being condemned to the stake by succeeding in persuading that arch-bigot, Archbishop Bonner, that he was perfectly orthodox in matters religious, so he was set at liberty in 1555. As a result, his contemporaries conceived a new respect for his magical gifts: no other power, they thought, could have persuaded so fanatical a bigot as the Archbishop. His run of ill luck ended when Queen Elizabeth came to the throne. He was taken into favour at court and was on many occasions consulted by the Queen. Elizabeth even condescended to visit him at his house in Mortlake, to inspect his museum of curios.

It was in this museum that John Dee, one November evening in 1582, had the vision of an angel, who said that he was Uriel. The Doctor was stunned and terrified, but the angel smilingly presented him with a highly polished black stone, convex in shape, telling John Dee that this stone would enable him to converse with beings on other planes of existence if he gazed at it fixedly. These beings would appear in the surface of the stone and would reveal all the secrets of the future. Dee said later that he had tried and been successful in doing this. There is, by the way, nothing legendary about the stone which, after the magician's death, was acquired by the Earl of Peterborough and then came into the possession of Horace Walpole. It is now in the British Museum.

*

This was the man to whom Edward Kelly showed the manuscript found in the Welsh bishop's tomb. After a brief examination of the text, John Dee thought that the first thing to do was to make certain of the quality of the transmutatory powder and so he took Kelly with him to visit one of his friends, a goldsmith. There he made the experiment on a piece of lead, and it succeeded beyond all expectation: before the astonished eyes of the goldsmith a pound of base metal was transmuted into an equal weight of the finest gold.

Dr. Dee therefore decided to join forces with Edward Kelly, and invited him to share his house. He told him about the angelic visitation, and promised to let him take part in a séance in which he would evoke beings from another world by means of the black stone. The séance took place on 2nd December following, and showed that Kelly was an even better medium than John Dee, for the spirits spoke only to him, while the Doctor stood by to transcribe all that his friend repeated. The record of this extraordinary conversation still exists in manuscript at the British Museum, but unfortunately the text is totally unintelligible. Nevertheless, this episode strengthened the bonds uniting the two men, for Edward Kelly soon became indispensable to Dr. Dee as the link between him and the spirit world.

Not long after this, Albert Laski, a Polish nobleman and Count Palatine, visited the court of Queen Elizabeth. She ordered her favourite, the Earl of Leicester, to show him round London. Count Laski had heard of Dr. Dee's reputation as an alchemist and believed him to possess the secret of transmutation. Actually, since meeting with Kelly, John Dee claimed that the elixir of life had been found in the bishop's tomb. Meanwhile, Laski's expenses were such that his fortune—though immense—no longer sufficed for his extravagant tastes, and he asked Leicester to arrange a meeting for him with the famous occultist. It took place sooner than had been expected, for the three men happened to meet in the Queen's anteroom at the royal Palace. Dee immediately invited the Count to visit him at Mortlake. Actually, he had not enough money to enable him to receive his guest in a suitable manner, and was obliged to appeal to the generosity of the Queen; she sent him twenty pounds by Leicester.

It seems clear that John Dee, who was by nature an honest man, allowed himself to be persuaded by Kelly to play on Count Laski's credulity, so that he might become the Maecenas for their alchemical researches, which still hung fire. They began by telling him about the vision of the angel Uriel, but refused to allow him to witness an evocation, on the pretext that the presence of a stranger would prevent the angel's manifesting. They kept him in suspense for several weeks, stimulating his eagerness to penetrate the spirit world and bringing him more and more under their influence. At last, on 23rd May 1583, a séance was arranged. The report that has come down to us about this makes it impossible to decide whether a supernatural apparition really presented itself or whether Dee and Kelly used some optical or hypnotic illusion. At all events, Laski declared himself to be absolutely satisfied, and thereafter placed unquestioning faith in Dr. Dee's magical powers. Through these, the Count learnt, among other interesting things, that he would become the fortunate possessor of the Philosopher's Stone, that he would wear the Polish crown, and finally that he would achieve immortality. Before these prophecies could be translated into fact, however, it was necessary that the two Englishmen should go to Poland with him, so that they might continue their Hermetic researches. Laski assented to the proposal enthusiastically, and the trio soon set off for central Europe.

After four months' journey they reached Laski's castle, near Cracow. Dee and Kelly had brought their wives and children with them, showing that they were in no hurry to return to England. As soon as they arrived, Laski equipped a laboratory for them and they set to work. Of course, no tangible results were obtained, except to accelerate Laski's ruin as he ran increasingly into debt to satisfy the requirements of the two Puffers. After a time he realised his mistake; but he did not choose to admit it by quarrelling with his guests, so he advised them to go to Prague to continue their work, where they would be near the Emperor Rudolf, to whom he would give them letters of introduction.

Seeing that no more was to be got from Laski, the two friends agreed at once, and by 1685 reached Prague, the capital of Bohemia. Until then, Dr. Dee had never used the remainder of the powder from the bishop's tomb, because he knew himself to be incapable of renewing the supply. But in Prague he could not count on the same liberality that he had enjoyed in London and Cracow, and he had to justify his reputation. He was by this time more than ever swayed by Kelly, who was now the only one honoured by the visits of Uriel. At the "request of the angel"—via Kelly—the Doctor was obliged even to agree to exchanging his wife for Kelly's, who was (need one say?) not nearly such a pretty woman.

Now Edward Kelly publicly performed a whole series of transmutations that dumbfounded the whole city. He became the pet of high society, he was invited to receptions held in his honour where he effectuated transmutations in full view of all and sundry, and distributed the resultant gold or silver to his audience. He went so far as to undertake a transmutation at the house of the imperial Physician, Dr. Thadeusz Hayek: with a single grain of his powder he changed a pound of mercury into gold. Louis Figuier says:

> "This story admits of no doubt whatever. It was reported by authoritative writers and corroborated by trustworthy witnesses, such as Nicholas Barnaud, another doctor who lived in the same house as Hayek, and who himself performed the operation with Kelly's help. A piece of the gold that resulted from this experiment was kept by Hayek's heirs, who were always ready to show it to anyone who was interested."

After this, Edward Kelly was invited to the court of the Emperor Maximilian II of Germany, who was also greatly interested in the Hermetic Art, particularly if it resulted in a golden bonus for him. Kelly did a public transmutation that was so successful that the Emperor conferred the rank of Marshal of Bohemia on him. This sudden access of fortune turned his head and he forgot the wise counsels of John Dee, who had always warned him not to claim to be an Adept, because he was not capable of reproducing the precipitate if his supply ran out. But Kelly behaved as though the supply were inexhaustible, lavishing it on public transmutations and telling anyone who would listen that he was perfectly able to renew his stock of the powder, since he was one of the great Masters of the Hermetic Art.

His bragging brought about his downfall. Jealous of the rapid rise to fortune of a plebeian, the nobles at the court never ceased to urge the Emperor to insist upon his revealing the secret so that the public treasury might be replenished. In the end, the Emperor called Kelly before him and ordered him to manufacture several pounds of the powder. There was nothing the unfortunate man could do but refuse; and so he was imprisoned.

One idea presented itself: Dr. Dee promised the Emperor that he would work with Kelly to produce the powder he demanded. The two men were sent back to Prague and shut up in a laboratory. Unfortunately they failed to create so much as a speck of the Philosopher's Stone. It is said that they invoked the help first of Uriel, and then of devils; but neither the angelic nor the infernal powers appeared to be familiar with the Art of Hermes. From day to day the situation of the two men grew more unpleasant. Kelly went mad with fury and ended by killing one of the warders. Once again he was imprisoned.

For a time he occupied his enforced leisure by writing a treatise on alchemy entitled *The Stone of the Sages*, and sent it to the Emperor, promising to reveal his secret if he were set at liberty. But this promise had no effect on Maximilian II, who had evidently learnt his lesson. Next, Kelly suggested to Dr. Dee that he should go to England and try to interest Queen Elizabeth in his fate, which his friend did. It appears that the Queen did intercede on behalf of her subject, but that she was informed that he was being held for a Common Law crime and could not therefore be returned to her. This, however, is uncertain.

One thing only remained to Kelly—to attempt escape. He tried to do this by tearing his bedclothes into strips and using them as a rope to slide down the side of the fortress. He was a heavy man, and the line broke, so that he fell to the ground and broke two ribs and both legs. He is believed to have died of his injuries in 1597. Dr. Dee was kindly received by the Queen, but an unpleasant surprise awaited him at his home. The mob, who believed him to be a sorcerer and a necromancer, had set fire to his library, burning four thousand rare volumes, and had entirely destroyed his laboratory. He was granted a meagre pension and spent the last few years of his life in poverty at his house in Mortlake, where he died in 1608 at the age of eighty-one.

*

This is a particularly interesting case—a man who, though not himself an Adept, was able to perform numerous metallic transmutations in public by means of what seems to have been a stock of the Hermetic powder. What could actually have been the substance found in the bishop's grave? Applying the nineteenth-century precepts of rationalism, Louis Figuier does not, of course, admit that it might have been the Philosopher's Stone. He says: "Either it was a large quantity of the Philosopher's Stone—or else, to put it more rationally, it was an auriferous compound in which the gold, disguised by some chemical combination, made it possible to reproduce all the marvels attributed to this famous mystery." This is, of course, simply nonsense. Some "auriferous compound" might no doubt have been concealed within the precipitate, but in that case no more gold could have been produced than was initially present. In other words, it could not have been used to transmute to gold a large quantity of any other metal. This point must be made, because all Louis Figuier's objections are biased by his desire to prove that experiments in transmutation were not possible unless some gold was present in the powder, which is impossible from the chemical point of view. If to one pound of mercury is added a pinch of the Philosopher's Stone, and this contains one gram of gold, at the end of the experiment will be found precisely one gram of gold in the pound of mercury, no more and no less. But in Kelly's demonstrations, as in others that we shall be discussing later, it was the whole substance that was transmuted into gold. So the nineteenth-century "scientific" explanation is inadmissible.

Besides, the stories of transmutations effected by Kelly are very

Comment & par quelles figures ilz figni-
fioient laage & les ans du temps.

Orus Apollo (Paris 1543). Depicting the dragon-serpent Ouroboros, symbol of the Great Work, in the light of the Philosophers'
Sun and Moon.

numerous indeed; Figuier's book contains a long list of similar public
demonstrations, and the one that took place at Hayek's house seems
particularly convincing. Yet it must not be forgotten that Kelly was
an impostor and, not to put too fine a point on it, a thorough-going
scoundrel. So it is not impossible that by some sleight of hand he
might have made it appear that he had really transmuted metals

when in fact he had done nothing of the sort. There would seem to be two possibilities: either he might have made some gilt bronze which at that time could have passed for gold, since analysis was much less accurate than it is now; or else it might simply be a case of legerdemain such as conjurors use, by which he might have replaced the base metal by real as it was put into the crucible, though in this latter case it would have been an expensive proceeding because the result was generally distributed to the audience.

I am not, therefore, entirely convinced by the activities of this gentleman. But it does put a second positive mark in the "ayes" column of my enquiry, to add to the one we had from Nicholas Flamel, even though one cannot count it as determinant.

6. The Cosmopolite

At the beginning of the twentieth century it was still thought that the Adept known as the Cosmopolite, author of the remarkable treatise *New Light on Chymistry*, was Michael Sendivogius. But, in view of the study written on him in 1742 by the Abbé Lenglet du Fresnoy, it should have been realised that the Cosmopolite was a Scot, probably named Alexander Seton, who when he died left a small quantity of his alchemical precipitate to this same Sendivogius. The latter appropriated the famous name Cosmopolite, and passed himself off as an Adept, although he was no more than a lucky amateur. His career will be reviewed later in this chapter. But let us first take Seton.

Actually, not a great deal is known about him—not even the date and place of his birth. His nationality only is certain. Lenglet du Fresnoy tells of him:

"Jacques Haussen, a Dutch sea-farer, having been shipwrecked in the German Ocean, was washed up on the coast of Scotland. He was rescued by Alexander Seton, who owned a house and some land along that coast. Seton nursed Haussen back to health and later helped him to return to his own country. Not long after this, in 1602, Seton thought he would like to see something of the world, and crossed over to Holland. He arrived at Enkhuysen, where Jacques Haussen welcomed him hospitably and gratefully. Unfortunately for himself, Seton was anxious to go on to Germany. But before proceeding, he wished to demonstrate his knowledge of the Hermetic Science to Haussen. He therefore transmuted a piece of base metal to gold in his presence. Haussen was so greatly impressed, that he could not resist telling the local doctor, a man named van der Linden. Georges Morhoff, himself a great authority on the art of transmutation, affirms that with his own eyes he saw a piece of gold owned by Jean-Antoine van der Linden, a grandson of the Enkhuysen doctor, who had carefully marked the ingot to say that the transmutation had taken place on 13th March 1602 at four o'clock in the afternoon."

Lenglet du Fresnoy's own researches did not permit of his going further into Seton's history. He says about him:

"We know nothing of his early life, and his story begins with the seventeenth century. He appears before us as a fully adept alchemist and, as we shall see, a Past Master in his Art, by whatever means he may have come by his knowledge. A quality for which he particularly deserves admiration is his disinterestedness. In every place to which the need he felt to make Hermetic propaganda took him, he justified his mission by successes that might in all conscience be regarded as miraculous. He made gold and silver whenever he was asked to do so, and this not for the sake of increasing his own wealth, but so that he might give it to sceptics and thereby dispel their doubts. This indeed is characteristic of most of the Adepts of the time. It appeared to them that alchemy had been evolved, not to pander to men's baser instincts but to be the glory of men of learning and high ideals. They went from place to place, preaching their Science as though it were a religion—that is, never neglecting anything that would demonstrate its truth, though never profaning its mysteries. In a word, it was a sort of apostolic mission carried out by Adepts during a century that bred critics and rationalists—a mission that was always difficult, often dangerous, and in which Alexander Seton was to find martyrdom."

This rather lengthy extract has been quoted because it contains a number of informative ideas on the position of alchemy during the seventeenth century. It is, indeed, shown in a completely different light from that of earlier centuries. In this period, Adepts such as the Cosmopolite, Philalethes or Lascaris are no longer found as isolated Seekers, concerned to carry out the Great Work alone; they are transformed, as it were, into emissaries of the Hermetic Art for the benefit of their fellow-scientists. It is impossible to say why

Adepts of the seventeenth and early eighteenth centuries acted in this way. The fact remains that they devoted themselves to proselytising, which often enough back-fired on them and brought about their downfall.

To return to Seton who, after leaving his friend Haussen, went on to Amsterdam, and thence to Germany by way of Switzerland, where he made the acquaintance of Wolfgang Dienheim, a Professor at Fribourg and a passionate opponent of alchemy. Dienheim has left an astonishing record of a transmutation which the Cosmopolite effected at Bâle in his presence and that of a number of local notabilities.

"In the middle of the summer of 1602," he says, "I was returning to Germany from Rome, and found myself travelling in company with a gentleman of remarkable intellectual gifts. He was short of stature and rather stout, with a high colour, and sanguine temperament, and wore his brown beard trimmed in the French style. He was dressed in a suit of black satin, and was accompanied by one servant only, who was distinguishable from everyone else by his red hair and beard. This gentleman was named Alexander Setonius. He was a native of Molia, a place on a North Sea island. At Zürich, where he collected a letter to Dr. Zwinger, we hired a boat and went on to Bâle by water. When we reached there, my companion said: 'You will remember that during the whole of our journey as well as on board the boat you spent your time attacking alchemy and alchemists. You will also remember that I promised to reply, not by argument but by a philosophical demonstration. I am only waiting for another person, whom I want to convince at the same time as yourself, so that two adversaries of alchemy may dismiss their distrust of the Art.'

"We went to find this other person, whom I knew by sight and who lived not far from our hotel. I learnt afterwards that he was Dr. Jacob Zwinger, whose family includes a number of well-known naturalists. All three of us went to see a man who worked in gold, taking with us some slabs of lead brought by Dr. Zwinger, a crucible that we borrowed from a goldsmith, and some ordinary sulphur which we bought on the way. Setonius did not touch any of these things. He asked for a fire to be lit, ordered the lead and sulphur to be put into the crucible over the fire, the mass to be stirred, and the lid to be put on. Meanwhile he chatted with us. At the end of a quarter of an hour he said: 'Throw this bit of paper into the molten lead, but make sure that it goes right into the middle, and that none falls into the fire.' In the paper was a heavy sort of lemon-yellow powder—but you needed good eyesight to see it. Although we were as doubting as St. Thomas himself, we did everything he told us. After the mass had been heated for another quarter of an hour and stirred continuously with little iron rods, the goldsmith was told to extinguish the fire by pouring water over it. We found not a vestige of lead remaining, only the finest gold which, in the opinion of the goldsmith, was of a quality better even than the excellent Hungarian and Arabian gold. It weighed exactly the same as the lead we had put in originally. We were struck dumb with amazement, and hardly dared to believe our eyes. Setonius teased us: 'Now,' he said, 'what about your cynicism? You have seen the truth of the matter, and that is mightier than all—even than your subtleties!' Then he had a piece of the gold cut off and gave it to Zwinger as a memento. I too was given a piece weighing about as much as four ducats, and I have always kept it in remembrance of that day.

"You may laugh at what I have written, but I am still living and am always prepared to testify to the truth of what I saw. Zwinger, too, is alive, and he will not hesitate to second my words. Setonius and his servant also remain on this earth, the former is in Germany and the latter in England. (*Note:* Actually Seton was dead at the time this was written, but Sendivogius had by then adopted the Cosmopolite's alias, which explains Professor Dienheim's mistake.) I could even give their exact addresses, but this might cause them to be pestered by enquiries from people anxious to know how this great man has fared—this saint, this demi-god."

Jacob Zwinger, the second witness to the demonstration, was a doctor and a Professor at Bâle, who has left a name famous in the history of German medicine. He was the ideal witness, of irreproachable character and in every sense trustworthy. He entirely confirmed

Professor Dienheim's statement in a letter to Emmanuel König, another Professor at Bâle, who published it among some *Ephemerides*. This letter says definitely that, before leaving the city, the Cosmopolite performed another transmutation at the house of André Bletz, a goldsmith, where he transmuted several ounces of lead into gold, a number of witnesses being present. No chicanery, such as that suggested in the case of Edward Kelly, could possibly be suspected on this occasion. The lead was brought by one of the witnesses, the equipment was supplied by the goldsmith, and Seton personally touched nothing. Clearly, no trickery was possible in these conditions. One is therefore bound to concede that here we have the first historically verified account of the transmutation of a metal. But of course one swallow does not make a summer.

Karl-Christoph Schmieder, a learned German, takes the story a stage further. In one chapter of his *Geschichte der Alchemie* (History of Alchemy) he follows the Cosmopolite to Strasbourg during the summer of 1603, into the shop of the German goldsmith Gustenhover. The Adept asked if he might use a crucible and the furnace for a particular piece of work. The man agreed, and when the Cosmopolite departed later he left him a small quantity of red powder as a reward.

The goldsmith immediately called together some of his friends and neighbours to watch him test the powder he had been given. The result was entirely convincing: a pound of lead was turned into gold. As a consequence, Gustenhover foolishly claimed to be an Adept and to have developed the Philosopher's Stone himself. After all, weren't they all friends together? But, as Schmieder said, every friend had a neighbour, and every neighbour a friend, and soon the whole town was ringing with the news: "Gustenhover is making gold!"

The Town Council of Strasbourg, hearing the rumour, sent three of its members to enquire into it. Gustenhover gave each of them a grain or two of the red powder, and made them try the experiment for themselves then and there. Herr Glaser, one of the Councillors, went to Paris and showed a piece of this Hermetic gold to Dr. Jacob Heilmann, who has left a report of the incident.

Gustenhover's renown was enormously increased when the three experiments came off successfully, and it travelled as far as Prague, reaching the ears of the Emperor Rudolf II who, as we know, was interested in the Hermetic Art. This potentate immediately sent three members of his police force to the pretended Adept, with orders to attach his person. Faced by the Emperor, the unhappy Gustenhover collapsed and was obliged to admit that he had not prepared the miraculous powder himself, and that he had no idea whatever how to do it. But Rudolf saw this simply as a disguised refusal and ordered him to be imprisoned until he should come to a more coöperative frame of mind. In the hope of saving himself, Gustenhover made the Emperor a present of the remainder of his powder. Rudolf tested it successfully; but, instead of satisfying him, this triumph only stimulated his cupidity, and he called upon the goldsmith to renew the supply immediately. Gustenhover was appalled and attempted flight, but was soon caught by the imperial police and was shut up in the White Tower at Prague, where he remained a prisoner for the rest of his life.

The Cosmopolite himself had gone to Germany, where he was careful to preserve his anonymity by using a variety of aliases. He stayed for a few days at Frankfort-on-the-Main, where he made friends with a businessman named Koch, who later wrote to Theobald de Hogelande, the historian, telling him that he had had the opportunity of watching the Cosmopolite carrying out a transmutation, and that he had kept a piece of the resultant gold:

"For some time an Adept had been living at Offenbach (near Frankfort), and had often bought things from me in the name of a French Count. Before leaving here, he wished to show me the art of transmuting metals. He did not put a hand to the work himself, but allowed me to do everything. He gave me a reddish-grey powder, weighing about three grains. I dropped it into two half-ounces of quicksilver in a crucible. Then I filled the crucible about half-way up with potash, and we put it over a gentle heat. After this I filled the furnace with charcoal, so that the crucible was entirely embedded in a very hot fire; I left it there for about half an hour. When the crucible was red hot, he told me to throw a little piece of yellow wax into it. A few minutes later, I cooled the crucible and broke it open. At the bottom I found a small piece of gold that weighed fifty-four ounces three grains. It was melted in my presence and submitted to an assay; twenty-three carats fifteen grains of gold resulted, together with six of silver— both of an exceptionally brilliant colour. I had a stud made for my shirt with part of the gold. It looks to me as though mercury were not essential to the operation."

After Frankfort the Cosmopolite went to Cologne, and spent some time there. This town had at one time enjoyed considerable fame from the point of view of alchemy, by reason of the fact that Albertus Magnus and later Denis Zachaire had lived there. He enquired discreetly about any persons of quality who might be interested in alchemy, partly in the hope of finding somewhere to live but also in order to gather information about any who might be worthy of benefiting by a demonstration of the Hermetic Art. Eventually, he took up residence at the house of a distiller named Anton Bordemann, who was understood to be interested in it. But Seton soon discovered that his work was held of little account in the ancient city of Cologne. Not only scientists and doctors, but also the mass of the people took a low view of the Hermetic Art—it was worth a laugh at best. The Cosmopolite had discovered that the highest scientific authority in the city was Meister Georg, a surgeon, who was a declared opponent of alchemy. A frontal attack on him would have been of no use, because news of Seton's fame had not reached him, and Georg would certainly not have agreed to try the effect of the Cosmopolite's powder. A more subtle method of making publicity was therefore indicated. On the 5th August 1633 Seton went to an apothecary's shop and asked to see some lapis lazuli. He pretended that none of the pieces he saw was good enough, and the shopkeeper promised to show him some better ones on the following day. While waiting, he had got into conversation about the Hermetic Art with an ecclesiastic and with another apothecary who happened to be in the shop. They were both making fun of alchemy and the folly of Adepts. When the Cosmopolite, without revealing his identity, told them that to his certain knowledge transmutations had been effected and that there was no reason to doubt them, he was shouted down with gales of laughter.

125

On his return to the shop the next morning, he bought some of the lapis lazuli he was shown and then asked for some glass of antimony. He professed to be dubious about the quality of what he was offered and proposed that it should be tested in a hot fire. The apothecary agreed readily and sent his young son to accompany the Cosmopolite to a neighbouring goldsmith, Johann Lohndorf. The antimony-glass was put into a crucible under which a fire was lighted. Meanwhile, the Cosmopolite had brought a little box out of his pocket with some reddish powder in it. He took a pinch of the powder and gave it to the goldsmith, telling him to wrap it in a scrap of paper and throw it into the melted substance. The goldsmith seemed surprised at the odd request, but shrugged his shoulders and did as he was asked. A quarter of an hour later to his immense astonishment, he found a small nugget of gold in the crucible instead of antimony. Besides the goldsmith, the apothecary's son, two men from the workshop and a neighbour who had turned up by chance, were present at the operation. They were all dumbfounded, more especially since the visitor had not himself touched anything. However, the reputation of alchemy was so low in the city that Lohndorf refused to admit the evidence of his senses and insisted that his guest should perform another transmutation immediately. The Cosmopolite was happy to agree to conditions imposed by the goldsmith, who chose to use lead this time instead of antimony. What is more without letting the Adept see, he introduced a piece of zinc into the melting pot with the lead, because he had an idea that the only metals alchemists could use for transmutation were mercury, lead and antimony. The mixture of lead and antimony was duly melted, then the Cosmopolite handed the goldsmith another pinch of powder, which again was wrapped in paper and thrown into the crucible. When the whole thing had cooled, Lohndorf was obliged to admit that the entire mass of metal had been turned into gold.

News of the marvel was soon spread abroad throughout the city, and Anton Bordemann, at whose house the Adept was living, became famous overnight. But this did not induce Meister Georg to watch a demonstration. Alexander Seton, therefore, asked for an interview with him, for the purpose of discussing surgery and anatomy. In the course of this meeting at which, incidentally, he proved that he had considerable medical knowledge, the Cosmopolite averred that he knew of a means of cutting away proud flesh without damaging the nerves. The surgeon asked with some curiosity to be shown the procedure. "Nothing easier!" replied the Adept. "Just let me have some lead, a little sulphur and a melting pot." He also asked for a heating apparatus with a bellows. Meister Georg's servants quickly produced the things he had asked for, all except the furnace. So it was decided to repair to a neighbouring goldsmith, Master Hans von Kempen, to carry out the operation.

In the absence of the goldsmith, his son received the visitors, who included Meister Georg and his servants carrying the ingredients, accompanied by the stranger. While one of the servants was putting the sulphur and lead into a crucible, the Cosmopolite got into conversation with four of the goldsmith's workmen, who were busy with some iron. He suggested that he might turn the iron into steel for them. The bewildered workpeople offered him another crucible, but the Adept refused to touch it himself and simply told them what to do. So then the two operations were in progress at the same time—one by Meister Georg's servants under his direction, and the other by the goldsmith's workers, supervised by his son. The Cosmopolite himself stood aside, touching nothing. When the substances in the two crucibles reached melting point, the Cosmopolite took a pinch of red powder from a box and, after mixing it in a lump of wax, made two little balls of it, one of which he gave to the surgeon and the other to the goldsmith's son, telling them to drop them into the crucibles. After a very short time one of Meister Georg's servants shouted: "The lead's turned to gold!" and simultaneously one of the workmen: "It isn't steel—it's GOLD!!" The two gold nuggets were cut at once to make sure that the original base metals had indeed been entirely transmuted. Which they had. The goldsmith's wife, who was accustomed to help her husband in assaying precious metals, was called by her son and tested the ingots in the usual way. She found that they were of excellent quality and offered to buy them for eight Thalers. The Cosmopolite, seeing that a crowd was gathering, intimated to Meister Georg that they had better get away. Looking thoroughly embarrassed, he followed the Adept out into the street and said:

—"So that was what you wanted to show me!"

—"Of course," said the Cosmopolite. "My host told me that you were a convinced opponent of alchemy, and I wanted to persuade you to the contrary by an irrefutable proof. I have done the same in Rotterdam, in Amsterdam, in Frankfort, Strasbourg and Bâle."

—"But, my dear Sir, surely it is very rash of you to do this so openly. If ever any of the Princes get to hear about it, they will make enquiries and you will be held prisoner to force you to give up your secret."

—"I am well aware of that," said Seton, "but we are in Cologne which is a free city, where I have nothing to fear from the mighty. And in any case, even if I were arrested, I would suffer a thousand deaths before I would reveal the mystery."

After a moment's silence, the Cosmopolite resumed:

—"If I am asked for proof of my Art, I will give it to anyone who asks. And if they want me to make large quantities of gold, I will still agree. I would gladly make fifty or sixty thousand ducats' worth."

From that day on, Meister Georg was utterly convinced of the reality of metallic transmutation and, when some of his friends suggested that he must have been tricked by a clever charlatan, he said: "What I have seen, I have seen. What Master von Kempen's men did themselves in the presence of witnesses was not a dream. The gold, of which they can still show you a piece, is not a chimera. I shall continue to believe my eyes rather than the nonsense you talk!"

Before leaving Cologne, the Cosmopolite did another public transmutation watched by Anton Bordemann, who asked him why he sometimes used sulphur and at other times mercury. Seton replied: "I do so in order to show that all metals, whatever they may be, can be brought to perfection. But never forget, my friend, that I am forbidden to reveal the really important part of the Work."

Alexander Seton next went to Hamburg where, as Georges Morhoff tells us, he again performed some successful transmutations. Then he went on to Munich; but here, contrary to his usual custom, he undertook no alchemical work. In fact, he met a girl there, with whom he fell in love. Her father, a substantial citizen, refused his consent to their engagement—so they eloped. The girl is said to have been very pretty and, once beyond the pursuit of her family, they were married, after which the couple continued their peregrinations together. In the autumn of 1603, he is heard of at Crossen, where the Duke of Saxony was living at the time. Hearing of the triumphs of the Cosmopolite, he invited him to perform a transmutation at the court. Seton, who appears to have been wholly preoccupied with his young wife, sent his servant to carry out the operation. It was done before the whole court, and was a complete success. The historian Guldenfalk tells that the gold obtained on the occasion stood up to all the tests to which it was submitted and proved to be of very high quality. Hamilton, the Cosmopolite's servant, who had hitherto accompanied him in all his wanderings, decided after this to leave him and return home. He may not have got on well with Seton's wife; or, perhaps more probably, he felt that his master's position was likely to become dangerous because, being totally absorbed in his love, he omitted to take precautions to protect himself against the cupidity of the great.

In fact, this is what happened to the unfortunate Adept. The Elector of Saxony, Christian II, was a cruel and avaricious young man. Up to that time, he had always thought that alchemical research was mere folly, not worth considering. But the transmutation carried out by the Cosmopolite's servant had completely changed his views. He invited Seton to come to his court and affected to be friendly disposed to him. But it was not simply a pinch or two of the philosophic powder that Christian hoped for—he wanted the secret of its preparation, and was quite determined to get it by fair means or foul.

At this point the story of the Cosmopolite will be interrupted, because the tragic end to his adventures is told in the document which follows. It describes the first appearance of Michael Sendivogius, and is more impressive in its stark factualness than any romanticised version could be.

Michael Sendivogius

This man brings us to the unusual story of a Puffer who was believed, not only by his contemporaries but also by posterity, to be one of the greatest Adepts in the Hermetic Art. Even today it is not always possible to disentangle his own writings from among the many that are attributed to the Cosmopolite, whose name he adopted.

A document, dated only five years after his death—which took place in 1646—will give some idea of how this paradoxical situation arose.

The following is an extract from the *Treasury of Gallic and French Researches and Antiquities* by Pierre Borel (1655), in the shape of a letter written to him by M. Desnoyers, secretary to the Princess Marie of Gonzaga, Queen of Poland and wife of King Ladislas.

"Dated from Warsaw, 12th June 1651.
"Sir,

Before leaving Paris, I undertook to do my utmost to collect the entire works of the Cosmopolite. I have made the fullest enquiries and, as far as I can discover, he wrote only the *Book of Twelve Treatises*, signed *The Cosmopolite*. But you will see from the rest of this letter that I found out a great deal about him, which I am now passing on to you.

"*The Cosmopolite* was an Englishman who, while he was in the Duke of Saxony's estates, scattered a powder he possessed over some metals which were thereupon converted to pure gold. One of those who witnessed the operation told the Duke of Saxony about it, and he, fearing lest such a man should escape him, immediately despatched members of his police force to the house where he was living with his wife, with orders to arrest him and bring him to the court. When the Cosmopolite arrived, the Prince asked if he were the man who had changed base metals into gold; he admitted it, for there had been too many witnesses to make denial possible. He tried to be evasive about it, but the Elector refused to listen to any arguments, and proceeded to threats and then to direct action. The Cosmopolite (I call him by this name because I was unable to discover his real name) was a Catholic who, finding himself in such a plight through his own fault, determined that he would suffer any torture rather than give so powerful a weapon into the hands of a heretic, and prayed that God would grant him the strength to carry out his resolve. The Duke, seeing that nothing was to be gained by kindness, condemned him to torture, to which he submitted with great fortitude, never so much as giving any hope that he would reveal his secrets. When he had recovered, it was begun all over again, and torture was applied many times over, until his body was torn and broken, fire being employed even on his dislocated limbs. But he never told anything of what the Duke wished to know.

"Michael Sendivogius, whom a Polish author accidentally listed among the Polish nobility, was a Moravian, born in Moravia but living in Cracow. He happened to be staying near where the Cosmopolite was incarcerated and, knowing a good deal about chemistry, he was anxious to get in touch with this man. In order to do so, he became an habitué of the Elector's court and made friends with many of the people there. Finally he managed to gain admission to the prison, and saw the Cosmopolite. He discussed chemistry with him in casual fashion. And, as he was most anxious to discover the real secret, he became sufficiently intimate with him after several visits to ask surreptitiously what he would give if means were found to set him free. The unfortunate man replied that he would give him enough to live on in comfort with his family for the whole of his life. Sendivogius, having this promise, soon afterwards took leave of his friends at court, pretending that some business he had been engaged upon was finished, and promising to come and see them again another time. He went to Cracow, sold a house that he owned there, and then returned to Saxony. Here he entertained his friends on the proceeds of the sale, and through them also the Cosmopolite's guards. And one evening when he had got them all thoroughly drunk, he went to the prison in a little carriage such as was used in that part of the country, and fetched the Cosmopolite, whom he had to carry out, because by now he was too weak even to walk. He insisted on going round by way of the house where his wife was living, because he wanted to take her with him; and when she came out he sent her back to find some of the powder that he had hidden, after which she made all speed to get into the coach. They set off at once and travelled throughout the night, taking the shortest possible route to leave the Elector's country. They reached Poland without adventure and, as soon as they were in Cracow, Sendivogius reminded the Cosmopolite of his undertaking, in fulfilment of which the latter gave him an ounce of the powder. Sendivogius asked him for the secret of its manufacture, to which the Cosmopolite replied, showing him the terrible condition to which his body was reduced, that since he had suffered every possible cruelty in order not to reveal it, he must not be surprised if he did not tell it now, and that he believed he would be committing a mortal sin if he were to reveal the great secret for which he had worked and prayed to God. This was all that Sendivogius could get from him. The Cosmopolite died soon afterwards, saying that if he had had an ordinary, natural illness the powder would have cured him; but that his body, weak and enfeebled by torture, with nerves cut and drawn, could be recovered by no means whatsoever.

"After his death Sendivogius thought that the wife might know something of her husband's secret, so he married her in the hope of getting it out of her. But he found that she was completely ignorant on the subject, and could do no more than give him the book entitled *The Twelve Treatises of The Cosmopolite*, containing the dialogue between Mercury and the Alchemist. Sendivogius interpreted this in his own fashion and began to work on it, hoping to increase his supply of the powder, the principal ingredient he used being ordinary mercury; but since he was not working with the proper substance he had no success. He tried again by other means, but always uselessly. Then he went to Prague to see the Emperor Rudolf and performed a transmutation before him or rather, he made the Emperor do it himself, giving him the necessary powder; in memory of the event, the Emperor had a marble plaque set into the wall of the room where the experiment was conducted, with the following words engraved on it: *Faciat hoc quispiam alius quod fecit Sendivogius Polonus*. And this marble tablet is to be seen to this day. Having given the Emperor this proof, he seems to have told him the truth of the matter, but on returning to Moravia he was arrested by a local nobleman who had watched the procedure, and was made a prisoner in the belief that he knew the secret. The story of what had happened while he was with the Emperor had lost nothing in the telling, quite apart from the fact that he really was a learned man. Sendivogius, fearing that the same fate as the Cosmopolite's would overtake him, found some means of obtaining a file, and cut through one of the bars on the window of his cell. Then he made a rope of all his clothes and escaped stark naked. He accused his captor to the Emperor, who imposed a large fine and made him give a whole village to Sendivogius, one of whose daughters later had it as a marriage dowry.

"On his return to Poland, Sendivogius protested to Wolski, the Grand Marshal of the Kingdom, that if he had had the means to do the Work he could have made a similar powder. M. Wolski, though a great boaster himself, believed him. But in order to explain how Sendivogius became a poor man, it will be necessary to go back a little way in the story, and to tell you that while the powder lasted he had lived merrily, being by nature something of a voluptuary. He lost part of the powder in trying to increase it, and wasted more in doing transmutations. A Jew who used to sell what he made is still living in Cracow. At last, seeing that he had practically none of it left, he decided to rectify some spirits of wine and put the remainder of the powder into this. He used the result as a medicine, putting all the other doctors in the town to shame by the marvellous cures he effected with it. It was in some of this same liquid that he turned a medal I have into gold, after heating it. The transmutation was performed before Sigismond III, whom Sendivogius also cured of a distressing illness with the same elixir. So, in one way and another, Sendivogius used up all the powder and the elixir, and that was why he told Marshal Wolski that he had not the means to carry on the Work, although he knew the secret. Wolski, upon this assurance, gave him 6,000 francs. He spent them, but produced no result.

"The Grand Marshal, finding himself defrauded of 6,000 francs, told Sendivogius that he was a rogue and that if he wished he could have him hanged; but that he would pardon him if he found some means of returning the money. Sendivogius had a considerable reputation as a scientist, and was approached by M. Mniszok, of the Palatinate of Sandomire, who also gave him 6,000 francs to carry on the Work. Of these he handed over 3,000 to the Marshal and used the rest for his experiments. Finally, having

133

nothing left, he took to charlatanry. He carefully soldered a gold piece to a silver one, stamped it as money, and then covered the whole thing with mercury. Then he pretended that he still had some of the elixir left, heated this coin over a fire, so that the mercury melted away. He coloured the gold part red, and made believe to have transmuted it. In this way he always kept up some sort of reputation among ignorant people, to whom he sold the coins for more than they had cost. Those who were more clear-sighted soon realised that he was not as knowledgeable as he would like them to believe.

"Having worked unavailingly on the Cosmopolite's memoirs, he proposed publishing the book to see if anyone could find out more from it than he was able to, and who would tell him what he discovered. In the hope that it would be thought to be his own work, he introduced into it a certain number of words that he felt might persuade readers that he was the author, so that they should not hesitate to communicate with him about it. But he had not quite the effrontery to sign his name to it openly, so he made an anagram of it: *Autore me qui* DIVI LESCHI GENUS AMO . . . (I am the author, who love the sacred race of the Lesch, who founded the Polish Kingdom.)"

Most of the rest of this letter is taken up by a list of texts, some of which M. Desnoyers attributes to the Cosmopolite and others to Sendivogius, which need not particularly concern us here. The letter ends with a note giving the date of the pretended Cosmopolite's death: "Sendivogius died during the year we arrived in Poland, that is in 1646, destitute, in poor health, and at a great age."

The personal adventures of Michael Sendivogius are interesting because as in the case of Edward Kelly, they show that the Philosopher's Stone retains its transmutatory power no matter who the lucky possessor may be, but that only a true Adept is able to create it. Much more than in the case of Edward Kelly, where some doubt might well be felt, here we know quite certainly the value of the Cosmopolite's powder.

One question remains open in the present case: did Sendivogius himself become an Adept in the long run? Personally, I do not think he did; I consider him to have been a fortunate Puffer. On the other hand, Eugène Canseliet, the contemporary Adept, who has made a close study of his life, believes that Sendivogius must have succeeded in interpreting the Cosmopolite's text, and have become a real Adept. As he died at the age of eighty, and we know very little about his last years, this is not wholly out of the question. In any case it adds nothing to the transmutations that he most certainly effected in public—and which therefore give another "aye" for my historical enquiry.

7. Transmutations Carried out by Scientists

So far we have been hearing about transmutations achieved by either Adepts or Puffers; but from a scientific angle it would seem more interesting, as well as more convincing, to be able to present instances in which they were carried out by well-known scientists of their day. Such cases do exist, and they are being grouped together in this chapter, although they sometimes lived at dates comparatively far apart.

The cases have a number of characteristics in common: in every instance the scientists in question started by being violently antagonistic to alchemy; the Adepts who contacted them remained strictly anonymous and said that they were acting solely "in the interests of science"; the transmutations were carried out by the scientists themselves, generally before witnesses; the tests to which the resultant gold was subjected were made by the foremost experts of the day and with very special care. This will show the interest for our particular enquiry of the accounts which follow and which may, indeed, be considered as quite determinant.

The first witness will be Jean-Baptiste van Helmont, a Belgian, born in Brussels in 1577. He was a physician and a chemist, and made one of the most important of scientific discoveries—that of gas. He first observed the presence of carbonic acid, and by deduction argued that some new chemical substance was involved. In effect he says: "Here is something that cannot be contained in a vessel nor reduced to a fixed volume. I shall give it a new name: gas." He also discovered the presence of sulphuretted hydrogen in the large human intestine; he observed that an acid fluid was secreted in the stomach; he prepared hydrochloric acid, ammonium acetate, and various sulphuric compounds. It would be hard to find a more reliable witness.

Louis Figuier, despite his constant endeavour to prove that transmutations did *not* take place, felt obliged to write:

"Hermetic Philosophers have always confidently quoted the testimony of van Helmont to support their claim to the truth of transmutations in general. It would certainly be difficult to find a more impressive and more trustworthy authority than that of the illustrious doctor-chemist, whose fame as a scientist was equalled only by his reputation as an honest man. The circumstances in which transmutations were operated were strange enough in themselves, and it is understandable that even van Helmont was prompted to proclaim the truth of the alchemical principles after the remarkable operation he was enabled to perform."

In 1618, while he was working in his laboratory at Vilvorde, van Helmont was visited by an unknown individual who was anxious, he said, to discuss a matter of interest to them both. Van Helmont thought at first that the visitor was a fellow-doctor who wanted to raise some medical point, but the man began immediately to speak of the Hermetic Art. Van Helmont stopped him at once, saying that he considered alchemy to be a superstition with no scientific basis, and that he was not interested in talking about it. The stranger said:

—"I quite understand that you do not wish to discuss it, Sir, but can you honestly say that you would not be interested in seeing it?"

With some surprise the scientist asked what exactly he meant by "seeing" it. To which his companion replied:

—"I am not talking nonsense when I tell you that the Philosopher's Stone does exist and that it possesses transmutatory powers. I am quite aware that you do not believe me, but if I were to give you a fragment of the Stone and let you perform the operation yourself, would you refuse?"

Van Helmont had by now decided that he was dealing with either a lunatic or a charlatan and said that he would be very willing to experiment with a piece of the Stone, as long as he was allowed to do the whole thing himself and in conditions chosen by himself. He expected to discourage the visitor by this, but far from it. The stranger dropped a few grains of powder on to a sheet of paper that lay on the table. Van Helmont described it in these words: "I saw and handled the Philosopher's Stone. It was a saffron-coloured powder, very heavy, and it glittered like splinters of glass."

Having done this, the unknown took his leave; and when van Helmont asked whether he proposed returning to hear the result of the experiment, the man replied that that would be unnecessary because he knew it would be successful. In seeing him off, van Helmont asked why he had wanted him of all people to make the experiment; the answer was that he wanted "to convince an illustrious scientist, whose work is an honour to his country".

Moved by these words, van Helmont decided to make the experiment. He sent his laboratory assistants to fetch a crucible and put eight ounces of mercury into it. When the metal had melted, he added a pinch of the substance given him by the unknown, first wrapping it in paper as his visitor had instructed him. Then he put a lid on the crucible and waited for a quarter of an hour. At the end of this time, he threw water over the crucible, so as to cool it abruptly, and then broke it open: in the bottom he found a lump of gold, of exactly the same weight as the original piece of mercury.

This is not an imaginary story—van Helmont wrote it himself and published it in his own name, guaranteeing the truth of what he said, under the title *The Garden of Medicine*. One is bound to admire the courage he showed, as well as his scientific integrity in publicly admitting his error and in proclaiming that he was thenceforward convinced of the truth of alchemy. In memory of the experience he named one of his sons Mercurius, and this boy in his turn grew up to be an ardent champion of alchemy, later actually converting the philosopher Leibnitz. Louis Figuier has this to say: "Van Helmont, the greatest chemist of his day, was difficult to deceive. He was incapable of imposture himself and had nothing to gain by lying about the affair. In view of the fact, finally, that the experiment was carried out in the absence of the alchemist, it is hard to suspect any fraud. Van Helmont was so thoroughly deluded by it, that ever after that day he was an avowed supporter of alchemy." The use of the word "deluded" by Figuier has its humour, for he offers no reasonable suggestion of any possible trickery. In other words, there's none so deaf as those who won't hear!

*

We now pass on to the year 1666 and to the home of Helvetius, physician-in-ordinary to the Prince of Orange. Johann Friedrich Schweitzer (Helvetius being, of course, the Latinised form of his name) was born in 1625 in the Duchy of Anhalt. He rose rapidly to fame as a doctor, and the Prince of Orange appointed him as his personal medical attendant.

Helvetius was an outspoken opponent of the Hermetic Art, and he carried on a violent altercation with Sir Kenelm Digby who appeared at the Prince's court with what he called a "sympathetic powder", that he claimed as a cure for all diseases. Helvetius went so far as to publish a pamphlet directed against him, that was soon being read all over The Hague.

On 27th September 1666 an anonymous person asked to see Helvetius, just as happened in the case of van Helmont. Helvetius described him as a little man, of dignified bearing, and aged about forty. The stranger began by complimenting him on his latest book, *The Pyrotechnic Art*, and then passed rapidly on to his castigation of Digby. After agreeing with the physician in his condemnation of the "magic powder", the stranger asked if he believed the existence of a universal medicine, capable of curing all illnesses, to be impossible. Helvetius replied that he knew alchemists claimed to possess a medicine of that description, which he believed they called "drinkable gold", but he thought it was only an illusion—though he admitted that it was every doctor's dream to discover such a substance. He then asked the stranger if he were himself a doctor. The man passed off the question, and said he was only a poor metal worker who had heard from a friend that it was not impossible to extract certain medicines from metals. The conversation continued along these lines, each doing his best to make the other man talk, while saying nothing himself. At last the stranger appeared to make up his mind, and asked Helvetius whether he would recognise the Philosopher's Stone if he saw it.

—"I have read," replied Helvetius, "a number of treatises by famous Adepts such as Paracelsus, Basil Valentine, the Cosmopolite and also the story of van Helmont. But I would not claim to recognise the philosophic matter if I were shown it."

The stranger then drew from his breast pocket a small ivory box, opened it, and showed Helvetius that it contained a powder the colour of pale sulphur.

—"You see this powder," he said, "well, Sir, there is enough of the Philosopher's Stone here to transmute forty thousand pounds of lead to gold."

He allowed the doctor to hold the box and to touch the powder with the tip of his finger, telling him as he did so of its wonderful curative properties. Then he returned the box to his breast pocket. Helvetius asked whether he would give him a few grains of the powder, so that he might test it; but the stranger refused, saying that he was not permitted to do so. But, as he asked if they could go to a room where they would not be overlooked, Helvetius hoped this meant that he was about to be given a fragment of the Stone. His hope was in vain, because all the stranger wanted was to show him some gold medals in his pocket. Helvetius was able to handle them and examine them closely, and he observed that the gold of which they were made was incomparably superior to anything he had seen before. When Helvetius pressed the question, the stranger refused to admit that he had himself made the Hermetic gold and said that the buttons had been a present from a foreign friend. Then he told Helvetius of a transmutation he had seen performed by the hypothetical friend, and also said that this Adept used a dilution of the powder to keep himself in good health.

Helvetius pretended to be convinced, but nevertheless said that only a demonstration would finally convert him. The visitor refused, still quoting a superior authority. Eventually he said that he would go and ask permission of this Adept, and if he agreed he would return in three weeks' time and operate a transmutation before the doctor's eyes. Helvetius saw him off, feeling convinced that he would never see the man again, and that he had been wasting his time on a charlatan.

Nevertheless, three weeks later, the stranger once more knocked at Helvetius' door. This time too he appeared to be in no hurry to perform a transmutation, but only to engage Helvetius in conversation on philosophic subjects. The doctor, however, always brought him back to the original theme, and as an added inducement asked the man to sup with him; but the stranger persisted in refusal.

141

Helvetius himself describes what happened, in his book *Vitulus Aureus*. The following extract was translated from the Latin by Bernard Husson and published in No. 59 of the journal *Initiation and Science*:

"I asked him to give me a little of his precipitate, if only enough to transmute four grains of lead to gold. He appeared to yield to my importunities and gave me a piece about the size of a turnip seed, saying:

—"Very well. With this, I am giving you the greatest treasure in the world, that even kings and princes have no more than looked at—and not many of them!

"I objected: But Sir, this minute speck will hardly be enough to transmute four grains of lead?

"He replied: Give it back to me.

"And while I thought he was going to give me a larger amount, he cut it in two with his fingernail, threw one piece into the fire and, having wrapped the other half in some red paper, handed it to me saying: This will still be plenty.

"In startled embarrassment, I asked:

—"But Sir, what does this mean? I was doubtful before, but now it looks to be absolutely impossible for it to transmute four grains of lead.

"He replied:

—"I am telling you the truth.

"Then I thanked him warmly and enclosed my diminutive but highly concentrated treasure in a small box, saying that I would make the experiment on the following day and would not tell anyone what the result was.

"No, no, he said, we must publish to all those who are ignorant of the Art whatever manifests the glory of Almighty God, so that they may live as theosophers and not perish as sophists."

At this point, Helvetius confessed to his visitor that during their first meeting he had slipped a few grains of the powder under a fingernail, and had recovered them after the stranger had left. Then, he continued, he had melted some lead in a crucible and had dropped the stolen scraps into it. No transmutation had taken place—all that remained in the crucible was the lead, with a slight admixture of some vitrified substance. The stranger laughed, without showing any resentment over the theft, and explained that an indispensable precaution must be observed if a transmutation were to succeed— the powder must be wrapped either in a lump of wax or in a piece of paper, so as to protect it from the fumes rising from the lead or other metal, which would otherwise take from it all transmutatory power. He added that he was in a hurry because he had another visit to make, so that he would be unable to witness Helvetius' experiment, but that he could come back on the morrow if the doctor cared to wait until then.

Helvetius agreed at once and saw his visitor off the premises, all the while asking him questions about the length of time it took to produce the Stone, how much it cost to become a Master, and the nature of the prime substance and of philosophic mercury. The stranger laughed again, and replied that he could not explain the whole Hermetic Art in a few moments; but he went so far as to say that the Work was not very costly to carry out and need not involve serious delays. As regards the prime substance, he said that it was extracted from minerals; and that philosophic mercury was a certain salt that had creative virtue and would dissolve minerals. He concluded by telling Helvetius that none of the materials required for the Work was costly and that if it were done by the short way the whole thing could be completed in four days. When Helvetius exclaimed in surprise, he added that there were two methods of carrying it out and that not all philosophers used the same; but that in any case Helvetius should not attempt the Great Work yet, because his knowledge was far from adequate, and he would succeed only in losing time and money. With these rather discouraging words he left, promising to return on the next day—a promise which, in the event, he was not to keep.

Helvetius was inclined to await the return of the unknown Artist, but his wife, to whom he had told the whole story, was too impatient and gave her husband no peace till he agreed to make the attempt. He was not in the least convinced that the operation would be a success, for he suspected that his visitor—despite his air of sincerity—

was no more than a clever talker who had preferred to seek safety in flight when it came to the decisive test. Without his wife's insistence he might never have made the experiment, because the reasons given by the stranger for the failure of his first attempt had not really satisfied him. He could not understand how a little wax or a scrap of paper could keep alive the transmutatory power of a tiny speck of powder. So it was actually with no feeling of certainty that he decided to try it.

He went and fetched an old piece of lead piping and put it in a crucible over a fire lighted by his assistants. When it had melted, his wife dropped the powder on to it, having first embedded it in wax. The pot began to bubble and they heard loud hissing noises. At the end of a quarter of an hour the whole of the lead had been transmuted to gold.

Helvetius shaped the gold into an ingot and took it to a neighbouring goldsmith who tested it with a touchstone and offered him fifty florins an ounce for it. Naturally, the doctor refused to sell, and began showing it round among his friends. The fact was soon known all over The Hague and beyond, and Master Povelius, the Controller of the Dutch Office of Assay, came to see him and demanded that the Hermetic gold should be tested under his own supervision in the official laboratories. He treated it seven times with antimony without its losing weight, then submitted it to all the usual tests with meticulous care, and in the end was obliged to admit that it certainly was gold, and that it was of the highest standard that he had ever seen.

Helvetius, determined to leave nothing undone to prove the success of the operation, took it to a celebrated goldsmith named Brechtel, who carried out the following test: after shredding the gold and dissolving it in nitric acid, he mixed it with some silver. Then he melted the whole mass and afterwards separated it into its two original components. Far from losing weight, the amount of gold had been slightly increased, because a small amount of the silver had actually been transmuted to gold by contact with the Hermetic metal. After further tests with antimony, the silver thus transmuted remained incorporated with the gold and was no longer discernible as a separate entity.

To support the incontestable evidence of Helvetius, there is another first-class witness in the person of that most sceptical of philosophers, Benedict Spinoza, who was staying in The Hague at about that time and who personally verified the facts. During the following year, in March 1667, he wrote to his friend Jarrig Jellis:

"When I spoke to Voss about the Helvetius affair, he made fun of me, and said he was surprised to find me interested in that sort of nonsense. To make sure of my facts, I went to see Brechtel, the man who did the assay. He told me that while it was being melted, the gold had actually increased in weight when they dropped some silver into the pot. The gold that changed that silver into more gold must have been of a very remarkable kind! Not only Brechtel, but other people who were present when the tests were made have told me that this is a true account of what occurred. After that I went to see Helvetius himself, who showed me the gold and the crucible, that still had some traces of gold on the inner surface. He told me that he had used a piece of the Philosopher's Stone about a quarter the size of a grain of wheat in the melted lead, and he added that he was going to tell everyone in the world about it. Apparently the Adept from whom he got it had already done the same sort of thing in Amsterdam, where in fact he was still to be found. This is all the information I was able to get on the subject." (From the *Posthumous Works* of Benedict Spinoza.)

So clear a case, and one which had also been most carefully checked, was awkward for opponents of the Art to explain away. It is always quoted in contemporary studies of alchemy, such as Professor Holmyard's *Alchemy*, in which he says that it is difficult to imagine that so cultured a man as Helvetius, who was learned and most discerning, would have lied or wilfully given an incorrect account of the remarkable events that form the subject of his narrative. In most reports of this type, it is easy enough to find the chink through which the fraud might have entered, but no one has yet found the loophole in Helvetius' case. Even Hermann Kopp, a nineteenth-century German chemist, and the author of a history

145

of chemistry, preferred to reserve judgment. Figuier attempts a "rational" explanation—which is unfortunately most improbable:

"The terms used by Helvetius and the minute details into which he goes in his account," he says, "prevent one's feeling that he himself was guilty of imposture. But if the truthfulness and the integrity of the learned physician of the Prince of Orange are above suspicion, the same confidence cannot be extended to the unknown hero of the adventure. It is obvious that to the crucible or to the lead ingot used by the operator, either gold or some auriferous compound must have been added without the knowledge of Helvetius."

The expression "it is obvious" shows very clearly that this nineteenth-century chronicler was prepared to accept any absurdity rather than admit that he was recording an absolutely certain case of metallic transmutation. Let us emphasise yet again—in case it should be necessary—that an "auriferous compound" might conceivably have dyed the lump of metal to make it look like gold, but subsequent tests would soon have shown the truth.

The pseudo-scientific spirit of modern opponents of alchemy has gone to even greater lengths of intellectual dishonesty than did that of their forerunners in earlier centuries. Since it was impossible to prove fraud in experiments carried out by men as eminent as van Helmont or Helvetius, they quite simply proclaimed that these two people were themselves alchemists. The reasoning is as follows: an alchemist is a man who claims to transmute base metals into gold, and you cannot have confidence in his testimony. Now, van Helmont and Helvetius both claimed to have transmuted base metals into gold, therefore they are alchemists in whom one cannot have confidence. Such an argument is not only dishonest, it is untenable, because it is immediately demolished by the evidence of Spinoza about Helvetius, and also by an analogous transmutation carried out by Berigard of Pisa, which will be described below. To avoid all possible confusion in the reader's mind it should be noted that these experiments were the only ones of their kind made by either van Helmont or Helvetius, neither of whom—although both were entirely convinced of the truth of the Hermetic Art—ever sought to go further in alchemical studies.

*

The Italian philosopher Berigard of Pisa, who also lived in the seventeenth century, was another person to have been presented with a piece of the Philosopher's Stone by an unknown Adept. He has left a circumstantial account of the transmutation he carried out with it:

"I used to have the strongest possible doubts," he says, "about the transmutation of mercury to gold. Then a learned scholar gave me a small quantity of some powder, its colour not unlike that of wild poppies, and it smelt of calcined sea-salt. In order to avoid any possible suspicion of fraud, I personally bought a crucible, charcoal and mercury from different merchants, so as to make sure that no gold had been concealed in any of these things, as is often done by alchemical charlatans. I added a little of the powder to the mercury, and placed the crucible over a hot fire; in a short time the whole lot was converted into about the same quantity of gold that tests by various goldsmiths showed to be perfectly pure. Had this not happened while I was entirely alone, with no witnesses, I might have suspected some trickery. But as it is, I can assert quite confidently that the operation went off as I have described it." (*Circulus Pisanus.*)

Here is Figuier's comment: "The Italian philosopher Berigard of Pisa was converted to alchemy by an event analogous to the previous one quoted above. All such things can be easily explained nowadays by agreeing that in the mercury or other ingredients used, or in the crucible itself, a certain quantity of gold, hidden with remarkable ingenuity, was concealed." This is purely and simply an insult to the reader's intelligence, for Berigard of Pisa was careful to specify that he had bought the necessary materials from different merchants and without the knowledge of the Adept. If anyone had managed to slip some gold into the crucible in this case, no one need believe in alchemy—the answer would simply be: "magic"!

147

It is interesting to see that Figuier, who devotes so much space to
Denis Zachaire or Bernard of Treviso, Adepts whose transmutations
might be considered doubtful, polishes off the story of van Helmont
in a page and a half, and that of Helvetius in a bare three pages.
Clearly, such brilliant successes would be very difficult to explain
away.

A transmutation has also been credited to the well-known chemist
and physicist Robert Boyle, who has left a name important in the
history of science by enunciating the law of the compressibility of
gases, and by discovering the part played by oxygen in combustion.

It was Jean-Jacques Manget, in his *Bibliotheca Chemica Curiosa*,
who described the circumstances:

"A shabby-looking stranger went to see Mr. Boyle and, after discussing chemical matters with him for some time in a general
way, he asked him for some antimony and other metallic substances normally found in a laboratory. He put these substances
into a crucible which he placed over a lighted furnace. When the
metal had melted, the visitor showed the laboratory assistants a
certain powder which he then dropped into the crucible. He went
away almost immediately after doing this, telling the assistant to
leave the crucible until the fire died down. He promised to come
back in a few hours' time. But the unknown did not return, so
Boyle told them to examine the crucible, and found that it now
contained a yellow metal having all the properties of gold. Its
weight was only slightly less than that of the original metals."

It is certain that Boyle was not convinced by this transmutation,
which allows Louis Figuier to score an easy point. He deduces
from it: "The experiment carried out by the stranger did not dispel
Boyle's incredulity, and he proved more able than van Helmont to
resist the seduction of this empiric demonstration." In 1661 Boyle
wrote his most important treatise, *The Sceptical Chymist*, which a
good many adversaries of alchemy regard as having been directed
against the Hermetic Art. Actually, it was not, and it is only necessary
to look at any good modern encyclopaedia to prove this. Boyle's
treatise is an examination of the Aristotelian theory of the four

elements, which he considers to be out of date and to have been superseded by the very modern idea of chemical elements. A single remark about alchemy occurs in it, but that is dubitative rather than negative: "I would very much like to know how gold may be resolved into sulphur, mercury and salt;" he says, "I would undertake to pay the full cost of any such research. I admit that, for my part, I have never been able to do it."

In fact, if Figuier had pursued his research a little further, he might have realised that Robert Boyle had never been present at a transmutation, and that Jean-Jacques Manget's story is inaccurate. Actually, a German chemist named Ettner—or, rather, an archimist, as he would have been called later—himself described his visit to Boyle and the experiments that he performed before him. These were "special" procedures, that were supposed to permit of the very partial transmutation of certain metals to gold. Clearly, in these circumstances, Boyle would not say that he was convinced of the reality of the philosophic Mystery—any other point of view would have been most surprising.

One may, therefore, unhesitatingly accept the last few cases of transmutation described above, for they were truly scientific demonstrations. It seems nevertheless essential to complete the picture by studying the lives of the most important of the remaining Adepts, and in particular that of one who is perhaps the greatest of all— the author of *The Open Door into the Secret Palace of the King,* Eirenaeus Philalethes.

8. The Real Philalethes

"To this day," writes Lenglet du Fresnoy, "England has never produced a man of this type more remarkable than the anonymous celebrity who called himself Eirenaeus Philalethes. His name, his appearance, his life, his works, all combine to form an insoluble mystery. It is known that he was born in England in the year 1612 because, in 1645, when he wrote his most important book, he was no more than thirty-three years old; but neither the town nor the district is known. He was taken, presumably at an early age, to the English part of America. This is stated by him in a short treatise called *Experiments in the Preparation of Philosophic Mercury*, published in 1668 by Daniel Elzevir in Amsterdam, and it is believed that his name was Thomas de Vagan."

The Abbé Lenglet du Fresnoy was, in fact, recording all that was known in his day about the antecedents of the Adept referred to as Eirenaeus Philalethes. A century later, the German historian Karl-Christoph Schmieder said no more than that "a miraculous phenomenon appeared in western Europe!" This alchemist had the same propensity as the Cosmopolite of appearing suddenly on the stage of history as fully Adept, and then of disappearing equally suddenly, with no indication of where—or even whether—he had died. The same will be seen to be true of Lascaris; and one may ask whether the imprisonment and murder (to çall it by its true name) of Alexander Seton did not prevent him from disappearing in the same fashion, once his mission had been accomplished.

The first chapter of his book *The Open Door into the Secret Palace of the King* (which is also sometimes called *The Real Philalethes*, whence the title of this chapter) will give some idea of this mysterious individual, in his own words:

"I am a philosopher, an Adept, who call myself by no other name than Philalethes, an anonymous name signifying *lover of truth*. In the year of the redemption of the world 1645, being then thirty-three years of age and having learnt the secrets of medicine, alchemy and physics, I decided to write this short treatise in order to teach apprentices to the Science what they should know, and to hold out a hand to those who are struggling in the labyrinth of error. I intend by this same means to let Adept Philosophers understand that I am their fellow and their equal in the Art, and to give light to those who are misled by the impostures of sophists, so that they may return to the true path if that is their desire; for I believe there will be many who are enlightened by my book.

"What I tell you are no fables, but real and successful experiments that I have myself witnessed and know for certain to be true, as every man who becomes a philosopher will understand from my text. And since I have studied this only for the advantage of my fellow-men, I declare unhesitatingly—and you must take my word for it—that of all who have written on the subject there is none who speaks as openly as I, though I have many times been tempted to abandon my design, believing that I should do better to disguise truth under the cloak of allegory; but God, Who alone knows all hearts and Whom I could not withstand, obliges me to act as I now do. This it is that causes me to believe that in this latest age of the world, there will be some who will be granted the joy of possessing this precious treasure, because I write with sincerity, and leave no uncertainties that I have not explained fully, that might trouble the minds of those who are beginning to study the Science.

"I know a number of persons who are as familiar with the secret as I am myself, and I have no doubt that there are many other Philosophers, whose acquaintance I hope to make ere long. May God in His Holy Will do as seems good to Him. I confess that I am unworthy to be chosen for this task. I shall not cease to adore His holy Will, to which all created things must bow since He is their Creator and it is for Himself alone that they are preserved; He is the centre and the point from which every line in the universe emanates and to which it will return."

It is from this first chapter that the date of the Adept's birth is deduced. He says that he is thirty-three years old in 1645, which would make the date of his birth 1612; but, as has been said before, Philalethes' "sincerity" is always suspect. Also, I am personally not by any means convinced that he really was thirty-three at that date. The statement adds nothing to the treatise, and it was not customary to give one's age at the beginning of an alchemical work. Remembering, on the other hand, that Philalethes was a deeply Christian mystic, and that thirty-three was the age at which Christ died, or rather the age at which He ascended to heaven, in other words the time of His perfecting, it would seem by no means impossible that the thirty-three years might be intended in an initiatory sense, in which case they would symbolise his attainment of Adepthood and not be a reference to his physical age.

What is more, the first Latin publication of *The Open Door,* gave the age as twenty-three and not thirty-three. The original English text, published two years later, also gives the age as twenty-three. The extra ten years were added only in subsequent editions. This might, of course, be due to a typographical error corrected afterwards by the author; but, in view of the fact that Philalethes had "disappeared" before the later editions of the book were published, it seems more probable that the alteration was made by the publishers themselves, doubting whether so young a man could have succeeded in achieving the Stone.

If that is so, then it would seem reasonable to apply the "twenty-three years" not to Philalethes personally but to the length of time it took him to complete the Philosophic Work. It is in fact very probable that it did take him this length of time to accomplish the Mystery, as was the case with Flamel, Zachaire and many others.

One thing, at all events, is now certain: that we have no idea whatever of the Adept's age in 1645, except that he was probably a good deal older than has been believed. The point is worth making, because it will be of importance when an attempt is made to decide who gave the samples of alchemical powder to van Helmont and Helvetius.

*

To return to the mysticism of Eirenaeus Philalethes, which is

153

particularly evident in chapter XIII of the same treatise, a few extracts
are given here:

"Let no-one accuse me of insincerity, because I write openly and
fearlessly, because I write of strange things that have never before
been written as I write them; and this I do for the Glory of God,
for the benefit of my fellow-men, and because I despise the world
and its riches. Already Elias the Artist is born and glorious things
are told of the City of God. I swear in all truth that I possess greater
riches than can be found in any part of the world we know, but
I may not use them because of the snares of the wicked.

"With reason do I despise and contemn gold and silver, so passionately sought by all the world, that are used as a standard of value
for all things, that are the instruments of its pomps and vanities.
Does any man think that I veil the Science for greed or jealousy?
No, no! I confess freely that I grieve from the bottom of my heart
to be a wanderer and a vagabond upon earth, as though I had
been driven from before the face of the Lord. . . .

"I hope—and I hope I may live long enough to see it—that within
a few years cattle will be used as it was in olden days instead of
silver and other means of exchange, and that this prop and stay
of anti-Christ (because it is opposed and contrary to the spirit of
Christianity) may come to naught. The peoples are crazed, nations
are bewitched, and recognise no other god but this heavy, insensate
concretion of metal. Can such things be a part of the Redemption
for which we have waited so long and that must soon come, when
the streets of the New Jerusalem shall be paved with gold, its gates
be all of precious stones, and the Tree of Life in the midst of
Paradise shall shed its leaves for the well-being of nations?

"I know, yes I know that what I write will be as the finest gold
to many, and that by this same text gold and silver will be shown
to be worthless as any dross. Yes—believe my words, all you
young students and apprentices to the Science; believe them, all
you old men and philosophers, for the time is at hand (I do not
write this in vain imagination but I foresee it in the spirit and by
revelation) when we who know and who understand the Science
will be gathered from the four corners of the earth, and our works

will be accomplished through the Grace of the Lord our God and for His glory. My heart conceives and says of itself things such as have never been heard, my spirit mounts up, beating in my breast with joy and gladness in honour of the God of all Israel.

"I proclaim these things throughout the world as a herald and a trumpeter, lest I die without doing it some service. My book shall be as a harbinger for Elias, who will prepare the royal road for the Lord. And may it please God that all men of good will in the whole world shall understand the Art. Gold, silver, jewels, will then be so common and so abundant in all places, that none will value them save as they manifest the Science. Then at length the essential value, the naked Truth, glorious in itself, shall be held in honour."

It is such passages as this which induced the Abbé Lenglet du Fresnoy to dub Philalethes a good Christian. The Abbé says, in effect: "Since I am proposing to make this Artist famous to the best of my ability, I am bound to say that he is morally sound; he seems to be a good Christian, though I cannot say to which particular sect he subscribes. Judging by his book, he appears to have been some kind of visionary or idealist."

Many guesses have been made about the true identity of the Adept. The one most frequently quoted is that he was the British scientist Thomas Vaughan, whom Lenglet du Fresnoy mentions, though misspelling the name. Other names suggested were probably pseudonyms that Philalethes adopted from time to time in order to avoid the persecution that had always to be guarded against. At one time or another he called himself Childe, Dr. Zeil, M. Carnobe.

Thomas Vaughan was a member of an ancient noble Welsh family, the head of which was a peer of the realm. Thomas Vaughan himself was a well-known scholar, a long-standing friend and correspondent of Robert Boyle, one of the small group of scientists who later formed the nucleus of the Royal Society. As he travelled a great deal and declared publicly that he believed in alchemy, it has been supposed that the gaps in his life-story might correspond with the appearances of the Adept known as Philalethes. One other suggestion has been added, apparently clinching the argument: the manuscript of a work on alchemy exists that is in the handwriting of Thomas Vaughan himself and is signed with the pseudonym Philalethes—which would appear to be conclusive. Unfortunately it cannot be taken as such. It is true that Thomas Vaughan was interested in alchemy and that he was the author of at least one treatise on the Art (*Anthroposophia Theomagica*, published in 1650); but he signed it as *Eugenius* Philalethes, and not Eirenaeus. Moreover, if the photocopies of extant manuscript texts of the two men are compared, it will be seen that the handwritings have nothing in common; and the contents of Thomas Vaughan's alchemical treatises are absolutely different from those by the real Philalethes. Only one conclusion is possible: the identity of the Adept, like his age, remains an insoluble mystery. Besides, Vaughan is known to have been born in 1622 and to have died in 1666, well before the final "disappearance" of Philalethes.

Some information has been preserved about the youth of Eirenaeus Philalethes, thanks to a biography written by a British writer named Urbiger—but this must be treated with some reserve, because Urbiger says that the Adept came to man's estate in the reign of Charles II. As this King came to the throne in 1660, by which time Philalethes would have been forty-seven years old according to the accepted tradition, it is more likely that he grew up under Charles I, say between 1625 and 1649, because Urbiger's account mentions that he was invited to the royal court, which would not have been possible later, while Cromwell directed the destinies of England.

Urbiger's story is that the transmutations effected by the young Philalethes were so numerous and so brilliant that news of them reached the King, who tried to induce him to come to court, which the alchemist carefully avoided doing. One fact that is repeated constantly in stories told by contemporary witnesses is that a minute speck of his powder was sufficient to transmute a very large quantity of metal.

On this point, Louis Figuier says:

"All historians are agreed that Philalethes' tincture was more powerful than any previously seen or that could have been found in the possession of other seventeenth-century Adepts. A single grain added to an ounce of mercury turned it into gold; and if this transmuted gold was added to ten times its own bulk of mercury, a tincture resulted that would transmute 19,000 parts of metal. This figure does not differ greatly from that obtained by van Helmont in the experiment that converted him to alchemy; and it has been argued from this that the minute portion of powder he received came from Philalethes himself. Support is given to the hypothesis by a positive assertion from Starkey, the friend and disciple of Philalethes."

Louis Figuier's acceptance of this idea is rather surprising, since he agreed 1612 was the date of Philalethes' birth. Van Helmont's transmutation was carried out in 1618—and one might well doubt whether Philalethes had succeeded in becoming a Master at the age of six! On the other hand if, as I believe, this date is wrong, and if Philalethes was already known during the reign of Charles I, it is highly probable that it really was he who visited van Helmont in 1618, and that it was again he or perhaps one of his disciples who—much later—went to convert Helvetius.

We shall return to this point, but first it will be necessary to follow the Adept's peregrinations outside Europe. It is known for certain that he spent some time in America. This journey, which he undertook at an early age, is one of the few historically reliable parts of his life. After his arrival on the far side of the Atlantic, he made friends with an apothecary named Starkey, whose name is known in chemistry for his discovery of a disinfectant made from the turpentine tree (terebinth) that remains in our pharmacopoeia to this day. Philalethes lodged with him, and often used his laboratory to make quite considerable quantities of gold and silver in the presence of this man and of his son George. He several times made them a present of a good part of the metals obtained. When the two men returned to Great Britain they published a book (*The Oil of Sulphur*) in 1665, in which they described their meeting with Philalethes and the astonishing transmutations he had carried out. It appears that the Adept left Starkey's house because, being a religious man, living an unostentatious and strictly moral life, he was shocked by the dissipations of young Starkey, who spent in riotous living the gold he received from Philalethes. Another likely reason for Philalethes' departure was that there was danger of his becoming known as a maker of gold and therefore of suffering the same fate as that which had overtaken the Cosmopolite, for whom he had a great admiration and a profound sympathy. The sudden access of riches to the Starkeys carried with it the risk of drawing attention to their guest, and he therefore chose rather to return to Europe.

Besides the evidence of the apothecary and his son, there is that of Dr. Michael Faustius, who issued a complete collection of the works of Philalethes and was in touch with several people who said they had known the Adept in America or had carried on a correspondence with him. Among these was Robert Boyle, and he was not the only scientist to take Philalethes very seriously. For nearly twenty years *The Open Door* was Isaac Newton's bedside book. His copy, annotated on every page, is now kept in the British Museum, and is full of loose sheets with Newton's comments on the operations described by the Adept. He and Boyle were so thoroughly convinced of the truth of alchemy that they petitioned Parliament to bring in a bill prohibiting disclosure of the process of transmutation for fear the market value of gold should collapse.

After his stay in America, all trace of Philalethes is lost for some years. According to Georges Morhoff, he went to the East Indies and performed a number of public transmutations there; but this statement has not proved verifiable. The date of his reappearance in Europe is, however, known for certain, because it was at Amsterdam in 1666 that he gave the English version of *The Open Door* to Jean Lange for translation into Latin. The work was published under its Latin title *Introitus Apertus ad Occlusum Regis Palatium*. Now 1666 happens to be the year in which an unknown Adept visited Helvetius at The Hague, which is not far from Amsterdam; and it will be remembered that in the course of the interview he told Helvetius that he had enough of the Philosopher's Stone in his ivory box to transmute 40,000 pounds of base metal to gold. Moreover, an identical declaration was made to van Helmont by his unknown visitor, and the prodigious power of the Stone was proved.

In the earlier chapters of this book it was shown that the difficulties of creating the Philosopher's Stone were immense, so that very few alchemists ever succeeded. It would therefore appear to be extremely improbable that there were in Europe at that time three or four Hermetic philosophers in possession of so perfect a precipitate. It seems far more likely that it was a sole and unique Adept with exceptional knowledge—Philalethes—who in his younger days visited van Helmont and, after his return from America, Helvetius, before he had the opportunity of converting the philosopher Berigard of Pisa.

It may be wondered why he never gave his name, since in any case his real name was prudently concealed under the cloak of the Hermetic pseudonym. But the danger run by an Adept increased as his fame increased, and that is why Philalethes insisted over and over again in his books on the absolute necessity for secrecy. He went so far as to say that it had grown very difficult to sell Hermetic gold or silver without being immediately denounced by the purchaser and prosecuted. "Merchants are not fools," he says, "even if they say they see nothing, like children playing a game with their eyes shut. If you are unwise enough to visit them, they will at a single glance find out more than enough to cause you a great deal of trouble." Further on, he adds:

"I can speak with certainty, because once when I was in a foreign country disguised as a merchant I wanted to sell an ingot of very pure silver of about six hundred pounds' sterling value (I had not dared to add any alloy, because each country has its own standards for silver and gold, that are known to all bullion dealers. So, if you expect to be able to tell them that a piece of gold or silver comes from this country or that, they can recognise it by touch, and will arrest you immediately). The people to whom I had offered this ingot for sale told me at once that it was artificial and when I asked them how they could tell, they said nothing except that they were not apprentices and could recognise silver coming from England or Spain or elsewhere, and that mine was not of the standard of any of them. Having heard this, I departed without saying another word, leaving my silver and any money I expected to have got for it. And I never went back or tried again."

Elsewhere he says:

"But, please God, these two great idols, gold and silver, which are at present worshipped by all the world, may soon become as cheap and common as mud or any refuse. For then I, who know how to make it, shall no longer be obliged to take as much trouble as I do to conceal myself; it is as though the curse of Cain had come upon me (the very thought wrings sighs and tears from me) and that I am, as he was, driven from before the face of the Lord, being deprived of the beloved society of my friends, with whom I was wont to converse in full liberty. Now I am, as it were, pursued by Furies, so that I can be nowhere in safety for any length of time; and this makes me often cry to God as Cain did: 'every man's hand is against me!'

"I dare not so much as cherish my family, being a wanderer and a vagabond, now in one country, now in another, with no sure abiding place. And although I possess all riches, they are of but little profit to me."

All this explains the difficulty of following the tracks of the Adept, who moved ceaselessly from country to country, under various aliases. But there may in his case be yet another reason for his incessant journeying. Like Paracelsus, it would seem that Philalethes was a high emissary of the brethren of the Rose-Croix. If the teaching he gives in his various treatises is compared with that professed by the Rose-Croix, complete identity of outlook is found, even to foretelling the advent of that Elias of whom Paracelsus had also spoken.

If possible, even less is known about the end of Philalethes' life than about the beginning. Quite simply, he disappeared one day, and no one ever heard tell of him again. A vague tradition suggests that he retired to France, but no proof has ever been given; he might just as well have vanished into one country as into another. He never made any secret of the fact that he used the Philosopher's Stone not so much to make gold that was difficult to sell, but as a medicine and an elixir of life; and numbers of convinced alchemists have always maintained that he had reached the state of immortality reserved for the higher Adepts. A well-known fortune-teller named Etteila even said that Eirenaeus Philalethes and the Count de Saint-Germain were one and the same individual. He declared in *The Seven Degrees of the Hermetic Philosophic Work,* published in 1786, "M. de Saint-Germain unites in his own person a perfect knowledge of the three classical sciences, and is the true and only author of Philalethes' *Open Door into the Secret Palace of the King.*"

Personally, I do not agree with this venturesome identification. The Count de Saint-Germain appeared in the second half of the eighteenth century, about a hundred years after Philalethes. Nevertheless, it may be that he, like Nicholas Flamel, attained wisdom and, after a life of wandering, spent a long and serene old age in some secret refuge.

There could be no better way of concluding the chapter on this very exceptional man than by quoting the last few lines of his own treatise *The Open Door*:

"This book was begun and ended in the year 1645 by me, who have professed and still profess the secret Art, without seeking the commendation of any man; but the aim of my treatise is to help those who search sincerely after knowledge of this hidden science, and to assure them that I am their friend and their brother, under the name by which I sign myself, Eirenaeus Philalethes, English by birth, a denizen of the universe.

GLORY BE TO GOD ALONE."

9. The Apostolate of Lascaris

The name Lascaris is unlikely to be familiar to many readers. The names of Nicholas Flamel or Paracelsus are known to a wide public, those of Albertus Magnus and Basil Valentine are still mentioned in books on metallurgy, and the pseudonyms of the Cosmopolite and Philalethes continue to be revered by enthusiasts of the Hermetic science. But no one ever mentions Lascaris, although his alchemical demonstrations were most remarkable; and his personality remains mysterious yet with something familiar enough about it to suggest some very bizarre questions.

Who was he? Where did he come from? What happened to him? All of them are points which must remain unanswered. Even the name Lascaris is only one of innumerable aliases. He passed for a Greek, and is thought to have chosen the name because it was borne by a great many Greek refugees in Germany. This fantastic personage —and fantastic is the word—appeared towards the end of the seventeenth century and during the first thirty to forty years of the eighteenth, carrying on the same mission as that undertaken by the Cosmopolite and by Eirenaeus Philalethes.

Lascaris seems to have had one aim only—to promote knowledge of the Hermetic science and to persuade all men to admit its truth. Yet he was hardly ever seen, though careful study of most of the transmutations carried out up to about 1735 will show that the tincture used by one or another pseudo-alchemist had been given him by the same individual, whose description somehow fitted that of Lascaris. Time after time, behind the operator, who turns out to be no more than a supernumerary, can be discerned the figure of this most unusual alchemist as the instigator of a brilliant demonstration performed by someone else to prove the truth of the Art.

Several descriptions of Lascaris exist, but they are not much help. Whether at the end of the seventeenth century or forty years later, he is always said to be a man of uncertain age, not young at his first appearance, but not old at subsequent ones. His face is, if anything even more elusive, because none of the descriptions agree. Apparently Lascaris looked different every time anyone saw him. Only a certain southern vivacity, an enjoyment of talking and dazzling his audience, allows the conclusion that it really was the same man each time. He said he was Greek—but was he?—and alleged that he was the abbot of a religious establishment on the island of Mytilene. He spoke several languages fluently, with a slight but indefinable accent, which people soon forgot in his volubility. This, at any rate, is how he was described at the very beginning of the eighteenth century by Councillor Dippel, one of the best known chemists of his time, who stated that he was a man aged between forty and fifty—which is exactly the way he was described at his last appearances thirty years later.

His expansive "southern" personality was probably the reason why he personally operated as seldom as possible, having no doubt realised that he risked talking too much and attracting to himself the attention of the ruling classes, who were always avid for gold. The unhappy examples of Seton, Edward Kelly and more recently of the goldsmith Gustenhover, must have been known to him, and have reminded him to be vigilant at all times. This, I believe, was the reason that made Lascaris adopt the principle of having operations conducted by his representatives rather than by himself—a practice that was very unusual. The fate that befell his first emissary could only impress upon him more deeply the need to keep out of the limelight.

It was in the dawn of the eighteenth century that a Prussian gentleman presented himself to Frederick I, saying that he knew the secret of transmuting metals and that he hoped to be able to persuade the King of the truth of his claim. Frederick agreed without making any difficulty, and asked that the demonstration should take place at once. The gentleman used powder given him by Lascaris and transmuted a pound of lead to gold before the eyes of the delighted monarch. Unfortunately this easy success turned his head and, repeating the mistake made by some of his predecessors, he gave the King to understand that he was himself an Adept and quite able to manufacture the Philosopher's Stone. He hoped to assure his position at court thereby, carrying out no more than a minimum of transmutations with what remained of the powder he had brought with him. But Frederick did not see it in the same way, and ordered him to make a large quantity of the precipitate "in the interests of the State", so as to replenish the Treasury. The man set to work but, not being an Adept, he got nowhere. By way of impressing the King, he had sworn "by his head" that he possessed the great secret; so Frederick took him at his word and had his head cut off when he failed. In order to give some show of legality to the summary execution, an old story of a duel was dug up in which this gentleman had killed his adversary; not that anyone was taken in by it.

It was in 1701, at Berlin, that Lascaris happened to meet the man who was to become the best-known of his disciples. The Adept was ill—or at any rate he pretended to be—and sent for an apothecary so that he might order some medicines. This man, Master Zorn, did not answer the call himself but sent a nineteen-year-old assistant, Johann Friedrich Böttger (*not* Bötticher, as the name has sometimes been spelt). Lascaris began talking to the young man on subjects connected with alchemy, and found to his surprise that the boy was passionately interested in the Art, knew the works of Basil Valentine intimately and had actually tried to put them into practice. Böttger added that he had never told anyone about it because at the time, as at others, anyone doing this kind of research was looked upon as a lunatic. Lascaris told him that he was himself an Adept, and gave him advice and some instruction. Before leaving Berlin, he made him a present of two ounces of the alchemical powder, imposing three conditions for its use: first, never to tell anyone where he had got it; second, to use it only for purposes of demonstration and not for his own profit; and third, to wait for a given length of time after the Adept's departure before carrying out the first transmutation. Finally Lascaris added:

"You will see—the result will be that no one in Berlin will dare to call alchemists fools in future."

The young man waited impatiently for the end of the period of delay enjoined by Lascaris, and then proceeded to make his experiment, watched by a group of young friends who had previously made fun of his efforts. Before their amazed eyes, two ounces of mercury was quite certainly turned into gold. Böttger was wild with excitement, gave notice to his employer, and determined to go to Halle to study medicine.

*

For the moment, we will leave Lascaris' story, and carry on with that of his new disciple which is in several ways particularly interesting. Young Böttger, then, proposed leaving his present employer who, however, thought well of his work, and tried to induce him to stay on. Before his departure, he asked him to dinner, and as fellow-guests invited two clergymen named Winkler and Borst, hoping that they would help to persuade the young man to abandon his wild ideas. The two Pastors delivered themselves of a severe criticism of the Hermetic Art in the course of the meal, and concluded their lecture by saying: "You will never make the impossible possible!"

The young man rose to his feet:

—"Come into the laboratory," he said. "I will do this impossible thing before your very eyes."

The whole party followed Böttger, watching his every movement carefully. First he took a crucible, and was about to put some lead into it, when Master Zorn, fearing that it might have been tampered with, told him that he would prefer to see the experiment made with silver, and fetched a piece from among his stocks. The young man had no objection, put the three ounces of silver given him into the crucible and heated it. When the metal reached melting point, Böttger took a little silver box out of his pocket and extracted a grain of the Philosopher's Stone from it. He embedded it in wax and then dropped it into the crucible. The guests said that they had seen the powder, which looked like tiny splinters of fiery red glass. When the crucible had cooled down, Böttger poured out the molten metal, and Master Zorn and the two visitors found to their amazement that it had really and truly turned into gold. As usual, Zorn took it to the nearest goldsmith, and it came successfully through all the tests.

Siebert, an old friend of Böttger's, who managed what would nowadays be called a pharmaceutical laboratory, heard about the transmutation performed by his erstwhile fellow-apprentice, went to see him, and asked if he might also witness the prodigy. The young man agreed willingly. Siebert himself brought a crucible and the mercury destined for the experiment, and then carried out the whole operation, Böttger's only part in the affair being to drop in the wax containing the necessary precipitate. Siebert had meanwhile prepared eight ounces of lead in a second crucible and that too had been brought to melting point. As soon as the mercury was exposed to the action of the Philosopher's Stone, it began to turn brown, and was immediately poured over the lead in the other crucible. A quarter of an hour later the two metals had fused into a single lump of gold.

Böttger's reputation spread throughout Berlin. The inhabitants were divided into two camps: those who had seen and were obliged to believe, and the others who had only heard it spoken of and thought it was just "another of those stories". These last nicknamed Johann-Friedrich *Adeptus ineptus*. Once more, and most unfortunately, rumours of the operation came to the ears of King Frederick William I. Like his predecessors in previous cases, he ordered Böttger to be arrested. But, luckily for him, Master Zorn knew a member of the King's suite, who warned him, and the young man had time to leave Berlin and make for Wittenberg, where he had an uncle. His departure soon turned to flight when, after crossing the Elbe, he saw a squad of Prussian soldiers in pursuit, and was obliged to take to the woods to avoid them. Once he had reached his uncle's house, Böttger thought he was safe; but the King of Prussia refused to relinquish his prey and, believing him to be a Prussian subject, demanded his extradition from the city of Wittenberg. Fortunately, Böttger had not been born in Prussia, but in Saxony; and, when the Elector of Saxony, Augustus II, King of Poland, claimed him as his subject, Böttger was only too thankful to turn his steps in that direction and put the greatest possible distance between himself and the King of Prussia.

As soon as he reached Dresden, the capital of Saxony, he was conducted into the presence of the Elector, who asked him to perform a transmutation while he watched. The young man agreed readily, and the experiment was completely successful. Augustus II was delighted, and dubbed him Baron on the spot. His sudden rise in the world rather turned poor Johann-Friedrich's head. He completely forgot about the medical studies he had planned to take up, and thought of nothing but drinking and amusing himself, paying for it with the gold he was able to manufacture by using what remained of Lascaris' powder. He bought a splendid mansion, where he kept open house, and it is said that at every meal the guests found a piece of gold in their table-napkins. He became the darling of the ladies, who had no hesitation in offering their favours in return for some jewel bought with the Hermetic gold.

This went on for two years. Certainly the mission with which Lascaris had charged him was successful in a way, because Böttger's extravagance proved that the Philosopher's Stone made it possible to have all the gold one wanted. But, alas, the stock of powder given him by the Adept was rapidly dwindling. Remembering his studies of Basil Valentine and the instruction given him by Lascaris, Böttger —as other emissaries had done before him in similar situations— set to work to try to renew his supply, feeling sure that he would somehow be able to do it. As always in such cases, he failed completely, and one day he found that not a single grain of powder remained. He faced ruin.

He was, of course, obliged to stop his extravagant parties, to reduce his expenses, and try to get help from the people whom he had so liberally entertained for two years. He did not understand the type of person he had to deal with; they were fundamentally venal and turned their backs on him as soon as they found that nothing more was to be gained by knowing him. All his pretty ladies dropped him, and even his own servants turned against him when he could no longer pay them, and circulated a rumour that he was planning flight. The Elector gave orders that he was to be kept under house-arrest.

Once again Lascaris comes into the picture. He was still travelling in Germany at the time, and had from afar followed the adventures of his young protegé. He had heard of the flight from Berlin, of the arrival in Dresden, of his being granted a title, and of his present difficulties. Lascaris believed himself to be morally responsible for the follies committed by the young man and for their consequences. He therefore felt it to be his duty to do all he could to extricate him and, with this in view, returned to Berlin in 1703. He remembered

Böttger's telling him that among his friends and acquaintance there was only one man who seemed to be entirely trustworthy—a Dr. Pasch—so Lascaris went to see this man and gave him details of Johann-Friedrich's experiences.

—"Do you realise," he added, "the danger he is in? You will have to go to Dresden and explain to Augustus II that Böttger has never been in possession of the Hermetic secret, but that he had been given a stock of powder by an itinerant Adept. In return for his liberty, you will offer a ransom of eighty thousand ducats."

—"Eighty thousand ducats!" exclaimed Pasch. "But where will I get such a sum? Nobody except a Prince could possess such riches!"

—"Come with me," replied Lascaris, "and I will show you something that will convince you."

When they reached the hovel where the Adept was living, he showed Pasch a bag weighing a good six pounds, and containing a bright red powder. He continued:

—"Here is my store of the powder and, thanks to my Art, I can renew it at any time and to any extent. Each one of these particles is capable of transmuting into gold anything up to four thousand times its own weight in base metal."

In order to convince the Doctor, Lascaris then and there transmuted a pound of mercury. Pasch, dazzled by such an irrefutable argument, agreed to leave for Dresden on the following day.

—"When you return," said the Adept, "if you have succeeded in freeing Böttger, I will make you rich for the rest of your life."

A few days later, Dr. Pasch arrived in Dresden, where he happened to have some distant cousins who belonged to a noble family and were in good standing at court. With their help, he expected to be granted an audience of the Elector, at which he planned to put forward Lascaris' proposition. But his cousins discouraged him from making the attempt:

—"Think for a moment," they said, "such a ransom would only make the King believe that Böttger knew the secret, and that you had made the eighty thousand ducats according to his directions. Far from releasing him, you would risk his being put to the torture to make him reveal his secret."

—"Then what shall I do?" exclaimed the Doctor.

—"It would be better to use the gold to bribe the guards holding your friend, and so give him the chance to escape."

It was a sound idea, and very nearly succeeded. Pasch took a lodging opposite Johann-Friedrich's house and, with the help of the servants, got to see him and told him of the plan. Unfortunately, just as the escape was about to take place, one of the guards gave it away. The Elector had Pasch arrested and interned in the fortress of Sonnenstein. Böttger himself was imprisoned in the castle of Königstein where, however, he was given private accommodation including a laboratory in which to pursue his researches. The unhappy Dr. Pasch was in prison for two and a half years before he managed to escape, but in doing so he had the misfortune to fracture his breast-bone and died six months after returning to Berlin. He told the sad story of his adventure to Councillor Dippel, who left a circumstantial account of it.

Johann-Friedrich Böttger himself had an unexpected stroke of luck. Knowing that he was incapable of producing the Philosopher's Stone, he was expecting torture and death when things suddenly took a turn for the better through the intervention of Count Tschirnhaus, the Commandant of the prison in which he was held. The Count was interested in the manufacture of porcelain, a Chinese art almost entirely unknown in Europe at that time. Böttger's reputation as an alchemist, despite his repeated failures, stood so high that Tschirnhaus decided to associate him with his own business.

Working at this new art, Böttger in 1704 discovered a means of obtaining a red porcelain, and finally in 1709 the way of making white porcelain, the most sought-after secret of the day. The Elector was delighted, for the possession of this secret was worth almost as much to him as that of the Philosopher's Stone, and he put up china factories all over his estates to produce it. Böttger took advantage of his changed attitude to admit that he had never possessed the secret of the Stone, and told him the story of his interview with Lascaris. The Elector freed him, restored to him the title of Baron, and appointed him director of the first porcelain factory in Dresden. He resumed his luxurious habits and lived a riotous life until he died at the age of thirty-seven, his health undermined by excesses.

*

This account is not complete without the mention of a study of the life of Böttger published at Leipzig in 1837: *J. F. Böttger, Originator of Saxon Porcelain*, by Karl August Engelhardt, archivist at the War Ministry.

As was to be expected from a nineteenth-century author contemporary with Louis Figuier, Engelhardt maintains that Johann-Friedrich never transmuted so much as an ounce of any metal into gold. According to his story, Lascaris was a beggar well known in that part of the town in which Master Zorn's pharmacy was situated, who one day gave a certain powder to young Böttger. The boy made his employer believe that it had something to do with the Philosopher's Stone, and pretended to carry out a transmutation; then left him. Engelhardt believed that the affair caused such a stir that Prussia was within an ace of making war on Saxony after Böttger had fled there. At the court of Augustus II, King of Poland, so he says, Böttger told the same tale, and thereupon the King ennobled him and provided him with the means to carry on his alchemical researches. It was after Augustus' patience gave out, and he had been imprisoned, that Böttger discovered the secret of the porcelain. The beggar Lascaris, Engelhardt says, died in a poorhouse in Berlin soon after Böttger's flight.

To make Engelhardt's thesis tenable, it would be necessary to suppose that a country would make war to retrieve the undistinguished nineteen-year-old assistant to an apothecary, and then give him a title for no ascertainable reason. As regards Lascaris, the learned archivist may very likely have found some record of a beggar named Lascaris, because, as we said above, it was a common name among Greek refugees in Germany. But this particular beggar can have had no connection with the Adept, whose history was far from complete. If Böttger's life is studied carefully and is submitted to the critique of reason, only one conclusion can be drawn: Lascaris' powder makes the story not only probable, but actually possible.

*

To return to Lascaris himself who, for his part, continued to carry on the propaganda campaign on behalf of Hermetic Philosophy. He chose two more young pharmaceutical apprentices as emissaries.

Actually, in the Germany of those days, apothecaries were all more or less believed to be alchemists in their spare time; even if they did not succeed in making gold they were thought to have more chance than most people of discovering the secret. This no doubt explains the Adept's choice, because the two young men who received his gifts of philosophic powder were in no way particularly interesting or remarkable.

The first was Hermann Braun, an assistant in the largest pharmacy in Frankfort-on-the-Main. After meeting Lascaris, he told all his friends that one of his relatives had on his death-bed given him a small quantity of a transmutatory tincture. In order to give it a particular character without altering its properties, he had mixed the powder with some copaiva balsam, which turned it a very characteristic colour. Dr. Eberhard, the owner of the shop, asked him to test his alleged tincture in the presence of himself and a few friends. Braun agreed to do so, and transmuted to gold first some mercury and then a lump of lead. The highest scientific authority in the neighbourhood, Dr. Horlacher of Münster, was then approached, and he agreed to watch an experiment on condition that he was allowed to be in charge of the operation himself. Braun agreed, and Horlacher took every precaution to prevent fraud. He bought a new crucible, acquired the mercury from one of his own friends and, finally, picked an old lead pipe that had lain in his shed for years. The experiment was carried out in his own laboratory, first with the mercury, in which Braun's only action consisted in dropping on to the molten metal a little ball of wax containing four specks of the tincture. Horlacher himself then closed the crucible and, after heating it for a further ten minutes or so, saw that the mercury had turned into gold. The same happened with the old lead pipe, which also turned into gold of the highest quality.

This double transmutation caused a great stir in the place. Braun, speaking from ignorance, said that the precipitate was obtained from phosphorus—a substance that had recently come to be studied and that seemed to him to be mysterious. Once the powder given him by Lascaris had been used up, Braun retired from the scene, having made his contribution to the Adept's Hermetic propaganda.

The second young man was named Martin, and is even less interesting, for he lost part of the powder by mixing it up with other substances for sheer curiosity, and then wasted the remainder by doing some transmutations to impress his girl friends. He entirely neglected to carry out experiments before the scientific notabilities of his town, despite the orders that Lascaris must certainly have given him.

The Adept himself was now in Bohemia, having made the acquaintance of a Councillor Liebknech on the way from Vienna. The Councillor described him as a middle-aged man, highly cultured, and speaking Greek, Latin, French, German and Italian fluently. Lascaris, realising that he was talking to a person of quality, adroitly brought the conversation round to the subject of the Hermetic Art. The Councillor proved to be a strong opponent, and refused even to listen to arguments, saying that he would believe only if he could with his own eyes see a piece of base metal changed into gold. Lascaris made no comment and spoke of other things.

After a night's sleep at Hasch-on-Legeir, and before getting back into the travelling coach, Lascaris proposed that he and the Councillor should go to a near-by blacksmith's, where he would show him an interesting experiment. Liebknech, having by now completely forgotten the conversation of the night before, agreed at once. So Lascaris put some mercury into a crucible and quickly transmuted it to gold with a speck of his powder. The Councillor uttered not a word, and Lascaris said he was going to do it all over again to make sure of convincing him. With the help of the blacksmith, he obtained another crucible, put some mercury into it and heated it to melting point. When the transmutation had been carried out, Lascaris, looking at the resultant gold, said:

—"This time the gold is not as good as the first lot; I will purify it."

This gold was put into a third crucible and re-melted. The Adept dropped a different powder into it, and the gold turned white. When it was poured out, it proved to be very pure silver. Lascaris presented the gold and silver ingots thus obtained to Councillor Liebknech, but decided not to pursue the journey in his company, no doubt to avoid awkward questions, and went on to France. The three crucibles used for these transmutations are to this day preserved at the University of Jena.

All trace was now lost of Lascaris in France, and it was not until 1707 that news of him came to hand, this time thanks to Councillor Dippel, mentioned earlier in this chapter.

In Amsterdam, Dippel had got to know a man who said he had in his possession certain tinctures required for the transmutation of metals, and that he had been given them by a Master who wished to remain anonymous. Councillor Dippel questioned this man closely, and in the end realised from the description that the person who had provided the powders must have been Lascaris, whom Dippel had already met. The stranger, as soon as he discovered that the chemist knew his benefactor, agreed to operate a transmutation in his presence, saying that he would do it in the same way as he had seen the Master do it recently.

He took Dippel and some other people to a neighbouring workshop, and there showed them a round copper plaque, some thirty centimetres in diameter. He put the plaque on to a stove, so that only a circle of about ten centimetres' diameter in the centre was heated. When the metal had reached a sufficiently high temperature, he scattered a few grains of white tincture on to this part of the plaque, which immediately turned into silver. The operator removed the disc and put it over yet another burner, so that only a circle of about four centimetres' diameter would be in contact with the heat. When this had reached a suitably high temperature, he dropped a speck of red powder onto it that transmuted this inner circle to gold. Then he offered the plaque, with its three concentric rings of gold, silver, and copper, to Dippel, who had watched the proceedings with enormous interest. To make it quite clear that there had been no chance of any fraud, Dippel said, "The Artist did not only show us the outside of the plaque, he cut it in pieces, so as to let those interested in alchemy see that the tincture had affected the whole thickness of the metal; he sold us the pieces at a very moderate price."

This anonymous operator was not quite as lordly as real Adepts such as Seton, Philalethes or Lascaris, who used to make a present to the audience of the results of their transmutations; but he was obviously a skilled operator, and worthy of the confidence Lascaris reposed in him.

For several more years, until 1715, the mysterious Adept continued on his elusive way. He was then heard of in Hamburg, at the house of Baron von Creuz, a man who had devoted thirty years of his life to searching for the Philosopher's Stone, without ever achieving anything except to be constantly laughed at. He had a long conversation with Lascaris, in which he told him that the only wish he had in life was to be able to perform a single transmutation before his friends, so as to put a stop to their everlasting jokes, and to be able to carry on his work with a new peace of mind and fresh confidence. Lascaris gave him no encouragement but, after he had left, the Baron was surprised to find on the seat of the chair lately occupied by his guest a little box containing a small quantity of red powder and a piece of jewellery. A note accompanying this explained that it was a transmutatory powder, and gave instructions for its use. The ornament was a silver buckle, one part of which had been transmuted to gold— no doubt to show that it was possible to transmute this sort of thing without having to melt the whole and thereby risk destroying the design. The Baron never doubted for a moment that what he had been given was the philosophic powder. He called together his family and friends and, despite their mockery, began to operate a transmutation. It succeeded beyond his most fervent hopes, bringing the audience to stunned silence. He was wise enough to explain that he had not made the marvellous tincture himself, content to have proved his point in the present triumph. The half-gold, half-silver buckle is to this day in the possession of his descendants.

In July 1716 Lascaris appeared in Vienna and set about arranging a meeting of well-known people there, including doctors and other scientists, in order to prove the reality of the Hermetic Art by a serious demonstration, so organised as to provide the fullest guarantee against any possibility of fraud. A very detailed report of the proceedings was drawn up by Councillor Wolf-Philip Pantzer of Hesse, which is interesting as being one of the very few official reports on the reality of metallic transmutation.

The meeting was held on 20th July 1716, beginning at about ten o'clock in the morning, at the house of Count Charles Ernest von Rappach, Commandant of the fortress of Vienna. Signatories to the report, who guaranteed its factual accuracy, were Count Joseph von Würben und Freudenthal, Imperial and Bohemian Vice Chancellor;

Count Ernest Metternich, Privy Councillor to the King of Prussia; his brother, Baron Wolf Metternich, Privy Councillor to the Prince of Brandenburg-Culmbach and Anspach; and Councillor Pantzer himself.

One of the visitors brought the philosophic powder, wrapped in a piece of paper—a minute quantity, Pantzer notes, and looking like sea-salt. A number of copper coins collected from various places—including a poor-box—were weighed and the weights carefully noted. The coins were melted a few at a time and the powder added in the usual way, some members of the audience helping—one of them burnt his fingers in his anxiety to fish one of the coins out of a hot crucible. The brothers Metternich, it is noted, were particularly keenly interested in the operations, the results of which were all successful. The report notes that one part of the tincture had transmuted ten thousand parts of metal, all to silver on this occasion.

*

Lascaris' next appearance occurred only after some considerable time had passed. It was reported by Lieut. Colonel Schmolz von Dierbach, who was then in the service of the King of Poland. His father had been a great enthusiast for the Hermetic Art and had ruined himself through his researches, which was the reason why his son had been obliged to take up a military career. One day Dierbach happened to be talking about his father to some of his fellow-officers in a public place; they made fun of him and of the absurd ideas of alchemists in general. The young man defended his father's memory warmly and appeared to be seriously vexed by the attitude of his companions. Among other people present, was a stranger who had listened to the discussion with great interest, though without taking any part in it. This man was, in fact, Lascaris who, when most of the others had left, approached Dierbach and got into conversation with him. The Adept told him now indignant he had been to hear what the other officers had said, and added that he himself had the means of showing how wrong they were and thereby rehabilitating the memory of his father. He then provided Schmolz von Dierbach with a small packet of the Philosopher's Stone, at the same time warning him not to attempt to make more than the equivalent of three ducats' worth of gold a week with it for the next seven years. At the same time he urged him to try to convince as many people as possible of the truth of alchemy. The officer agreed, and went back to his quarters fully determined to hand in his resignation.

So Schmolz von Dierbach left the army and wasted no time before astonishing his friends by operating repeated and successful transmutations. The news came to the ears of old Councillor Dippel, who went to Frankfort-on-the-Main, where Dierbach was now living, called on him and asked if he might see the powder. They gave each other descriptions of the mysterious person from whom the powder had come, and Dippel was amazed to find that the picture given by Dierbach corresponded exactly with what he remembered of the man. Dippel, being a chemist, was able to examine the Adept's powder very minutely. He looked at it under a microscope and ascertained that it consisted of a very large number of tiny reddish-orange crystals; but he tried in vain to analyse it. Then he attempted a series of transmutations with it in order to determine its exact power, and came to the conclusion that one part of the powder would transmute at least six hundred parts of any metal to gold.

Schmolz von Dierbach was an ideal Hermetic emissary. With the greatest generosity he operated transmutations for any who asked to be convinced, always handing over to them the products of the transmutations and never keeping anything for himself. When the seven-year period imposed by Lascaris ended, he was startled to find that his whole stock of powder was spent, because he had not remembered to keep to the conditions. His mission was therefore over, and he was no more heard of.

Despite the greatest care, Lascaris ended by attracting the attention of the Elector Palatine, who sent men-at-arms to arrest him. He sought safety in flight, but was reduced one night to asking for asylum at the home of the Countess Anna-Sophia von Erbach. The lady refused at first to admit him, thinking he was an escaped criminal, but was eventually persuaded to allow him to spend the night at her house, though warning the servants to keep a careful watch on him. Lascaris spent several nights there, long enough for his pursuers to believe that he had left the country. Before his departure, and by way of showing gratitude to his benefactress, he offered to transmute all her household silver to gold. At first this offer revived the Countess's original suspicion of him; but when he pressed the point she sent for a battered old silver bowl and gave it to him to see what would happen. To her great relief, but also to her intense astonishment, the bowl was melted and transmuted to the finest gold. At Lascaris' request, the gold ingot was examined with all the usual tests by a goldsmith in the nearest town; the servant who took it there returned with the goldsmith's certificate to the effect that it was of the highest standard. Fully reassured by this time, the Countess agreed to hand over all her silver to the Adept who, incidentally, promised to reimburse her in full should he be unsuccessful. However, the operation went off perfectly, and very soon the Countess found herself the owner of a very satisfactory number of gold ingots, their weight corresponding exactly with that of the old silver. After spending another few days at her home, all danger being now past, Lascaris said farewell to the Countess who—bless her innocent heart!— offered him a purse containing two hundred Thalers as a reward for his alchemical operations. The Adept refused it with a friendly smile.

The authenticity of this adventure is quite certain, because it led to legal troubles. The Countess and her husband, Frederick Charles, had lived apart for some years. When news of the remarkable transformation of the silver reached him, he bethought him that in law he was still the Countess's husband, and demanded half the Hermetic gold, as representing an increase in the assets included in goods shared in common. His wife refused to agree, and the Count took up the matter legally; but the Leipzig court disallowed his claim: since "the silver had belonged to the wife, she was also entitled to the gold". (*Enunciata et consilia juris Leipsicae, 1733.*)

This was Lascaris' last recorded appearance. He vanished as if by magic between 1730 and 1740.

At the beginning of this chapter I said that Lascaris' image, his vivacity and other characteristics were somehow reminiscent of another and more familiar historical personage. It is this individual who appears on our stage soon after 1740, as though Lascaris were carrying on living in him. I will say no more for the moment, because we shall meet this very well-known character in a later chapter. Meanwhile, the identity and the fate of Lascaris must remain uncertain.

10. The Story of Sehfeld

This eighteenth-century alchemist is almost entirely unknown—even Figuier ignores him completely, though Karl Schmieder gave him quite a fair amount of space when he published his *History of Alchemy* at Leipzig in 1832. It was not until 1963 that Bernard Husson rescued him from oblivion in Nos. 56 and 57 of the journal *Initiation and Science*. After pointing out that, at a time when "scientific" explanations were demanded for all phenomena, it was useless to mention anything that could not be backed up with chemical facts, Husson proceeds:

> ". . . Sehfeld's case precludes any attempt at a scientific type of comment, and this no doubt is the reason for Figuier's decision not to refer to him, despite the narrative interest of his life.
>
> "The story of Sehfeld is, as it happens, given support by the fact that it has been reported by writers whose veracity is beyond question and who obtained first-hand information from witnesses to the events they described."

Two such writers were, first, Johann von Justi, a German mineralogist in the service of the Austrian Ministry for Mines, and a member of the Academy at Göttingen; and second, Karl-Christoph Schmieder, Head of the Kassel High School, whose *History of Alchemy* is regarded as a standard work. Here is a résumé of Justi's story:

Born in the first half of the eighteenth century, Sehfeld was early attracted to the study of chemistry and to research along alchemical lines. His first attempts ended in utter failure, and he was obliged to leave the country to escape the mockery and resentment of certain rich people who had financed his youthful efforts. He did not return to his native land for some ten years, but then came back and settled in the little Spa of Rodaun near Vienna, hoping to enjoy peace and quiet in its pleasant valley. He lodged with a man named Friedrich, the Manager of the thermal bathing establishment there. He was on excellent terms with his host and hostess and their three daughters, and decided to prove his gratitude by transmuting a pound of tin to gold while they watched. It was very necessary for him to have Friedrich's help as an intermediary in buying the various utensils and substances he needed for the practice of his Art, and also for the disposal of ingots from time to time at the Mint or to dealers. This fact, which is a certainty, leads one to assume that Sehfeld had succeeded in qualifying as a Master during the intervening years or, at all events, that he had become possessed of a stock of the Hermetic powder.

Friedrich, who expected to earn a good commission on the deals, gladly accepted his lodger's proposition and arranged a number of transactions for him with Viennese goldsmiths and with the Austrian Mint. Unfortunately, the four women of the establishment did not manage to hold their tongues, and soon the whole village knew of Sehfeld's alchemical activities. Rumours of possible arrest were rife and alarmed the alchemist. He decided to ask for a safe-conduct from the Emperor through the intermediary of a friend, on the pretext that he was working on the production of artificial dye-stuffs that would bring large profits, and alleging this as the origin of the foolish tales current about him. In order to obtain the protection of the authorities, he went so far as to offer a considerable annual payment. The offer was evidently accepted, because Sehfeld showed the safe-conduct to the Friedrich family. Justi says that Sehfeld spent several months in this peaceful spot, and made a lot of gold. He performed transmutations at least twice a week, and Friedrich's wife, who told Justi about it after her husband's death, said that she and her daughters often watched the proceedings and that he invariably used tin for transmuting. They told Justi that, after the metal had melted, Sehfeld dropped a red powder into the crucible. A sort of iridescent froth then formed on the surface, rising almost to the top of the vessel. Effervescence lasted for about a quarter of an hour and during this time the metal boiled and bubbled furiously. Then the foam died down, and what remained was the purest gold.

These people had some curious ideas about Sehfeld. They thought he knew what went on in his absence, and also that transmutation could take place only if he willed it. He had on one occasion given them some of the precipitate powder and told them that it was a potent remedy in case of illness. But they had been too anxious to try its transmutatory power, and one day when he had gone to Vienna they decided to make the attempt in his absence. They melted some tin and dropped their powder on it, but it stayed on the surface without sinking in, and caused neither foam nor transmutation. Despite their efforts to efface all traces of the attempt, Sehfeld noticed when he returned that someone had been using the laboratory and his equipment. They admitted it, but begged him to let them try again when he was not in the room with them. He seemed to yield to their entreaties, so they once more melted some tin while he remained in another room. At first the precipitate again would not mix with the metal, so they went to ask his advice. He smiled and told them to look again and transmutation would certainly take place. Hardly had they crossed the threshold when froth formed and all went well. This was what gave them the idea of his occult powers. Yet they were far from believing him to be a sorcerer. No doubt he had before going to Vienna somehow arranged his utensils so as to be able to see if anyone meddled with them during his absence. The fact that the powder had not been effective while he was away could be explained by his not having given them the right kind; and when he came back he could have given them a mixture that would delay its action just long enough for him to have time to return to the laboratory.

His peaceful existence did not last. One night the Bathing Establishment was surrounded by a detachment of police from Vienna. Sehfeld was arrested and taken to the capital, attention having been directed to him by the amount of gold he had sold to the Mint and elsewhere. True, the power of princes was no longer absolute at this date, but various old complaints were resurrected from people who had supplied him with money in his early days, more than ten years before, when he had spent it to no effect. He was accused of cheating and imposture, and was condemned to life imprisonment in the fortress of Temesvar. It was asserted that his present alleged transmutations were nothing but frauds that would delude a fresh lot of innocents.

Sehfeld's situation was, however, not as bad as might have been expected. The commandant of the fortress, General Baron von Engelshofen, had some long discussions with his new prisoner and took a liking to him. He decided that Sehfeld had been the victim of an intrigue and arranged for a counter-investigation to be made in Vienna. Meanwhile, he did his utmost to make Sehfeld's life at Temesvar as little unpleasant as possible, exempting him from fatigues and allowing him all possible liberty within the regulations. And when he went to Vienna a year later, he got to see the Emperor and told him the full story of his prisoner. Von Justi continues:

"Although His Imperial Highness was not entirely convinced, his attention had at least been directed to the person of Sehfeld and when, not long afterwards, the Emperor chanced to be boar-hunting in the forest of Rodaun, he remembered the case and sent for Friedrich, the Manager of the Baths. When he presented himself, he was made to tell all about Sehfeld's stay at his home, down to the smallest details. He did so with the candour and spontaneity that are the hallmark of truth. He described the many occasions on which he and his family had watched transmutations carried out by his guest. When he had finished his story, His Imperial Majesty did not conceal his scepticism, and suggested that they must have been mistaken. But Friedrich burst out: 'Your Majesty, if the good God in person were to come down from heaven and say to me: You're wrong; Sehfeld cannot make gold. I would answer: Lord God, it is true all the same, and I am just as certain of that as I am that You created me!' This anecdote was told by one of the members of the hunt who was present at the whole interview. The certainty evinced by Friedrich, whose frank, open countenance radiated sincerity, and who in any case had the reputation of being an honest man, undoubtedly induced His Majesty to think better of Sehfeld."

When he decided to set Sehfeld free, the Emperor, Francis I, asked him if he would like to take up his alchemical research again, on his (the Emperor's) behalf. Sehfeld, he added, would be given complete freedom of action, but he would at all times be accompanied by two officers chosen for their absolute trustworthiness. Sehfeld agreed to these conditions thankfully, and undertook several journeys in company with his two guards before returning to see the Emperor and carry out a number of chemical experiments in his presence. Nothing is known about these experiments, but Francis I expressed himself as entirely satisfied.

What pleased him less, however, was that one day Sehfeld and the two officers simply disappeared. Von Justi remarks: "A great many discerning people believed that the defection of the two officers was the best argument in favour of Sehfeld's having really been capable of making gold; that he had proved it to the two men and had taught them the secret." The fact remains that Sehfeld never went back to Austria and was thereafter obliged always to maintain the most absolute anonymity. It is only by deduction that Karl Schmieder claimed to find a trace of him in the person of an itinerant Adept, who appeared first in Amsterdam and then at Halle, where he made a present of some precipitate to a chemist's assistant. Bernard Husson, who has studied Sehfeld's case very minutely admits that Schmieder's hypothesis is, as he says, ingenious and attractive; in fact it would seem that, without being prepared to say so definitely, he is strongly inclined to agree with Schmieder.

The story of what happened at Halle is given by Bernard Husson in No. 59 of *Initiation and Science*, quoting from an earlier account published in 1774.

The anonymous author of this earlier account says that a man whose name he was never able to discover was a customer at a chemist's shop in Halle, and always spoke to the same assistant. He went to see him frequently, although he certainly did not need the things he bought, because he was observed throwing them away in the street afterwards. One Sunday the unknown man found the assistant deep in an alchemical treatise, so much so that he did not even hear his customer coming in. He apologised, saying: "It is not surprising that when you are reading alchemical books you lose all sense of what goes on around you; the authors write so obscurely and so confusingly that the greatest concentration and the hardest thinking will not help you to get at their meaning."

The customer rallied to the defence of Hermetic treatises which,

183

he said, were absolutely true and should be treated with respect. He suggested that he might be able to show the young man some interesting experiments if he cared to come and visit him. The assistant accepted gratefully and went that very evening. He found his customer living in absolute squalor. On a wretched pallet bed lay a little box which his host handed to him; he found it astonishingly heavy for its size—a piece of lead of the same dimensions would have been much lighter, he thought. The alchemist, to call him by his proper title, then presented him with a few grains of the powder contained in the box. The young man exclaimed at being given so little, and the alchemist took back some of it—thinking, perhaps of the story of Helvetius. He had not mentioned that the substance was the Philosopher's Stone, and the visitor asked what exactly he was supposed to do with it.

—"Melt some silver," replied the alchemist, "and when it has liquefied drop in the powder just as it is, wrapped in paper, and let it go on boiling for a time; then pour it into a mould, and when you come back we will talk about it again."

"When the young chemist returned to his lodging," the anonymous writer continues, "he waited until everyone else had gone to bed, then went to the laboratory and lit a furnace. As nothing else was handy, he took a silver spoon weighing about an ounce and a quarter. He melted it in a crucible, and when it had liquefied completely, he dropped the paper with the powder into it. The metal began to boil up immediately and a thick froth appeared, with red bubbles in it. The effervescence was so strong that the young man kept pincers within reach to take the crucible off the fire in case it should boil over. But when the bubbles had reached the top of the pan, they subsided. The fire round the crucible blazed gloriously with all the colours of the rainbow; at the end of a quarter of an hour it had died down. He poured the liquid into a flat mould and saw by the light of his candle that what had been white metal an hour earlier was now yellow. The time had grown late, so he put off making any tests until the following day. Next morning, as soon as he awoke, he went to look at the result of his midnight operation, and found that it had become a very dense metal of brilliant colour and highly malleable. He rubbed it on a touchstone and found that the mark was not affected by nitric acid but was removed by a mixture of nitric and hydrochloric acid (aqua-regia). Other tests convinced him that the metal was indeed pure gold. It weighed one and a half ounces, though the original silver had been only one and a quarter ounces. The speed with which the young man rushed over to see the alchemist to tell him how astonishingly successful his powder had been may be imagined. He knocked several times at the door of the room where he had been the night before—but there was no answer."

Doubts might well be expressed of the authenticity of an anonymous story about an Adept and a chemist's assistant, both anonymous too, sited in an unknown place at an unknown date; and the rest of the story might have been copied from that of Helvetius and Philalethes. On the other hand, Schmieder knew the writer of the account personally, and was able to give the following particulars:

"The anonymous writer was Dr. von Leysen, a Councillor at the War Ministry, and Manager of Mines and Salt works in the Saal district, founder of the Society for the Advancement of Natural Sciences in Halle, a man with important connections in all branches of natural science, whom even the great Linnaeus honoured with his friendship, as is shown by correspondence carried on between them. His *Flora halensis* puts him among eminent botanists, and he also won high opinions as a zoologist and mineralogist. But his real preference was for chemistry and metallurgy, and lectures he gave on these subjects at the University won high commendation.

"Leysen had first-hand information about the transmutation carried out by the chemist's assistant, whose name was Reussing. Some years after his adventure he set up as a pharmacist in Löbgune, in the Saal district, some four hours' journey from Halle, and his daughter married Leysen. Reussing was a quiet, reserved man, who carefully avoided drawing attention to himself, especially about this affair. But he told the story with full details to his son-in-law, and when they were alone together the conversation infallibly turned to this subject. I was myself honoured by the paternal friendship of Leysen."

Farther on he adds:

"Reussing went to see Lemrich, the goldsmith in Lurich Street, because he was far and away the best of his kind. Lemrich said that that gold was the finest he had ever seen. He particularly noticed, no doubt, the little star-shaped red marks in it that promised—to anyone who understood—the possibility of prolonging its transmutatory power. The Adept was never seen again in Halle, and his name has never been known. But he left his mark in the crucible, with the scarlet bubbles that are characteristic of Sehfeld."

This is the last material trace found of the alchemist who, like many of his fellows, disappeared completely after this episode. It may have been observed that all through the present chapter Sehfeld has been called an alchemist and not an Adept. This is because details known about his life and the use he made of his supply of the Philosopher's Stone make it very doubtful whether he ever solved the Mystery personally and hence whether he was truly an Adept. Sehfeld was certainly not a bad man, but he was none the less something of a charlatan in his youth, and was too greatly occupied in making gold for his own benefit when he did discover the secret. It seems very possible that during the ten years he spent outside Austria he might have met Lascaris, who was in and about Germany at that time, and have got from him a stock of the precipitate; this would explain his later course of conduct. It will have been noticed in particular that after his liberation from prison he took up his alchemical work again and, as Justi says, carried out a number of experiments with which the Emperor was very well satisfied. Since Sehfeld's reputation as a maker of gold was established, it would seem likely that, if he had really carried out a transmutation in the presence of the Emperor, the higher court officials, at any rate, would have been told. More probably, Sehfeld let him see one of the stages of the Master Work, to show the progress he was making; but I personally do not believe that he was himself capable of renewing his stock of the powder. No doubt he bribed the two officers with some gold that he had secreted in anticipation of such an eventuality. Or else he got rid of them in some other way (since they had been specially chosen by the Emperor as the most incorruptible members of the Guard), while he travelled about Europe searching for Lascaris. Mention has been made above of the kindness of Lascaris when one of his emissaries, like Böttger, got into difficulties, even if it was due to his own carelessness. So one may suppose that Sehfeld succeeded in finding the Master, and obtained from him a fresh supply of powder after he had told him about his misfortunes.

Bernard Husson is inclined to think that Sehfeld may have attained Adepthood towards the end of his life, following a road like that of Michael Sendivogius, who got the Philosopher's Stone before he had even looked for it!

11. The Count de Saint-Germain

It is hardly necessary to go fully into the story of this enigmatic individual here, because whole books have been written about him. We shall only try to decide whether he may properly be included among alchemists, or indeed among Adepts, as many have claimed.

The Count's historical existence begins in London in the year 1743. In 1745 he was in trouble with the Law, suspected of being a foreign spy. Horace Walpole pointed out that he had been in England for two solid years, and had refused to say who he was or where he came from, though he admitted that he was living under an assumed name. The Count was described as a man of medium height, aged about forty-five, very urbane, and a great talker. The name was obviously a pseudonym, for he once told his friend and benefactor, the Landgrave of Hesse: "I call myself Sanctus Germanus, the Holy Brother."

It is also known that, after spending some years in Germany, he went to France, in 1758, to the court of Louis XV. Madame de Pompadour left a description of him: "The Count seemed to be about fifty years of age; he was refined and intellectual, and dressed simply but with good taste. He wore some splendid diamond rings, and had these stones also on his snuff-box and his watch." Although an unknown foreigner, his title of nobility more than doubtful, and his name uncertain to say the least, he became a member of the inner circle at court, and was often granted private audiences by Louis XV. The influence he exerted over the King was a source of considerable exasperation to the Minister Choiseul, and ultimately became the reason for his disgrace and banishment. Finally, it is known that Saint-Germain spent the last years of his life at the castle of the Landgrave of Hesse, where—so it was said—he died on 27th February 1784. It should, however, be noted that his "death" occurred during one of the Landgrave's rare absences, when the only people left at the castle were some women, who might have been bribed to agree to the story.

*

This ends our very brief sketch of the known episodes in the life of Saint-Germain; but a great deal was thought, rumoured and said about him that makes it extremely difficult to decide how much to believe. Was he considered to have been an alchemist? Was he ever an Adept?

According to one story, he boasted at court and in the presence of numerous witnesses that he knew how to increase the size of diamonds; according to another that he had on two occasions turned silver objects to gold; or again, that he possessed the elixir of life and was a great deal older than he looked. And there were even more fabulous tales: the Count, it was averred, had known Pontius Pilate and Julius Caesar personally. Actually, he was in the habit of telling stories of historical events in past centuries as though he had been there and seen it all himself, going into details that even a well-informed historian would hardly know. Sometimes he would stop himself (or appear to do so), and instead of saying: "So-and-so said to Henry IV . . .", he would begin: "So I said to Henry IV . . ." and then correct himself. This might well have been just a game he played, and in any case he never pretended to be a thousand years old, as some people said.

Taking the various points in detail: first, was it ever proved that he could increase the size of diamonds? An account was given by Madame du Hausset, lady-in-waiting to Madame de Pompadour, which may be taken as quite truthful, unlike the famous memoirs of the Countess d'Adhémar, which are certainly apocryphal, since she was born in 1760 and the Count had left Paris a year earlier. One day, Madame du Hausset being present, the Count was talking to the King of his ability to increase the size of diamonds, and to remove blemishes from them. Louis XV sent for a stone he had, of medium size but spoilt by a flaw. Showing it to the Count, he said:

—"This diamond has been valued at six thousand pounds; but it would be worth ten thousand without a flaw. Will you undertake to make four thousand pounds for me?"

M. de Saint-Germain examined the stone carefully, using a strong magnifying glass, and said it could perfectly well be done, but that it would take about a month. The King agreed to this.

"A month later," wrote Madame du Hausset, "he brought back the diamond, wrapped in a piece of asbestos cloth. The flaw had gone. It was weighed and found to be practically the same as before. M. de Gontaut was at once sent with it to the court jewellers, who offered £9,600 for it. But the King decided to keep the stone as a curiosity.

"But was it really the same one? In the course of a month M. de Saint-Germain could have sent it to Amsterdam, could have chosen another one and if necessary have had it cut as nearly as possible like the original but without the flaw. Thanks to his occult resources, the price would be a small matter to him. The King was greatly astonished and remarked that, with his knowledge of this secret, the Count must be a millionaire, especially if, as was said, he could fuse several small diamonds to make a single large one. To a question put by Louis XV on this point, he gave no direct reply, but he claimed to know how to make pearls increase in size and to give them the most beautiful sheen. Pearls, he also said, were the result of a sickness in the oyster, and he knew how to induce the disease."

Clearly, Madame du Hausset's doubts and those which presumably the King also felt, were fully justified. But, however that may be, two words in Madame du Hausset's story are worth noting, where she refers to his "occult resources". It is quite certain that the Count de Saint-Germain had no regular income, that he never at any time received the kind of bills of exchange that enabled nobles living at court to collect the revenues from their estates. It is no less certain that M. de Saint-Germain lived in the greatest luxury. Besides, it would appear that the Count, who was always on the move, possessed neither lands nor property; so the supposition that his ever-renewed wealth was Hermetic in origin is not in the least absurd.

As regards stories of transmutations effected by the Count, there are two of them, one of which is pretty certain to be true, because it comes from the Chevalier de Casanova, who disliked Saint-Germain intensely. The other is at best a matter of hearsay, as it is taken from the memoirs of the Countess d'Adhémar, in which the noble lady says that she knew M. de Saint-Germain well at the court of Louis XV (before she was born!). Casanova's account, on the other hand—although he was an unpleasant person and detested the Count—cannot be called in question.

Saint-Germain was at the time living in Tournai, where Casanova also chanced to be just then, no doubt busy seducing some young local beauty. Casanova had met the Count at the French court, so he went to call on him. M. de Saint-Germain having for some reason shown him a little bottle containing a certain tincture, the Chevalier asked him what it was to be used for:

"It was a white liquid," he writes, "contained in a well-stoppered phial. He told me that it was the universal spirit of nature, and that the proof of this was that the spirit would come out of the phial immediately if the slightest perforation were made in the wax stopper. So I asked him to let me try.

"He handed me the phial and a pin. I pricked a tiny hole in the wax—and, sure enough, the phial was entirely empty in a moment.

—"'That is marvellous,' I said to him; 'but what is the point of it?'

—"'That is just what I cannot tell you. It is my secret.'

"As always, he did not wish me to leave until he had made some deep impression upon me, and he asked if I had any loose change. I pulled out a few coins and laid them on the table.

"He got up without saying what he proposed doing, picked up a piece of glowing charcoal, which he placed on a metal slab. Then he asked me to hand him a sixty-centime piece which lay among the coins. He put a small speck of black powder on it, then laid the coin on the charcoal and puffed at it through a glass tube; in less than two minutes I saw that it was red-hot: 'Wait', said the alchemist, 'until it cools', which it did almost at once. 'Take it', he said, 'for it is yours.' I picked it up. It was gold. I never doubted for a moment that he had somehow juggled away mine and substituted the one I now held, which had probably been whitened beforehand. I did not want to quarrel with him, but neither did I wish him to think he had deceived me, so I said: 'Very clever, Count; but another time you should warn people of what you are going to do, so that you may be the more certain of surprising even the most clear-sighted, and that they may watch the operation attentively and examine the silver coin before you lay it on the hot charcoal.'

" 'People who question my Art,' said the mountebank, 'do not merit my attention.'

"This sort of arrogance was typical of him—I had met it before."

Further on he adds: "The coin was pure gold, and two months later I showed it to Field Marshal Keith whom I met in Berlin; he seemed interested, so I gave it to him."

Casanova's doubts seem to me to be much less convincing than Madame du Hausset's, for the Chevalier's pride could not bear anyone to be cleverer and more brilliant than he was himself. Besides, he knew Saint-Germain's ways well enough to have kept a very watchful eye on his manipulations.

So it would seem certain that the Count was in possession of the philosophic tincture. If so, Saint-Germain no doubt also had the elixir of life, which would account for the stories of longevity current about him. Quite a number of positive facts exist on the subject. His history is well established between the years 1743 and 1784. So trustworthy evidence would be needed from people who could have known him before or after these dates. Such witnesses do, in fact, exist. The first story comes from Madame de Gergy, French ambassadress to the State of Venice. She met Saint-Germain at Madame de Pompadour's house one day, and looked really startled. She said she remembered meeting a foreign nobleman in Venice in the year 1700, who was astonishingly like the Count, although he bore another name. She asked him if it could have been his father or some relative.

"—'No, Madame,' replied the Count calmly. 'I lost my father much longer ago than that. But I was myself living in Venice at the end of the last century, and at the beginning of the present one I had the honour of meeting you, and you were kind enough to enjoy some songs I composed and that we sang together.'

"—'Excuse my frankness, but that is quite impossible. The man I knew in those days was about forty-five years old, and I am sure you are no more than that now.'

"—'Madame,' replied the Count smiling. 'I am very old indeed.'

"—'But in that case you would be nearly a hundred.'

"—'It is not impossible.'

"And the Count began telling Madame de Gergy a mass of details about the time when they had both been in Venice. He offered, if the lady still doubted his word, to remind her of various happenings, of things that had been said. . . .

"—'No, no,' the old ambassadress interrupted, 'I believe you; but you are a queer man . . . a queer devil . . .'" (Quoted by Touchard la Fosse in his *Chroniques de l'oeil-de-boeuf.*)

Concerning the time after 1784, there is the record of at least one occasion on which the count appeared that seems to leave little room for doubt. In the year following his reported death, he attended the Masonic Congress in Paris that was held on 15th February 1785. It included members of the Rose-Croix, the Illuminati, the Cabalists and the Humanitarians. The Free Masons' archives show quite certainly that the Count de Saint-Germain was present, as also were Mesmer, Lavater, Saint-Martin, and others of their kind, and that he spoke at it. Finally, before leaving the subject, one other fact must be mentioned that is an absolute certainty: the Count never ate anything. He refused to take any food whatever at the dinners he attended, but was quite happy to go on talking and dazzling the other guests with his stories and his wit. This again smacks of the philosophic elixir, that allows high Adepts to live without experiencing material needs. As was mentioned above, an alchemist who reached this stage never ate but for pleasure; and Saint-Germain may well have got beyond enjoying earthly food. It was also observed that in this licentious century the Count was not in the least interested in women (nor, for that matter, in the dainty boys of the period), but lived a notably chaste life.

What can be made of all this? It seems probable that the Count de Saint-Germain possessed a store of the Philosopher's Stone that he used not only to cover his financial needs, but also to keep himself in good health and to prolong his life beyond the normal span. Even if the exaggerated stories of his longevity are rejected, it is certain that the Count was about forty-five in 1743 and at least eighty-six in 1784, which was greatly in excess of the average expectation of life in that century.

Actually there was in 1687 a certain Signor Geraldi in Vienna who bore a striking resemblance to the Count, and who for three years excited the interest of the inhabitants of the Austrian capital before vanishing suddenly. Then came Lascaris, who caught the attention of his contemporaries soon after Geraldi's disappearance. What connection had he, you may ask, with the Count de Saint-Germain? Frankly, I do not know; but one wonders. Personal descriptions of the three men are remarkably similar. All three were of medium height and middle aged; they all spoke several languages, and enjoyed talking above all else; all three would appear to have possessed the Philosopher's Stone. True, Geraldi, Lascaris and Saint-Germain did not operate in the same surroundings, but the eclipse of one corresponded pretty closely with the irruption into fame of the next.

All trace of Geraldi is lost in 1691, and Lascaris appeared two or three years later; in his turn he vanished between 1730 and 1740 just before the Count turned up in England. . . .

There is no doubt whatever that Saint-Germain was connected with the Rose-Croix. It has even been suggested that Saint-Germain was Christian Rosenkreutz himself, the founder of the brotherhood, who, having discovered the Hermetic secret, acquired immortality and throughout history appeared under different identities, including that of Philalethes. Personally, I would not go so far; but it does seem extremely probable that Saint-Germain was one of the high emissaries of the Rose-Croix, and that it was the Masters of this secret and always mysterious Society who initiated him. It may be that he succeeded to Lascaris, who himself followed on Geraldi, in the work of keeping alive and promulgating the knowledge of alchemy in different classes of society and in different countries. Or else, perhaps it was the same individual who bore, one after another, different names until his death at the age of over one hundred years. In any case, if he was not himself an Adept, the Count de Saint-Germain was certainly a Hermetic emissary, for his story can be explained only in the light of the Philosopher's Stone.

12. Twentieth-century Adepts

Despite the remarkable demonstrations described in preceding chapters, alchemy sank into disrepute at the end of the eighteenth and the beginning of the nineteenth centuries, chiefly as a result of the influence of the French chemist Lavoisier, whose new theories were soon accepted everywhere, and made any belief in transmutation impossible. Stories of transmutation were at first stigmatised by official science as fraudulent, and afterwards simply ignored. Adepts, therefore, realised that their attempts to promote the Art were now useless, so they gave up the struggle and returned to working in solitude.

Hence only very few practitioners of Hermetic science are known in the nineteenth or the early twentieth centuries. Furthermore, those few surrounded themselves with a wealth of precautions in order to avoid publicity and to remain anonymous. One might have heard of Cyliani in 1832, or Fulcanelli in our own day; but no one has ever discovered who was concealed under those pseudonyms.

Cyliani stated that he had succeeded in carrying out a transmutation at seven minutes past ten o'clock on Maundy Thursday in 1831. Here is the beginning of the preface to his *Hermes Unveiled*:

"Heaven having permitted me to create the Philosopher's Stone after thirty-seven years of research, after spending at least fifteen hundred sleepless nights, after suffering misfortunes without number and irreparable losses, I believe it to be my duty to present to the young, who are the hope of their country, the harrowing record of my life, so that it may be a lesson to them and at the same time dissuade them from pursuing an Art that at a first glance appears to offer as it were glories of red and white roses with never a thorn—but in which the path to the spot where they may be gathered is full of pitfalls.

"Since the universal medicine is a treasure more precious than

197

the gift of riches, students—thinking to be more fortunate than most of their predecessors—will surely be inspired to search for it. This is the reason why I am passing on to posterity in the fullest detail, omitting nothing, the operations that must be carried out, to prevent the ruin of good men and at the same time to render a service to suffering humanity.

"Any reader who is stimulated by my writings has but to discover the prime substance, the fire and the labours of Hercules. All philosophers have been instructed that it is their duty to keep the knowledge hidden. I myself have sworn before God to carry the secret to the grave, and I shall not be forsworn, though I were to be stoned; for I prefer to rouse the wrath of man rather than that of the Eternal."

It is not really certain whether Cyliani was correct in claiming to have succeeded in the Great Work. His treatise seems straightforward enough, except in so far as it concerns the prime substance which he designates metaphorically as gold. It has never been known who he was, but his *Hermes Unveiled* is regularly republished and is regarded as a classic.

The other nineteenth-century alchemical workers have preferred to remain in the shadows, with the exception of the archimist Tiffereau and J. F. Cambriel who says himself that he never solved the mystery. The twentieth century, on the other hand, boasts a brilliant array of Hermetists.

*

Fulcanelli

In 1926 a book entitled *Le Mystère des Cathédrales* and signed with the pseudonym Fulcanelli, was published in Paris by Schemit.* It aroused little interest at its first appearance, but was followed two years later by a second volume, double the length of the first, called *Les Demeures philosophales et le symbolisme hermétique dans ses rapports avec l'Art sacré et l'ésotérisme du Grand Oeuvre*. These two books are regarded by students of the Hermetic Art as being of the

* English translation is published by Neville Spearman Ltd., London.

same calibre as *New Light on Chymistry* by the Cosmopolite and Phila-lethes' *Open Door*. They are, in fact, two of the best, clearest and most soundly based of all treatises on the subject.

Who is, or was, this Adept who managed to keep aloof from the machine world of today and to devote long years to maturing the Philosopher's Stone? Despite the fact that he is a contemporary, despite the existence of living persons who have known Fulcanelli, despite modern methods of investigation, one is thrown back upon hypotheses, none of which seems to fit the case.

Prefaces to the two books by this unknown Adept were written by Eugène Canseliet, who was quite a young man at the time. But M. Canseliet is sparing of biographical details, and cannot be reckoned upon to solve the enigma. In his preface to the first edition of the *Le Mystère des Cathédrales* he says:

> "For a disciple it is a difficult and thankless task to introduce a book written by his own Master.
>
> ". . . The author of this book has for a long time not been among us. The man himself has faded out; only his work survives. I find it hard to evoke the spirit of this studious and scholarly Master, to whom I owe everything; I deplore the fact that he left us so soon. His many friends, unknown brethren who hoped he would resolve the great mysteries for them, join with me in mourning him.
>
> "Could he, having achieved full knowledge, refuse to obey the dictates of fate?
>
> ". . . My Master knew. He disappeared when the fateful hour struck, when the signs were fulfilled. Who would venture to flout the Law? I myself, despite the distress of a grievous but inevitable separation, if I were to win the victory that prompted this Adept to shun the world's homage, I should not act otherwise."

In the preface to the second edition, Eugène Canseliet declared: "When *Le Mystère des Cathédrales* was written in 1922, Fulcanelli had not yet received the gift of God, but he was so near to supreme illumination that he thought it necessary to wait and to preserve his anonymity—as, in fact, he had always done, possibly rather because his character tended towards it than because he wished to obey rigorously the law of secrecy." From these two excerpts we can at any rate gather two or three positive facts. Fulcanelli discovered the Philosopher's Stone between 1922, the date when he wrote the books, and 1926, when his first work was published; and he retired from the world, as every true Adept is encouraged to do—which does not necessarily mean that he died. These explanations, Hermetic in the traditional sense, though expressed in every-day terms, did not satisfy the anonymous Master's readers. A great number of writers and journalists have suggested answers to the puzzle. The four main theories put forward were: that Fulcanelli was the author J. H. Rosny, Senior; the learned writer Pierre Dujols; the painter Jean-Julien Champagne, who illustrated Fulcanelli's books; or, finally, Canseliet himself.

Only two of these suggestions are worth following up. To begin with, not so much as the shadow of any proof has been adduced to identify the alchemist with the elder Rosny, whose life is well known, nor with Dujols, who wrote alchemical articles under the name Magophon, and had therefore no need whatever to hide behind yet another pseudonym.

The reasons for linking Fulcanelli with Canseliet are as follows: M. Canseliet has the manuscripts of the *Demeures philosophales* and of *Le Mystère des Cathédrales*; he arranged for their publication and draws the royalties on them; he is himself an alchemist, and professes opinions identical with those of Fulcanelli. But Eugène Canseliet describes himself simply as Fulcanelli's disciple and the executor of his spiritual testament. Actually, there seems to be to be, firstly, an excellent reason for rejecting this identification, and secondly, clear proof that the two men are not one and the same. M. Canseliet would have no ground for disguising his name under a pseudonym unless he wished to conceal the fact that he is an alchemist. Not only does he not conceal it, but he has in his own name written several books on the Hermetic Art. So, simply to *pretend* that he was not the author of the Fulcanelli books would be absurd and quite pointless.

As regards the proof, it can be found by a comparison of the two men's styles. There can be no doubt whatever that the writings do not come from the same pen.

Anyone reading Eugène Canseliet's work will realise that his literary style is reminiscent of the classicism of past centuries, whereas Fulcanelli's is plain and straightforward; and this is why I consider that the identification should be definitely rejected.

The second suggestion—Jean-Julien Champagne—has been advanced by a good many people. The whole argument is well summarised by Pierre Geyraud in his book *Occultism in Paris*, as the following quotation will show:

"This man Champagne was short of stature and wore long Gallic mustachios; he spoke very largely in cant, which he maintained was a secret language or a code. Even before the appearance of Fulcanelli's two books, he had been heard to profess the ideas contained in them. From the beginning of 1925 he and Canseliet lived at the same address in Paris, No. 59 rue Rochechouart, where both had attic rooms on the sixth floor. Champagne is believed to have stayed there until he died, apparently in utter poverty and squalor, belied by the fact that he was in regular receipt of a large monthly pension. It was never known who provided this positively princely subsidy, nor for what reason; Canseliet would undoubtedly have said it was Fulcanelli, though without explaining why he did not benefit likewise. At all events, the two men lived there in close friendship, but nothing ever indicated that the actual work of preparing the two books for publication was a joint effort.

"And it is undeniable that during the seven years they spent next door to one another while the two books were coming up for publication, it was always Canseliet who worked at the National Library, while Champagne never left his room, where no doubt he had more important things to attend to. Canseliet, living in the adjoining room, professed the greatest regard for his old friend, who was rumoured to be a Healer, and who also carried on alchemical research with passionate enthusiasm, though his laboratory boasted no more than a domestic stove capable of developing a gentle heat, and a few retorts. He is believed to have been brilliantly successful, and to have discovered the prime substance. In any event, he was predestined to this triumph, for his

201

horoscope—recently cast by an astrologer—is 'that of an alchemist who finds the Stone'. He was also interested in secret societies. He founded the Brotherhood of Heliopolis, which many occultists believe to be a powerful and widespread Society, though actually it never had more than a very few members, M. Canseliet being one. (Fulcanelli's books, by the way, are dedicated to the Brotherhood; and the name of Helios, the Sun, is found phonetically linked with that of Vulcan, Fire, in the pseudonym Fulcanelli.)

"Champagne helped to organise a Luciferian Society in the Saint-Merry district, with a strictly limited membership, and himself designed the Baphomet—a male-female demon with the head and feet of a goat—for the inner sanctum, where ritual meetings were held. To this Templar figure, whose right arm hangs down while the left is raised in the traditional alchemical gesture of 'solve, coagula', he added a mitred rump under the right hand, while the left hand brandished an emblem impossible to describe. This fearsome image was later modified to eliminate its anti-religious and grossly sexual features.

"Some time later, in 1932, Champagne is said to have died a horrible, lingering death, at this same address, for having betrayed the Society. After a long-drawn-out struggle, his body tortured by fearful abscesses that seemed like some form of leprosy, he was buried in the cemetery of Villiers-le-Bel, where M. Canseliet piously tends his humble grave. A Latin inscription, stressing his anonymity so as to prevent any charge of posthumous vanity, tells us that here lies an apostle of the Hermetic Science: *Apostolus hermeticae scientiae.*—Is not the care with which M. Canseliet looks after this grave significant? Moreover, M. Jean Schemit, the publisher of the two books, never knew of any third person in the friendship that existed between M. Canseliet and Champagne; and the caretaker at 59 rue Rochechouart never saw anyone among M. Champagne's visitors except Canseliet, M. D. (a young man much interested in alchemical subjects) and M.S. (a young man intended for an important post in the Luciferian Society).

"Obviously, there can be no doubt about the identity of Fulcanelli."

To this quotation may be added revelations made by various people to whom Jean-Julien Champagne is said to have confided verbally, and even in writing, that he was himself Fulcanelli. Unfortunately this identification is no better founded than the last. Champagne's mysterious occupation and his ghastly death had a very simple explanation—absinthe. His pension, it is now known, really was given him by Fulcanelli, who realised that his unfortunate friend was condemned to a more or less short span of life. Eugène Canseliet received as his share the Master's manuscripts as well as the right to the royalties, because Fulcanelli believed that Canseliet would have a long career devoted to alchemical science. In any case, Jean-Julien Champagne could never have written Fulcanelli's books, because they demanded knowledge that could have been acquired only after long years of study. He would have had neither the time nor the physical energy to carry out the enormous amount of research that must obviously have gone into the writing of *Le Mystère des Cathédrales* and the *Demeures Philosophales*. As regards his "confidences", I do not in the least doubt their having been made; on the contrary! Champagne, a student at the time, was well known as a leg-puller and a practical joker, and this, added to his alcoholism, more than explains his claiming to be Fulcanelli. Finally, for him as for Dujols or Rosny there is an excellent reason why none of them could have been the celebrated Adept: they are all quite certainly dead.

*

One question now arises: did Fulcanelli carry out a transmutation during the present century? The following sentence occurs in Eugène Canseliet's book *Alchemy*: "A little while after the successful experiment at the gas works, that is to say, the demonstration of the Master Work carried out before three witnesses, only one of whom has died, Fulcanelli etc. . . ." So I wrote to Eugène Canseliet, to ask him whether he could tell me anything about that "successful experiment". His reply ran as follows:

"I referred in *Alchemy* to an experiment made at the gas works at Sarcelles, which now no longer exist. The experiment consisted in transmuting a piece of lead to gold, which I carried out in my little laboratory at the factory with Fulcanelli's precipitate and according to his instructions. The other two people present were Jean-Julien Champagne, who died in 1932, and Gaston Sauvage, who is to the best of my belief still alive."

The next piece of information about Fulcanelli's alchemical work comes from Jacques Bergier, who was in June 1937 visited by an unknown man who gave no name but said he was the author of two books that were not known to Bergier at the time—*Le Mystère des Cathédrales* and the *Demeures Philosophales*. In *The Dawn of Magic* Louis Pauwels describes the interview:

"One afternoon in June 1937 Jacques Bergier thought he had good reason to believe himself to be talking to Fulcanelli.

"My friend met this mysterious personage at the request of André Hellbronner in the prosaic setting of a test laboratory at the Paris Gas Company. The conversation ran as follows:

"—'M. André Hellbronner, whose assistant I believe you are, is researching into nuclear energy. M. Hellbronner wished to keep me informed about some of the results, and in particular about the appearance of radio-activity in connection with polonium when a bismuth thread is volatilised by an electric charge in high-pressure deuterium. You are very near to success, as of course some other scientists are too. Will you allow me to give you a word of warning? The work that you and your contemporaries are undertaking is appallingly dangerous. It imperils not only you personally—it is a threat to the whole of humanity. To release nuclei is easier than you think, and artificial radio-activity can poison the atmosphere all over the earth within a very few years. Atomic explosions can be created with a few grammes of metal, but can destroy whole cities. I am telling you this point blank. Alchemists have known it for a long time.'

"Bergier was just going to interrupt indignantly: alchemists and modern physics! He was about to burst into sarcastic strictures, when his visitor interrupted:

"—'I know what you are going to say, but it is of no interest to me—you think that alchemists do not know the structure of the nucleus, do not understand electricity, have no means of detection. So they have never achieved a transmutation, nor ever managed to release nuclear energy. I am not going to try to prove what I intend telling you now, but I would like you to repeat it to M. Hellbronner. Geometrical arrangements of extremely pure substances suffice to loose atomic forces without the use of electricity or the vacuum technique. I will say no more, but will just read you a few lines.'

"The man picked up off a desk Frederick Soddy's book *An Interpretation of Radio-Activity*, opened it and read: 'I believe that in the past there were civilisations that understood atomic energy, and that they were utterly destroyed by making a wrong use of it.'

"Then he continued: 'I ask you to agree that certain techniques have partially survived. I also ask you to remember that alchemists have always taken religious and moral issues into consideration in carrying out their researches, while modern physics were born in the eighteenth century from the spare-time amusements of a few lords and rich libertines. Science without conscience . . . I believe that I am doing my duty by warning a few research students here and there; but I have no hope that my warnings will bear fruit. Taking it all in all, I have no reason to hope.'

"The memory of that precise, metallic, dignified voice can never have left Bergier.

"—'May one ask a question?' he said. 'If you are an alchemist yourself, Sir, I cannot imagine that you spend your time trying to make gold like Dunikovski or Dr. Miethe. For the past year I have been doing my best to find out something about alchemy, and I am swamped by charlatans or by interpretations that seem to me to be quite nonsensical. Can you, Sir, explain to me what your work really consists in?'

"—'You are asking me to give you a summary in four minutes of four thousand years of philosophy and of my whole life's work. Furthermore you are asking me to put into plain words concepts for which no plain words exist. But I can at any rate say this: you will not be unaware that in present-day official science the part played by the observer becomes more and more important.

Relativity, the principle of contingency, demonstrates how important is the rôle of the observer nowadays. The secret of alchemy is that there exists a means of manipulating matter and energy so as to create what modern science calls a field of forces. The field of forces acts upon the observer and puts him in a privileged position over against the universe. From this privileged position he has access to realities that space and time, matter and energy, normally conceal from us. This is what we call the Great Work.'

"—'But what about the Philosopher's Stone? The making of gold?'

"—'Those are only applications of it, special cases. The vital thing is not the transmutation of metals, but of the worker himself. It is an ancient secret, discovered by a few persons in each century.'

"—'And what happens to them then?'

"—'I may perhaps find out some day.'

"My friend was never to see the man again; but he had the indelible impression that he had been talking to Fulcanelli. All we know of the Adept is that he survived the War, but disappeared completely after the liberation. All efforts failed to find him again. They were very real efforts, for they were conducted by the 'Alsos' Commission, run by the American C.I.A., who had strict orders to track down anyone at all concerned with atomic science in Europe after 1945. Bergier was called upon as a witness, but was unable to give any help to the Major who interrogated him. The Major allowed him to see the first report issued about the military use of the atom. Jacques Bergier discovered from it that the atomic pile was indeed described as a 'geometrical arrangement of extremely pure substances', and also that—just as Fulcanelli had told him—its functioning depended neither upon the technique of the vacuum nor upon electricity. The report ended by referring to the risk of atmospheric pollution that might extend over the whole earth. It is understandable that both Bergier and the American officers were anxious to trace a man who was the living proof that alchemical science was ahead of official science by decades. But, if Fulcanelli was ahead in atomic knowledge, he was likely also to be in other matters, and so all efforts to find him came to nothing."

This is all that is known about the anonymous Master who, none the less, takes his place among the greatest Adepts of all time, and who—in this century, in which the doctrine of scientific omniscience is splitting in every direction—remains a beacon for all unorthodox Seekers.

*

Armand Barbault

The case of this contemporary alchemist is interesting on several counts. First, because it is astonishing that, well on in the second half of the twentieth century, a man who strictly applies mediaeval instructions to his Hermetic work, in particular those of the *Mutus Liber* and the *Emerald Table*, should succeed in discovering a material that is impossible to analyse by even the most modern scientific methods; and then, because Armand Barbault does not hesitate to describe his process fully, to reveal what his prime substance is, and what kind of liquid he used for its distillation.

Armand Barbault's avowed aim was to discover a new medicine, comparable with Paracelsus' drinkable gold, by purely alchemical means, and with reference also to astrology. This was why, as he says himself, he chose a prime substance that was not like the mineral bodies used by traditional Hermetic philosophers: in point of fact, he used *earth*. As regards the secret fire he needed for distilling and at the same time for maturing his prime matter, he decided upon the sap of plants and early morning dew. He was inspired to do so by a picture in the *Mutus Liber* showing a couple of alchemists wringing out cloths that had been stretched between poles overnight to gather the dew. Armand Barbault used to drag sheets across grass so as to soak them in dew. His Work, carried out with no more than 1800 grammes of earth (*less than four pounds*), lasted for twenty-two years—in which one may recognise the traditional delays always suffered by Hermetic students. The elixir that he eventually obtained was tested in German pharmaceutical laboratories, where it was agreed that it would be efficacious for certain maladies, among them affections of the heart and kidneys. So the incredible happened—incredible, that is, to the scientific mind, though familiar in the

Hermetic Art. Raymond Abellio tells the story in a preface he wrote to Armand Barbault's book *The Gold of the Thousandth Morning*:

"When, at the beginning of the 'sixties, Armand Barbault obtained his first tincture, he submitted specimens to well-equipped pharmaceutical laboratories for analysis. After exhaustive tests, they enquired how a similar product might be obtained by industrial methods, that is to say in large quantities and cheaply. Twelve long years of preparation for the prime matter, endless manipulations, the need for the producer to rise each morning before the dawn for months on end in order to collect dew from the fields or from young plants with rising sap, the tentative procedures, the enormous amount of labour involved, all appeared to the laboratory workers to be not only very expensive but unnecessary: there must be some way of simplifying it, of accelerating the process, of finding syntheses. All in vain. Not only did the liquid prove impossible to analyse, but nothing even vaguely resembling it could be discovered. Yet Armand Barbault concealed nothing."

Elsewhere Raymond Abellio says: "Faced with the liquid, that had taken on the colour of gold and that was impossible to analyse by any of the usual methods, it was they—the industrialists at the laboratories and not the alchemists—who came to speak of a new category of matter, endowed with mysterious, possibly vital, properties."

This is the real essential—the proof that it is perfectly possible to obtain by alchemical means substances that cannot be analysed in even the most up-to-date laboratories and that are impossible to reproduce synthetically by modern chemical means. This recent and irrefutable fact answers the assertion by official science that—because scientists are themselves incapable of doing it—alchemists have never been able to discover the secret of metallic transmutation. Alchemy and chemistry, so scientists maintain, are in no sense branches of the same discipline; they are completely separate and indeed irreconcilable faculties.

The other particularly remarkable point about Armand Barbault's case is that he describes in plain language all his methods and the prime substances that he has used. He justifies this by asking:

"Are we over-estimating the mystery and the danger of explaining it to the laity? All writers have said that the prime substance is to be found everywhere in Nature, that the ignorant tread it underfoot, that it is only necessary to stoop and collect it. Actually, if the prime substance is so carefully concealed from the eyes of laymen, it must be because it is much more difficult to find than is admitted and possibly, too, the elements constituting it differ from one Adept to another, so that what is right for one may not necessarily do for another. I propose, for my part, to attack the problem from this angle, because I fully intended to tell you all I know about the prime substance."

Finally, this contemporary alchemist has now begun work on the philosophic Mystery proper, no longer with the aim of producing a golden medicament but the Stone itself. The earth he used as his prime substance has, after twenty-two years of work on it, been transformed little by little to what the author calls the first degree of perfection. Since then, Barbault has for the past two years been working to bring it to the second degree of perfection, which will ultimately—after a necessarily indeterminate period of time—lead to the Philosopher's Stone. At the end of his book he says:

"In this year 1969, the sap is not very plentiful nor sufficiently rich, because two eclipses of Aries and the conjunction of the new moon with Saturn coincided with a frost that damaged plants on which we had been relying. It is therefore not certain that I shall succeed in bringing the substance to the second degree of perfection this year. At the same time, I discovered to my surprise that that part of my Stone which I was able to preserve promised well—it was a dark mass, its surface covered with little crystals, and within the mass were quantities of stellate specks. Tradition leads me to believe that this means that there is mercury ready to emerge from its matrix."

*

There could be no better conclusion to this study of the lives of the principal Adepts than the picture of an alchemist hanging over his prime substance like a father over the cradle of a new-born baby watching for the first smile. The Hermetic philosopher does not seek to break up nuclei nor to split atoms like modern physicists, he does not want to provoke reactions in order to study the chemical properties of one or another substance. Instead, he aspires to enter into spiritual communion with Nature, from whom he acquired his own particular prime matter, that he saw and recognised, and that he will, with patience and humility, develop to the highest degree of perfection of which it is capable. Is the alchemist a scientist? No, he is a farmer working to bring his corn to golden ripeness.

Now that the existence of the Philosopher's Stone has been abundantly proved by our study of the lives of the best-known chymical philosophers, all that remains is to try to discover the secret of its preparation. And it is proposed to do so in the last part of this book.

Book III

The Philosopher's Stone

THE DRAGON OF CHAOS

In the midst of the plate is a three-headed dragon whose heads by one interpretation are ignorance, superstition and fear; and by another interpretation wrong thought, wrong feeling, and wrong action. The dragon with its tail in its mouth represents eternity or ageless chaos, the slime of space from whose dark womb Cosmos or order is born. The cross, the solar face, and lunar crescent together make the symbol of Mercury, the proper hermetic figure for the adept or perfected man. From the lunar crescent rise the rose of Sharon and the lily of the valley. By the rose is here meant the red tincture, the elixir of life. By the lily, the white tincture or transmuter of metals. The whole figure is a Rosicrucian rebus.

1. Grudging or Generous?

An alchemist is said to be "grudging" if he knowingly gives wrong information about his Art, and "generous" if he reveals a truth. So one of the first things a student has to learn is to recognise whether an alchemical work comes from the pen of a "grudging" author or from one who is "generous", and it is no use hoping that he will ever be able to distinguish them by rule of thumb. In the main, there are two kinds of books on alchemy—those in which the writer says that he is convinced of the futility of alchemical speculations and therefore that the creation of the Philosopher's Stone is an impossibility; and those in which the author, introducing himself as an "amateur" (in the true sense of the word, a "lover") of the Art or an "initiate", says that he is bound by the traditional vow of secrecy, and therefore that any revelations about substances or processes used in the Work are not only worthless but actually dangerous. Some of those in the second category, no doubt hoping to appear "generous", adopt the system employed by Dom Pernety in his *Mytho-Hermetic Dictionary*: they quote series of extracts from the best treatises, grouped under various heads such as prime matter, secret fire, philosophic mercury, etc. Obviously such quotations, taken out of context and deriving from all manner of different authors, can only put the finishing touch to the perplexity of the unhappy student. I know two such works that indicate quite plainly the nature of prime matter. The drawback is that it is not the same in the two books. Also, it is a dangerous procedure, for the choice of texts can easily brain-wash the reader into adopting some particular mental attitude.

I personally intend to go further: I consider that the time has come for "revelation" (a word derived from the Latin *re-velare*, meaning to remove a veil). I am inclined to think that the supposed need for secrecy is a relic of the past, and I hold with Isaiah where he says,"The crooked shall be made straight and the rough places plain; and the glory of the Lord shall be revealed and all flesh shall see it . . ." (Isaiah XL 3) and Raymond Abellio in his preface to *The Gold of the Thousandth Morning* asks:

"Why is secrecy imposed upon those who engage in the quest, and why the dire threats against any who dare to make a disclosure? Nothing is more deceptive than books professing to teach esotericism, whose authors hint that they could say very much more than they do—but that we are unworthy to receive it! One's instinct is to reply: 'Then why write the books? Hunt your secret knowledge in secret and don't talk about it!' And one is tempted to add the well-known gibe: 'What you understand, you do; what you don't understand, you teach!' In truth, the secrecy that is supposed to be obligatory according to a decree that is itself obscure, appears to rest upon misconception. We are living in a time when categorical imperatives one way or the other are no longer accepted and when the motto is 'Nothing venture, nothing win!' Would not the prospect of danger act rather as a spur than otherwise in the search for knowledge? In the last analysis, the best defence lies in the intrinsic difficulty of the subject."

To be fair, one must examine the reasons advanced by those who wish to keep alchemical knowledge tucked away among the secret files. Bernard Husson, for example, is an enthusiast and has himself carried out two years' work in a laboratory, so his opinion is worth listening to:

"As we know, fifteenth and sixteenth century Adepts used unvarnished, coherent and precise language to describe the preparation and purification of a small number of substances that were used in the early stages of the Work, although these were not, properly speaking, essential to the final operations. Beginning from the seventeenth century, they relied on explanations given by their predecessors as well as by chemists of their own day, and felt it to be unnecessary to repeat them; so they disguised them under the veil either of allegory or of symbolism (siting them in another plane of existence). As a result, it was believed that the 'secret of alchemy' consisted in knowing what were the mineral substances to be manipulated, and in understanding how to carry out the manipulations. But of course, a 'secret' of this description was bound sooner or later to be found out. So why has silence, or at any rate extreme discretion, been enjoined right up to the present day? It was not, let it be emphasised, due to mere childishness; but as far as traditional alchemists are concerned, it was a point of honour, as it was among the ancients, who swore never to betray the 'secret' of the Eleusinian mysteries—which could not properly be called a secret at all, because almost everyone in the higher walks of life underwent initiation."

Can such an answer be considered convincing? Surely not. Bernard Husson recognises that the secret does not lie in knowing the nature of the substances used in alchemical work. And Raymond Abellio is right when he says that alchemy is quite capable of itself preventing penetration of its secrets because of the inherent difficulties of the Master Work. Knowledge of the substances used in the Work is obviously necessary, but it is by no means all that is needed for creating the Philosopher's Stone. This is where alchemy differs from chemistry and from any other science, in which experiments made in given conditions can always be repeated. To put it quite bluntly, this can never be done in alchemy. The Art may more truly be likened to agriculture, in that it aspires to raise a particular substance to a higher degree of perfection, to what may be called a certain degree of maturity; and in another way it may be said to need a "knack", just as two cooks may use the same materials and the same recipe, yet only one of them has the right "touch", and so the results will be different.

So there seems to be no obvious reason to go on hiding the secrets of the Work from the public and from the scientific world. When I said as much to Bernard Husson, the substance of his reply was: "I have been initiated, I have sworn secrecy, and it is a point of honour for me to keep silence." Obviously this answer is valid for him; but it would not be for me. I fully intend to discuss openly the different substances that are used in the alchemical Mystery; and then to pass on to the practical work of creating the Stone. I am obliged, of course, to make the same reservations as Jacques Bergier, who said: "I can only give my own opinion. I am not an initiate, and I am not a member of any secret society, but I have studied alchemy for nearly forty years. I have discovered a few things. I have carried out some experiments." My own study of the Hermetic Art has lasted for only about twelve years—a relatively short time in view of the difficulties of the subject; it has, nevertheless, allowed me to arrive at certain conclusions.

To begin with, I read what people who were not themselves "amateurs of the Science" had to say about materials used in the Work. Here are a few extracts from their opinions. Louis Figuier:

"... the two germinative substances used in the Work are *ordinary gold*, which represents the male principle, and philosophers' mercury, also known as the prime agent, which represents the female principle. ... The only difficulty in the preparation of the Philosopher's Stone consists in obtaining philosophers' mercury. Once this has been found, the operation is the simplest thing in the world. ... But the preparation of this mercury is no easy matter. All alchemists realise that its discovery is beyond human skill and can be attained only by divine revelation or through the generosity of an Adept who has himself received enlightenment from God."

Figuier then lists a number of bodies in which he says alchemists have sought their mercury. In reading his text it is clear that he has confused Philosophers' mercury with philosophic mercury; he believes that gold is the prime matter in the Work; he thinks that the Mystery is easy to solve as soon as the necessary substances have been found; and finally, he confuses Puffers with Adepts, for only the former are ignorant of the materials that must be used. It would seem, therefore, that Figuier did not pursue his research into practical operations very deeply. In any case, he was convinced that the enterprise was vain and doomed to failure from the outset.

Next on the list is Albert Poisson:

"The prime matter of the Great Work," he says, "consisted of gold and silver, united by mercury, all prepared in a particular way.

Gold was used because it is rich in sulphur, silver because it contains a very pure form of mercury, while quicksilver represents salt, a general unifying agent. These three substances, prepared according to certain processes, were enclosed in a glass matrass known as the philosophic egg, hermetically sealed. The whole thing was then heated in a furnace called an athanor."

It appears doubtful whether Poisson, who himself worked in a laboratory to the point of losing his health and dying of tuberculosis at an early age, was really sincere when he wrote the words quoted above. I would rather think that he was being intentionally "grudging", because I cannot see how he could genuinely be so mistaken.

Serge Hutin is a contemporary of our own and in his book *Alchemy* he writes:

"Gold and silver (to which quicksilver, or ordinary mercury, was sometimes added as being particularly rich in salt, to act as the unifying agent between sulphur and mercury) constituted the original, unpurified, substance of the Stone. But they could not be used in their natural state; they had first to be purified and made ready to serve for the next part of the Work, as a mixture of sulphur extracted from the gold and mercury extracted from the silver (though, according to some writers, natural gold might be used directly). . . . This was followed by a whole series of operations destined to procure the two opposing principles from gold and silver, the two perfect metals. 'Gold is the most perfect of all metals; it is the father of our Stone, and yet it is not its prime matter: the prime matter of the Stone is the germinative power contained in gold.'" (Philalethes, *Fountain of Chymical Philosophy.*)

Serge Hutin, who is not himself a laboratory worker, has evidently allowed himself to be misled by Poisson and by the tendentious words of Philalethes. Actually, Philalethes is perfectly correct in saying that the germinative principle of gold is the prime matter of the Stone, but that does not mean that the essence must be extracted from gold itself.

217

Guillaume Salmon, author of the *Dictionary of Chymical Philosophers*, was himself an alchemist although he did not describe the broad outlines of the Master Work from his own experience but as a historian of the Art. This is what he says:

"Philosophers tell us that the Work is carried out as follows: Philosophers' mercury (which they call the female) is added to and amalgamated with gold (the male), purified and laminated or in filings; these are put into the philosophic egg (a small oval matrass, which must be hermetically sealed, so that none of the matter evaporates). This egg is placed in a bowl filled with ash, and this is itself stood in the furnace. Thereby the mercury, stimulated by the heat of its intrinsic sulphur and by the fire lighted by the Artist, tended by him and kept continually at the proper temperature—this mercury, I say, gently dissolves the gold and reduces it to its prime constituents."

These few lines are the very archetype of a text that is both true and "grudging". What Salmon says is, in fact, true only at one particular stage; actually it refers to the last part of the Work, though he suggests that it is the beginning. Moreover, he does not say exactly what he means by "Philosophers' mercury" nor by "gold"; and so, without telling lies, he manages to mislead the reader.

Next comes Jacques Bergier who, among non-initiates, certainly has the soundest knowledge of alchemical subjects. And the *modus operandi* that he describes is certainly the nearest to the truth that I have been able to discover among modern writers. I would not like to say that he has actually given the "recipe", but the processes he describes—in plain language—are very near indeed to the real Master Work and may therefore be taken as the point of departure for a critical examination of traditional texts.

"We shall now," he writes, "try to describe exactly what an alchemist does. We cannot claim to reveal the alchemical procedure in its entirety, but we believe we have made some interesting discoveries about the process. We do not overlook the fact that the ultimate aim of alchemy is the transmutation of the alchemist himself, and that the manipulations represent a slow advance towards the 'liberation of the spirit'. It is about these particular manipulations that we are hoping to give fresh information.

"To begin with, the alchemist will have spent years in deciphering ancient texts in which 'the reader has been involved without Ariadne's thread to guide him through a labyrinth in which everything has been intentionally and systematically arranged to plunge the novice into inextricable mental confusion'. Patience, humility and faith will have brought him to a certain level of understanding herein, and at this level he will be enabled to begin the real alchemical experiment. This experiment can and will be described; but one element is lacking. We know what goes on in the alchemist's laboratory; but we do not know what goes on in the alchemist himself. It may be that it is interconnected.

"Our alchemist begins by preparing, in an agate mortar, a close combination of three constituents. The first, which makes up ninety-five per cent. of the whole, is a mineral such as arsenic pyrites, a ferrous mineral containing especially arsenical and antimonial impurities. The second is a metal—iron, lead, silver or mercury. The third is an acid of organic origin: tartaric or citric acid. All these must be pounded by hand in his mortar, and the constituents left to blend for five or six months. Then the whole mass must be heated in a crucible, the temperature being raised progressively for ten days. Certain precautions must be observed, because toxic gasses will be given off—mercury vapour and especially arsenious hydrogen—which have killed many an alchemist at the beginning of his labours.

"Finally, the contents of the crucible must be dissolved by means of an acid. It was in their search for the solvent that old-time alchemists discovered acetic acid, nitric acid and sulphuric acid. The dissolution should be carried out under a polarised light, either weak sunlight reflected in a mirror or moonlight. It is known nowadays that polarised light vibrates in a single direction, whereas normal light vibrates in all directions round an axis.

"After this the liquid must be evaporated and the solids recalcined. This particular operation must be carried out over and over again, thousands of times, for years on end. Why? We do not know.

Possibly it is so as to make sure of catching the right moment, the moment when all the conditions are exactly right—cosmic rays, earth-magnetism, etc. Or it may possibly be in order to obtain a lessened response to stimulus ('fatigue') in the interior structure of the substance which as yet we do not understand. The alchemist speaks of 'divine patience', of slow condensation of the 'universal spirit'. There must surely be something more behind this para-religious language. . . .

"To continue the description: at the end of several years' continuous work along the same lines, by day and by night, the alchemist will decide that the first phase of the Work is finished. He will add an oxidiser, such as potassium nitrate, to his mixture; so his crucible now contains sulphur from the pyrites, and charcoal

Roger Bacon's Gunpowder Anagram (13th century)

from the organic acid, together with the nitrate. It was from this phase of the operation that early alchemists discovered gunpowder.

"Dissolution, then calcination, must be repeated ceaselessly, for months and years, awaiting a 'sign'. Alchemical writers differ as to the nature of this sign, but it may be that there are several possible phenomena. Some alchemists expect stellate crystals to form on the surface of the mixture; others note that an oxidised film appears on the surface, which then parts to discover the luminous metal, reflecting in miniature the galaxy or some constellation.

"Once the sign has appeared, the alchemist removes his amalgam from the crucible and leaves it to 'mature', kept well sheltered from air and moisture, until the early Spring. When he begins work again, the operations will be directed towards what older texts call 'preparation for the tenebrae (*shadows*)'.

"The mixture is placed in a transparent container of rock crystal, securely sealed. Not very much is said about this form of closure, which is described as 'hermetically sealed'. The work now consists in heating the container by increasing the temperature very, very gently. It must be brought to a particular degree of incandescence, every care being taken to avoid an explosion. Many cases have occurred of alchemists being seriously burned or killed. Such explosions are exceptionally violent, and develop temperatures much higher than would normally be expected.

"The aim of the operation is to obtain an 'essence', a 'fluid', which alchemists sometimes call the 'raven's wing'. . . .

"The alchemist heats, leaves to cool, heats again, for months or years, watching the formation in his container of what is also known as the 'alchemical egg': the mixture having changed to a blue-black liquid. Finally, he opens the vessel in semi-darkness, by the light only of his fluorescent liquid, which, when it comes in contact with the air, solidifies and crumbles.

"In this way completely new substances are obtained, unknown in nature, and having all the characteristics of chemically pure elements, that is to say of substances that cannot be broken down chemically. . . .

"The alchemist has, therefore, by opening his crystal container, and cooling the fluorescent liquid by contact with the air, obtained one or more new elements. Some residue will be left; this he will steep in thrice-distilled water, for several months. Then he will keep the water shielded from light and in an even temperature. This water will have remarkable chemical and medical properties. It is the universal solvent, the traditional elixir of life. . . .

"The alchemist now possesses a certain number of elements, unknown in nature, and several bottles of an alchemical liquid capable of prolonging life considerably by rejuvenating the tissues.

"He will next try to re-combine his new elements. He will mix them in his mortar and liquefy them at a low temperature by the use of catalysts about which the texts are very vague. This work will again take some years.

"By this means, we are told, he will obtain substances that are exactly like known metals, and in particular metals that are good conductors of heat and electricity. These will be alchemical copper, alchemical silver, alchemical gold. . . . Some other, even more remarkable substances will result from alchemical manipulations. One of these is said to be soluble in glass at a low temperature and before glass itself is fusible. When this substance comes in contact with slightly softened glass, it will disintegrate within it and turn it to a ruby-red colour, that shines with a sort of mauve phosphorescence in the dark. If this tempered glass is pounded in the mortar, the result is what alchemical texts call the Philosopher's Stone or 'precipitate powder'." (*The Dawn of Magic.*)

The man who wrote the above has clearly worked in a laboratory and has reached a certain stage in the Master Work. Some inaccuracies about the time when the potassium nitrate is added, and the stage at which the universal medicine is obtained, prove that the Work was not wholly completed—which, in fact, Bergier never claimed to have done. With these reservations, I consider the book to be essential for the student who will be able to use it as "Ariadne's thread" to prevent being lost when he begins on the traditional treatises.

Now that a starting point has been reached that is sound, if not absolutely assured, it is time to discover the real chemical identity of prime matter, the secret fire and philosophic mercury.

2. Philosophers' Raw Material

Prime Matter

"There is a mineral known to true scientists who disguise it under various names in their books; its constituents are at once abundantly stable and volatile."

So says the eighteenth-century alchemist Le Breton in his *Keys to Spagiric Philosophy*; and in saying it he is only repeating the unanimous opinion of all philosophers, which is that the prime matter of the Mystery, the raw material of philosophers, is a single, unique body. This is the point from which our enquiry can properly begin: the substance exists and it is unique, we cannot get away from these two facts. It will be interesting to see what some of the Adepts who are known to have achieved the Philosopher's Stone have to say on the subject. The Cosmopolite, in his *New Light on Chymistry* writes:

"It is and is not a stone. It is called a stone because it looks like one; first, because it really is stone when it is extracted from the depths of the earth—it is hard and dry and can be broken up and pulverised like stone. Secondly, because, after the stinking sulphur and other impurities in which it is embedded have been eliminated, it can be reduced to its essence by slow degrees, as by a natural process, making it an incombustible stone, resistant to fire, and as easy to melt as wax: which implies that it has regained its universality."

All philosophers agree too that the substance is to be sought in the mineral kingdom, any other being too far removed from the perfection of metals to be suitable for the ultimate production of transmutatory powers in the Philosopher's Stone. Clearly, therefore, the prime matter must be a metallic mineral.

Much the same emerges in one of the *Discourses between King*

223

Khalid and Morien the Philosopher: "It is a worthless stone, black and evil-smelling; it costs practically nothing; it is heavy for its bulk . . . this is the first thing that must be known by any Seeker." In an anonymous seventeenth-century book entitled *Light out of Darkness* we read: "The substance is unique, and the poor possess it as well as the rich. It is known, but unrecognized, by everyone. In his ignorance, the ordinary man thinks it is rubbish, or sells it at a minimal price, although it is most precious to philosophers." Eugène Canseliet, in his preface to the *Demeures Philosophales*, says: "We no longer think it unwise to publish the fact that Fulcanelli told us he had spent twenty-five years searching for the philosopher's gold although it was around him all the time, under his hand, before his eyes. His confession, made in all frankness and humility, almost in a spirit of self-reproach, left us momentarily speechless. But, truth to tell, his experience is not unusual."

So we know that it is a mineral, and an ordinary mineral. But we must not allow ourselves to be misled by the mention of its low commercial value, because prices have changed considerably since the days when a good many of these books were written. This, incidentally, allows us to reject the identification of the substance with any metal properly so-called, whether it be gold, silver or mercury.

Which mineral, then, should we choose? In studying even the most "generous" of texts, it will be found that many Adepts have given their prime matter the name of various known minerals, or at any rate have indicated that the substance was of the same type as one or another of them. I am going to give a series of quotations to help us reach what I believe to be a most important conclusion—indeed one might call it a "revelation"—because I think it has never before been stated clearly and definitely: the prime matter is *a form of cinnabar*.

Please note, I do not say that it *is* "cinnabar", which is sulphide of mercury, but "*a form of* cinnabar", which means that the prime matter is a metallic sulphide. This is the reason why the Cosmopolite speaks of the stinking sulphur that must be eliminated; and this should not be confused with "philosophers' sulphur", which is also contained in the mineral.

To this extent, then, the problem is limited, the more so since in the Middle Ages, as also in antiquity, only seven metals were known, to which, however, zinc, arsenic and antimony must now be added. So there are ten possible kinds of sulphide. We shall briefly examine each of them and try to reach some effective decision.

*

Cinnabar, or sulphide of mercury (HgS).

The name cinnabar is derived from a Persian word meaning "dragon's blood", which is also one of the names used for prime matter. A number of authors have left their readers to infer, or sometimes have actually stated, that sulphide of mercury was in fact the prime matter; and this seemed reasonable enough because it contains both sulphur and mercury. Unfortunately it was rather too obvious a choice, as Dom Pernety points out in his *Mytho-Hermetic Dictionary*: "A good many chymists have mistakenly decided that ordinary, natural cinnabar is the material for the Great Work: but only ordinary mercury can be extracted from it, while alchemical cinnabar contains sublimated, purified mercury, red in deposit, which they call sulphur." And the contemporary alchemist Kamala-Jnana, in his *Dictionary of Alchemical Philosophy*, says: "Cinnabar: sulphide of mercury, from which commercial sulphur and mercury can be extracted. Mercury and sulphur in this form are dead matter, killed by the fire used to remove them from their matrix. Some philosophers (like Hermes) have referred to it as the prime matter, but this must be taken only as a standard of comparison—analogous, but not the same; similar, but not identical—because the mineral used by philosophers is not manipulated in the same way." Which is more or less what we said earlier in this chapter.

Argentite, silver-glance or native sulphide of silver (Ag$_2$S).

This mineral is rare and expensive, so may be eliminated from our list. The same is, of course, true of any sulphides of gold.

Galena, lead-glance or native sulphide of lead (PbS).

One sentence in Fulcanelli's *Demeures Philosophales* rather seems to indicate this mineral: "The symbol has the same significance as the letter G, seventh in the alphabet, initial letter of the common name for prime matter." (Note: Here G stands for *Ge*, Earth, one of whose

225

constituents is the prime matter. It is shown in one of the illustrations in the book as the centre of a radiant star.) Eugène Canseliet, in his own book *Alchemy*, says much the same:

"To understand the letter G is simply to show oneself capable of adding to it the remaining letters forming the name of the raw material. Obviously galena jumps to one's mind, for it designates natural sulphide of lead, the only source of the base metal, and is also favoured by the twelfth-century philosopher Artephius: 'Antimony comes under Saturn, and this Saturnian antimony also has an affinity with the sun, as it contains quicksilver with which no metal except gold can be fused.'"

These are the only two pointers to this substance that I have found, and they appear to me to be "grudging", that is to say, intended to mislead the student, because all other philosophers regard lead as being too far removed from the perfection of gold for it ever to be raised to the degree of transcendance required for the Philosopher's Stone.

Copper Sulphide, cogelite or copper-glance (CuS).
There are, in fact, several copper sulphides, some in combination with iron, like copper pyrites. None of them was normally used by alchemists in past centuries, and I have never found any allusion to them.

Tin (Sn).
This metal does not contain ordinary, natural sulphur, and I should have eliminated it, but for the fact that Roger Bacon referred to it by name in his *Mirror of Alquimy*. He tells us exactly what the nature of tin is: "It is a pure substance, imperfect, composed of a pure form of mercury, stable and volatile, bright, externally white, internally red. Its sulphur has the same characteristics. All that tin needs is to be heated and worked on a little more." And farther on he says: "A substance must be chosen that contains pure, bright, red and white mercury, a substance not wholly perfect, to be smoothly blended with a similar type of sulphur in the proportions required by the Work." Was Bacon being more "generous" than his colleagues? No, I am

226

afraid he was being "grudging", for no one except he himself has ever recommended tin.

Orpiment, or arsenic tri-sulphide (As_4S_6).

Its colour has tricked many a seeker, for it is a clear golden yellow. And of course some of the workers knew that arsenic played a part in the Master Work; but they did not realise that it was only one of the philosophic synonyms for a salt. This is why orpiment has often been believed to be the prime matter.

Zinc-blende or sphalerite, native sulphide of zinc (ZnS).

Only Fulcanelli has suggested that . . . possibly . . . But, as in the case of galena, the Master was laying a false trail.

Pyrites, or sulphide of iron (FeS_2).

This is the mineral referred to by Jacques Bergier in the excerpt quoted in the last chapter, but it is one that philosophers have either ignored or regarded as unsuitable for the Work. Might this not imply that they were being "grudging"? Bergier has identified iron pyrites with prime matter as a consequence of what he has read and of laboratory experiments that he has carried out. I myself have done some research along the same lines and have found indications here and there showing that iron is not really inconsistent with the requirements of the Work. For instance, Fulcanelli says in the *Demeures Philosophales*:

> "Considering the profound chemical affinities of these bodies, it is reasonable to suppose that the same element, used in the same circumstances, will yield the same result. This is what happens with iron and gold, which are very closely allied. When Mexican prospectors come upon very red, sandy soil, largely composed of iron oxide, they feel pretty sure that gold will be found not far off. They regard this red earth as the *womb of gold* (*my italics,* J.S.), and the best indication of a near-by vein. This seems curious when the physical differences between the two metals are considered. Normally, gold is among the rarest of metals; iron, on the other hand, is certainly the commonest, it is found everywhere, not only in

great seams in the mines, but even on the surface. . . . Of all classified ores, iron pyrites is the most ordinary and the best-known."

This passage is important, because it follows upon various more or less allegorical or veiled allusions by the older philosophers. I am thinking particularly of Sendivogius, where he says: "And to put it more clearly, it is our lodestone, sometimes called our sword (steel) . . . It is named magnesium, because its magnetic and occult characteristics attract to itself the son of the Sun from the very moment when it comes into effective existence." Magnet, steel—iron again!

One last mineral remains to be examined before we make up our minds, and one which also has a good claim to the honour of being philosophy's prime matter.

Stibnite, native antimony trisulphide (SB_2S_3).

Another variety of this metal is kermesite, a cherry-red mineral sometimes allegorically named as oak (because the kermes insect, used as a red dye-stuff, breeds in the kermes-oak).

To begin with, it should be noted that Artephius' words about galena, quoted above, might equally well be applied to antimony. It should also be remembered that Basil Valentine devoted a whole treatise to this mineral—*The Triumphal Chariot of Antimony*—and that Philalethes gave one of his works the title *Experiments in the Preparation of Philosophic Mercury by the Regulus of Stellate Ferrous Antimony and Silver*.

Fulcanelli, in his *Demeures Philosophales*, says:

"The most learned among our traditional Cabalists have no doubt been struck by the resemblance between the *way*, the *path* traced by the hieroglyph which forms the figure 4, and mineral antimony or stibium, that is clearly indicated by this topographic name. Natural oxisulphide of antimony was called *Stimmi* or *Stibi* in Greek; and Stibia is the *road*, the *path*, the *way* taken by the *explorer* (Stibeus) or pilgrim on his journey. This is what he walks on, tramples under foot (Steibo). These considerations, based upon the exact correlation between the words, did not escape the attention of the older Masters nor of more modern philosophers who, lending them the support of their authority, have contributed to the spread of the unfortunate heresy that ordinary antimony is the mysterious substance used in the Art; a most regrettable misunderstanding, an invincible obstruction, against which hundreds of Seekers have striven in vain."

We must not be too hasty in believing that Fulcanelli definitely condemned the use of antimonic sulphide, without first reading Eugène Canseliet's comment on the same passage in his edition of the *Mutus Liber*: "The student must, above all, be watchful. Fulcanelli's stern, five-page-long warning about this same problem could well be no more than his intention to prevent unworthy readers from having a firm, easily understandable base from which to begin the Work." And he adds almost immediately: "We might fairly quote the words of Pierre Dujols and say that we had almost given way to the temptation to reveal the secret!"

We have now come to the parting of the ways—do we decide for iron or antimony? I feel almost certain that both these minerals were used by alchemists, and that neither of them is wholly unsuited to the Work. Nor—apart from the uniqueness of the prime matter—must we lose sight of its most frequently mentioned characteristic, the one to which the old philosophers attached the greatest importance: its *universality*. It could be found everywhere, everyone saw it or touched it constantly, it was a constituent of the animal, vegetable and mineral kingdoms. This cannot be said to apply to antimony, but fits iron admirably. On the other hand, why should one say iron *or* antimony? Why not iron *and* antimony? Which, in fact, is what Bergier does say when he suggests taking as prime matter iron pyrites with some antimonic impurities. That would also be my own conclusion—a conclusion reinforced by the following fact: in 1616 an anonymous Adept published a Hermetic work called *Chymical Marriage*, in which he claimed to give the key to alchemy by a cabalistic calculation. He replaced the letters of the Word ALCHIMIA by their numerical value according to their position in the alphabet: A-1, L-12, C-3, H-8, I-9, M-13, I-9, A-1, which gives a total of 56. Now 56 happens to be, near enough, the atomic weight of iron (actually 55.84), which is the more remarkable since the theory of atomic weights had not

229

been discovered at the time. Or should one not rather say *re-discovered*?

*

The Secret Fire or Prime Agent

"In answer to your question," said the Philosopher Morien replying to a remark by King Khalid, "I must tell you that there is only one single body or essential substance which is the prime matter in the Master Work; that this (male) substance becomes one and unique by conjunction with the female; and that nothing whatever is added or subtracted."

Similar statements are frequently made by Adepts. Seekers have sometimes mistakenly thought that no substance apart from what is contained in the prime matter must be allowed to enter into the Work. This is another of the pitfalls lurking in the path of the neophyte. It is true that, strictly speaking, nothing must be *added* to the substance, but it is equally true that, in order to extract the philosophic mercury, the secret fire must be *applied* to it; and this fire is itself partly alien to the Stone. I say "partly" because, when alchemists are asked whether the secret fire has the same constituents as the prime matter, they reply "yes and no". And they are quite right, as we shall try to demonstrate.

What exactly is this secret fire, the dry water that does not wet one's hands, the substance that burns without fire? One thinks of various chemicals, such as acids, strong diluents, or certain salts. We can exclude acids and the usual diluents because they are liquids, which leave us with weak organic acids and some of the salts. Basil Valentine tells us: "Salt is the fire, the water that does not wet one's hands." So we conclude that the secret fire is a salt that we meet in the form of crystals, but that it can be liquefied, because it can be transformed to a "water". Elsewhere Basil Valentine describes it as "doubly fiery", and he is not the only one to draw attention to the dual nature of the salt. Once again the inference is clear: it is a two-fold salt, metallic in substance, contained—probably in the form of an impurity—in the prime matter, since alchemists say that one of the constituents of the prime matter also forms part of the secret fire.

The next thing to do is to find out whether Adepts have been on the look out for a salt of this type. The illustration to Basil Valentine's twelfth Key, for example, shows a fire burning round something that is not in the least like a furnace but very much like a cask; elsewhere he speaks of "concentrated lye resulting from the ashes of oak logs, or potassium carbonate". But the cask also makes one think of tartar which may be deposited on its inner surface; and it must not be forgotten that the mediaeval name for potassium carbonate was tartaric salt. Which brings us back to Jacques Bergier, who used tartaric acid as the prime agent in his Work.

In the first volume of *Demeures Philosophales*, where Fulcanelli is describing philosophers' mercury (which, one need hardly say, has no connection with the secret fire) we find these words: "This is why a number of Adepts, seeking to create confusion, have called it nitre or saltpetre (*sal petri*, stony salt)." Later, in the second volume, he adds: "Those who know the characteristics of the substance are aware that the universal solvent is a real mineral, dry and fibrous in appearance, of firm consistency, hard and crystalline in texture. It is, therefore, a salt and not a liquid nor fluid mercury (quicksilver), but a stone or a stony salt, whence its Hermetic description as saltpetre, salt of wisdom or sal alembroth. . . . ."

In his turn, Eugène Canseliet refers to saltpetre, that is to say potassium nitrate, also mentioned by Jacques Bergier:

"Among the salts that may properly be said to enter into the composition of the secret philosophic fire, saltpetre would appear to be important. At all events its etymology would make one think so. The Greek word *nitron*, which means azotic potassium, commonly called nitre, is derived from a word meaning "to wash" (*nipto* or *nizo*). All philosophers, as we know, prescribe washing with fire; all their purifications, their sublimations, are done by fire-washing, by lixiviation, according to Nicholas Flamel. On the other hand, saltpetre, when it operates by contact with substances in fusion, is, by fusing with them, partially transformed to potassium carbonate and becomes alkaline."

So we come back to the tartaric salt referred to above. Hence the

231

Fourth Plate from the *Mutus Liber* (Silent Book)

secret fire might well be a dual salt, potassium nitrate and potassium tartrate, potassium itself figuring as an impurity in the prime matter, that is to say in antimonic iron pyrites. It would therefore represent the unifying principle, uniting sulphur and mercury, because potassium is the only ordinary stable metal that is generally slightly radio-active.

It should be noted, however, that these substances cannot be used in their natural state; what alchemists call *philosophic* saltpetre and *philosophic* tartrate must be used. This is another of the mysteries that alchemists have never been willing to elucidate. One of them did go so far as to tell me on one occasion that the way to make a substance "philosophic" depended on physics and not on chemistry. If we go back to what Jacques Bergier says about the necessary operations, with this in mind and paying particular attention to his statement about polarised light, we shall not be very far from finding the solution.

*

Philosophic Mercury

Puffers and many alchemists have identified philosophic mercury with pretty well everything, down to and including the most revolting, such as distilled urine, the blood of new-born babies, and so forth. In fact, anyone who tries to discover what substance is meant by philosophic mercury will never get anywhere, because this mercury is in no sense external to prime matter, but will in fact be extracted from it by the action of the secret fire. We have seen that nothing must be added to the prime matter once the prime agent has begun to operate: this is an absolute rule. It is, therefore, obvious that philosophic mercury can only come from the prime matter itself. All alchemists whom I have questioned on the subject have agreed with this and have admitted that, on this particular point, the difficulty does not really lie in identifying the substance but in the knack of extracting it from the prime matter. And this is what is to be discussed in the next chapter, which is concerned with the practical execution of the Great Work.

3. The Great Work

First and foremost, one extremely important point must be made: the Great Work is not a single operation, but consists of three completely separate parts. Most alchemical treatises describe one of these sections, or possibly two, as though each were in itself the whole Work—and they do so without ever mentioning that anything has been omitted. This fact alone makes them impossible to use as textbooks for the creation of the Stone. Not a single treatise exists that gives the chronological order in which the three parts of the Work have to be carried out. In saying this, I am laying myself open not only to the charge of being unduly "generous", but actually to that of making a "revelation". Yet being convinced of the factualness, the truth of the Art, and wishing therefore to simplify it, to make it intelligible, I feel that it is essential to clear up the confusion.

In a single treatise one or at most two of the three separate operations may be described; and in addition the student is liable to find that what is called sulphur in Part II may well have been called mercury in Part I; so it is impossible to rely on a single writer to see one through the Great Work, because one or more stages in the operation will be missing. Does this mean that it will be necessary to make a sort of mosaic of several treatises, to use them like pieces in a jigsaw puzzle? No—certainly not; each philosopher has his own ideas, his particular methods, his personal bent, and they cannot be reduced to a common denominator. We are not dealing with scientific experiments that may be reproduced at will, but acting rather as though we were working out cookery recipes, the results of which depend largely upon the temperament of the worker.

Since the three sections of the Great Work are quite distinct, it is always possible to use a different guide for each part. So one might begin with Nicholas Flamel, take Part II under the aegis of Basil Valentine, and let Bernard of Treviso see one through to the finish.

235

Then all that remains will be to sort out the different names given to the materials by the various philosophers; this certainly demands meticulous care, but is by no means impossible. In an extreme case, one might even make appeal to a second Master to elucidate some point that had been left too obscure by the guide of one's choice; but this is already a much more complicated process, and is not really to be recommended to a beginner.

We shall therefore study each section of the Mystery according to the directions given by the philosopher who has in my view provided the clearest and best founded explanations; and we shall be following in turn Fulcanelli, Cyliani, and finally Philalethes.

An Alchemist and his Laborant at Work (*c.* 1520)

The First Work

The first thing to do is to procure the prime matter. This may seem to be self-evident and to present no difficulty once the right substance has been decided upon; but in fact it is not so easy in practice. As things are nowadays, all minerals undergo preliminary chemical treatment when they are first mined, with a view to increasing their metallic content, and this treatment makes them quite unsuitable for the Work. Even in his day, Basil Valentine said in *The Twelve Keys*: "Anything that comes from the mines . . . loses its value and becomes unfit for the Work if it is tampered with." The only hope is to get permission to visit the mine and go down the pit oneself.

As Armand Barbault says in *The Gold of the Thousandth Morning*, the alchemist's "taking possession" of his prime matter is a truly magical act. The operator must go to the place in person and allow himself to be "guided" to the substance that is destined for him—I had almost said *predestined*. Barbault insists that guidance by astrology is necessary at this stage, which I am quite prepared to believe; and he is of opinion that it is almost indispensable to have the help of a medium in choosing the location of the stratum from which the material is to be taken. In any event, whether one is guided by instinct, by a study of one's horoscope, or by a medium's interpretation of the spirit world, it is as necessary to be chosen by the prime matter as it is to be making the choice of it oneself.

The next question is, what quantity will be needed? Armand Barbault himself worked with no more than four pounds of earth, while an alchemist friend of mine bought about four hundred and fifty pounds as a preliminary. In any case, once the matrix has been discarded, only a very small amount of the intrinsic metal will be left. I would therefore think that something like two hundred and fifty pounds of ore would be needed to begin with.

The furnace that must be built should traditionally be suitable for prolonged heating by charcoal. Nowadays alchemists are often told not to use gas or electricity, but this ban seems to me to rest simply upon a superstitious desire to imitate slavishly the methods of the past. Personally, I would think that electric heating, being steady and particularly easy to regulate, would be better than any other. Next, the secret fire must be created, as described above. This, of course, is a chemical and not an alchemical operation; and it would be wise to consult one of the eighteenth- or nineteenth-century manuals about the preparation of cream of tartar and other requirements. On this point, Eugène Canseliet says in his edition of the *Mutus Liber*: "One piece of advice which should not be neglected is never to use artificial means in the hope of making the tartaric solution more speedily.

237

The double factor of time and patience plays a great part in the process; and it will be well to read the work of Nicholas Lémery on the subject." (Paris, 1756)

Can the Work be begun at any time? No, because there are two definite times of year, clearly indicated in the *Mutus Liber*, that delimit not only the most favourable season for carrying out the Work, but in fact the only possible one. The writings of every philosopher confirm this. Eugène Canseliet is particularly clear on the point in his comment on the fourth illustration in the *Mutus Liber* (reproduced here on page 232):

"The fourth plate definitely reveals one of the deepest secrets of the physical side of the Work. The cosmic influence, shown as a great stream of direct rays, marked alternately as straight lines and dots, fans out from a central point in the heavens, between the sun and the moon.

"No other writer has so clearly shown the ultimate cause of movements and transformations, on the surface of the earth as at the centre. It is this cosmic influence which differentiates alchemy from the vain-glorious empiricism of the parallel art of chemistry. The secret is of such vital importance that it was no doubt very hard indeed for Magophon (Pierre Dujols) to overcome his reluctance to disguise it when he wrote the following highly significant words: 'Without the help of Heaven, man's work is vain. Trees are not grafted nor seeds sown at every season of the year. There is a time for everything. The philosophic Work has been called celestial agriculture; it is not for nothing that one of the greatest of writers signs himself Agricola, and that two other high Adepts are known as the Great Peasant and the Lesser Peasant.'

"Yes, of course: the ram and the bull in this picture correspond to the zodiacal signs, that is to say they indicate the Spring months during which the operation whose purpose is to gather the celestial essence can be carried out exactly as is shown here. . .

"It is clear that what Jacob Sulat intends us to collect is indeed dew and nothing else, and that it would be useless to try to be too clever over the interpretation of a picture that is almost naïvely clear, on the assumption that it is really abstrusely allegorical. It portrays without any disguise the simple method that we used ourselves hardly fifty years ago, the only difference being in the way we fixed the cloth to the poles."

Armand Barbault, too, has told how, in imitation of the two alchemists in the *Mutus Liber*, he went out to gather the dew every morning at dawn during the months of the ram and the bull (that is from 21st March to 20th May), in order to steep his prime matter in it. After the end of the period, say in late May—and at that time only—the Great Work should be begun, because earth and air are charged with the celestial regenerative influence. This is an absolute rule, and disregard of it will mean that any effort is doomed to failure.

So now we have provided ourselves with the raw material of the Stone, the secret fire, a certain quantity of dew, and a furnace. We still need some utensils, a mortar made of agate or some other very hard substance, a crucible, and some retorts and matrasses. The season of the year is favourable; it is time to begin.

First of all, the dew of May must be made ready, because it cannot be used in its natural state as Armand Barbault suggests. This is what the Cosmopolite says about it in his *New Light on Chymistry*: "You must extract what exists but is invisible, until the Artist is satisfied that he has what is required. The saltpetre of philosophers, by which all things increase and multiply, is obtained from the dew." And Eugène Canseliet rounds it off: "Under the effect of heat carefully applied, and thanks to its subtle nitre, the dew changes and matures all salts, whatever they may be, and especially those destined for the Great Work." The substance thus obtained is what is called "Virgin's Milk". (It will be remembered that saltpetre, or potassium nitrate, is commonly known as nitre.)

And now operations can be begun. The first thing to do is to put lumps of the prime matter into the mortar together with the dual salt that constitutes the secret fire and to pulverise them, then to steep the result in the salt extracted from the dew. Fulcanelli, in the first volume of his *Demeures Philosophales*, explains the process as follows:

"If you wish to obtain the griffin, our astral Stone, by extracting

239

it from its arsenical matrix, take two parts of virgin earth—our scaly dragon (*raw material*)—and one of the fiery agent that is the valiant knight armed with lance and shield (*the dual salt containing the secret fire*). Ares is stronger than Aries and must be employed only to a very limited extent. Pulverise it, and add to it one-fifth of its bulk in our pure, white, peerless salt (*Virgin's Milk*), washed several times and crystallised, which of course will be familiar to you. Mix all thoroughly. Then, in memory of the grievous passion of Our Lord, crucify it with three iron nails (*that is, triple dissolution; solve*), so that the body may die and be resurrected. This done, remove the coarser sediment; crush and pound what remains; stir it over a gentle fire with a steel rod. Throw into the mixture half the second salt that has been extracted from the dews that fertilise the earth during the month of May, and you will obtain a substance that is finer than the former one. Repeat the same operation three times; you are approaching the mine from whence comes our mercury (*that is, philosophic mercury*), and you will have climbed the first rung of the ladder of the Sages. When Jesus returned to life on the third day after His death, the sole occupant of the empty tomb was a shining angel robed in white. . . ."

By way of comparison, I am going to quote a few lines by Philalethes on the same subject: "Four parts must be taken of our fiery dragon who holds the magic steel in his belly; nine parts of our magnet; stir them over a fire until they bubble, and remove the scum that forms on the surface. Leave the husk and put the kernel to one side; cleanse it and dry it three times by fire and salt; this will be done easily if Saturn has seen and considered its beauty in the mirror of Mars." Though in different words, the two philosophers have, in fact, said exactly the same thing. It should be noted that, after the three dissolutions, the operation should be carried on in a crucible, particular care being taken to avoid flying sparks that may cause serious, sometimes fatal, burns. To return to Fulcanelli: "When you hear a sound from the vessel as if water were boiling, turning to a hollow roar like fire tearing the entrails of the earth, be ready to do battle; and keep calm. You will see smoke, with blue, green, and violet flames, and hear a series of explosions. . . ." Elsewhere he says:

"Limojon de Saint-Didier enunciates an elementary truth when he declares that 'the Philosopher's Stone is born of the destruction of two bodies'. To which we would add that the philosophic Stone —that is, our mercury as it is at the end of the first part of the Work—is also born of the conflict, mortification, and destruction of two opposing principles. Thus, in all essential operations of the Art, we see that there are two elements that produce a third, and that this genesis results from the dissolution of its begetters."

The use of the word "mercury" by Fulcanelli in this context is misleading. Actually, the two bodies derived from the prime matter that are to be resolved into their elements are philosophers' mercury and sulphur, and the third body that we have to obtain in the course of this first part of the Work is *philosophic* mercury. In the second volume of his *Demeures Philosophales*, Fulcanelli explains how he extracts this latter:

"The operation is the more important because it leads to the acquisition of philosophic mercury, a living, vital substance, issuing from pure sulphur wholly fused with primeval, celestial water. . . . The two methods of the Work need different means of vitalising the original mercury. The first is for the short way, and consists of a single operation, by which the solid part is moistened gradually —for all dry matter drinks its humidity avidly—until the reiterated fusion of the volatile with the solid makes the mixture swell and turns it into a pasty or syrupy mass as the case may be. The second method consists in diluting the whole of the sulphur with three or four times its weight of water. Pour off the solution into a bottle, then dry out the residue, and begin again with a proportionate amount of fresh mercury. When dissolution is complete, separate any sediment there may be, and collect the liquids in an open vessel to undergo slow distillation. Any superfluous liquid will thus be eliminated, leaving the mercury at the desired consistency, without the loss of any of its virtue, and ready to undergo Hermetic coction."

It must not be forgotten that philosophic mercury takes the form of a salt, and it is this salt that must be saved after the repeated sublimations.

*

The Second Work

Our prime matter has now reached the second stage of the Work, and the next step is to turn it into the dual substance—essentially under the influence of its philosophic mercury and of Virgin's Milk—so that in the third part of the Work it may be brought to the highest state of perfection.

The operations for this second section of the Work have been described by a number of philosophers, though the reservation must be made that they appear to be referring to the *beginning* of the Work. Among these treatises, I have chosen to quote from Cyliani's *Hermes Unveiled,* for he seems to me to explain the process more clearly and more accurately than most.

"*First operation: making the azote (nitrogen) or philosophers' mercury.*

"I chose a substance containing the two metallic elements. I first steeped it in astral spirit, very gradually, in order to re-kindle its two interior fires which seemed to be dead, by drying it slowly and pounding it in the mortar with a circular movement, all in the warmth of the sun. I repeated this work a number of times, moistening it increasingly, drying and pounding, until the whole had become a fairly thick paste. Then I added a fresh quantity of astral spirit, enough to cover the solid matter, and left it to stand for five days, at the end of which I carefully poured off the liquid into a bottle and stored it in a cool place; then, again in the warmth of the sun, I dried the substance that remained in the glass jar, which came about three fingers high; I steeped, pounded, dried and dissolved as before, and continued until I had dissolved everything possible, each time pouring the new solution into the same well-stoppered jar that I put into the coldest place I could find, where I left it for ten days. When the ten days had passed, I put the whole quantity into a pelican (*a special kind of alembic used for continuous distillation*) for forty days, at the end of which time a black substance had been deposited as a result of the internal heat of the fermentation. After this I distilled, as well as I could without a fire, the precious liquid that covered the matter containing its own interior fire, and put it into a white glass jar, with a ground stopper, to be stored in a cold, damp atmosphere.

"I took the black substance and dried it in the heat of the sun, as I said before, repeated the soaking in astral spirit but stopped as soon as I observed the matter to be drying out, and so left it to dry by itself. I repeated this as often as necessary, until the substance became pitch black and shining. When putrefaction was complete, I removed it from the external heat, so as not to damage the substance by burning the delicate essence of the black earth. In the end, the matter became like horse manure. According to

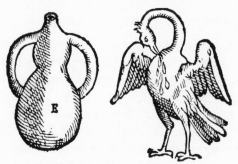

The Alchemical Pelican

what philosophers say, the internal heat of the matter itself must be allowed to bring it to this stage.

"At this point, external heat must be applied again to coagulate the matter and its essence. After leaving it to dry of itself, it is once more humidified gradually, but to an increasing extent, with the liquid that was distilled and reserved and that contains its own fire, until it has absorbed all the liquid. In this way all the water is changed to earth and this last, by desiccation, is turned into a white powder, sometimes called air, which falls as softly as ash, and contains the salt or philosophers' mercury.

"By the end of this first operation, the solution, or water, has been changed to earth, and this in turn, by subtilisation or sublimation, to air.

"This ash is taken and is gradually dissolved in a fresh amount of astral spirit which, after dissolution and decanting, leaves a black residue containing the fixed sulphur. But when the operation is repeated with this last solution exactly as has been explained, the solid now obtained is whiter than before, and this operation must be repeated seven to nine times. Thus the universal solvent or philosophers' mercury is obtained, that is the azote by means of which the active principle of any substance whatever can be extracted. . . ."

(Note: It should be observed that this "philosophers' mercury" is not the same as that contained in the prime matter, but is a different salt produced by the operation described.)

"Second Operation: Preparation of the Sulphur.

"The tincture extracted from ordinary gold (the male element in the compound) is obtained by the preparation of its sulphur, the result of the philosophic calcination that makes it lose its metallic quality and changes it into a pure earth. This calcination cannot be carried out by ordinary fire, but only by the secret fire that exists in philosophers' mercury as a result of its dual character; and it is by virtue of this celestial fire, seconded by trituration, that it penetrates to the core of natural gold, so that the dual mercurial and sulphuric internal fire of the gold, that seems to be lifeless and imprisoned, is released and brought back to life. This same celestial fire, having extracted the tincture of the gold, fixes it by its coldness and its congealing power, and makes it perfect, capable of multiplying itself in both quality and quantity. . . .

"Ordinary gold must therefore first be resolved into its generative elements by our mercury-water or azote. To do this, the gold must be reduced to a calx, a clear, red-brown oxyde; and, after washing this several times in rain-water well-distilled over a low fire, it must be slowly dried in the heat of the sun; at this point it should be calcinated with our secret fire. This is where philosophers say that 'chemists use fire for burning; we use water'.

"Soak and pound the well-calcinated gold oxyde repeatedly, then add its liquid and, having let it absorb its own weight in salt or

Alchemical literature abounds in cryptic descriptions and pictorial representations of the blending of sophic sulphur and sophic mercury.

'dry water which will not wet one's hands', and having thoroughly mixed all the ingredients, they must be steeped again, increasing the quantity successively, until the whole mass becomes a fairly thick paste. Then enough mercury-water must be added to cover the solid part; the whole mass must then be left in the gentle heat of a bain-marie for five days, at the end of which the solution should be decanted into a well-stoppered jar and stored in a cold, damp place.

"Any matter not dissolved should be dried at a temperature equal to full sunshine; when it has dried sufficiently, the process should be begun all over again as before, and the new solution added to the first; and this should be repeated until nothing remains except dead matter that is of no value. Dissolution being finished, and all collected in the airtight glass jar previously mentioned, its colour should be that of lapis lazuli. The jar should be put into as cold a place as possible for ten days, and then the substance should be left to ferment as was explained earlier; and through its own internal heat a black precipitate will be generated. This precipitate must be distilled without the use of fire, putting the liquid separated by distillation, that floated above the black earth, into a well-sealed jar and in a cold place.

"The black substance, separated from its liquid by distillation, should be left to dry out, and then it should once more be steeped over an external fire, that is to say in philosophic mercury. . . .

"What we said in describing the first operation, about cutting off the external fire at the right moment when putrefaction is complete, so as not to volatilise the spirit or burn the efflorescence, should now be remembered. The dark colour obtained after forty or fifty days provided that the external fire has been properly regulated, is proof that natural gold has been turned into black earth, which philosophers call horse manure.

"Just as horse manure works through its own heat, so our black earth dries up its own oily liquid by its own double fire and, after having absorbed all its distilled water and being turned into ash, it changes into a white powder that philosophers call air; and this is what constitutes coagulation, as described in the first operation.

"When the substance is white and coagulation complete, it is fixed by using external fire to desiccate it even further, exactly as was done in the preceding operation, until at last the colour changes from white to red, which philosophers call the element of fire. . . .

"Following this, the pure must be separated from the impure, which is the final stage of the regeneration of the substance effected by solution. To reach this stage, the matter must be well-pounded and then placed for sublimation into a good white glass jar of double the normal thickness, to a depth of some three or four fingers, as we said above. Mercury-water, our azote, dissolved in the requisite amount of astral spirit, must be poured over the substance, the fire being graduated so as to keep the heat at a moderate level, and finally enough philosophic mercury must be added to cover the substance. In this way, all the spirituous elements will be absorbed into the water, and the earthy parts sink to the bottom. The extract must be decanted and put on ice, so that the quintessence rises above the water to float on top of it like oil. The solids remaining at the bottom are useless and can be thrown away, for it is in these that the medicinal virtue of the gold was imprisoned.

"This floating oil should be removed by means of a white pigeon's feather, well washed and still damp. Great care must be taken to lose none of it, for this is the true regenerated quintessence of natural gold. In it the three principles are united and can never again be separated.

"The oil thus set apart is the tincture, the sulphur, the essential fire of the gold, seen in its true colour; it is the actual drinkable gold, the universal medicine to cure all the ills that afflict humanity."

(Unfortunately, Cyliani is being "grudging" here—this is not, in fact, the panacea, but a less potent medicine.)

But to continue:

"At the two equinoxes a few drops of this oil, enough to give a faint colour to a tablespoonful of distilled red or white wine, may be swallowed; any larger quantity of the medicine would destroy a man's natural fluids and so kill him.

"The oil may take any form whatsoever; it can be turned into a powder, or a salt, a stone or a spirit, using its own fire for desiccation. This oil is also called the blood of the red lion; and the ancients represented it symbolically as a winged dragon resting on the earth.

"Finally, this never-wasting oil is auriferous mercury. When produced, it should be divided into two equal portions, one half to be kept in the oily state in a small white glass phial with an air-tight stopper, to be used medicinally during the ascendants of Mars and of the Sun, as I shall explain at the end of the third operation. The other half must be dried until it becomes powdery, using the same means that I indicated earlier to desiccate and coagulate the stone. This powder should then also be divided into two equal parts, one part to be dissolved in four times its weight of philosophic mercury, to be used for steeping the other half of the powder."

*

The Third Work

We now have our *rebis*, ready to be brought to perfection by coction
—or, to use a simpler word, by cooking. The operation would appear
to be quite easy, but it is actually one of the most difficult to carry
out in practice: the heat must be kept regularly adjusted, and either
to make the fire too hot or, on the other hand, to let the matter cool
off, may result in total failure. Plenty of alchemists have come to
grief here, after spending years toiling over their furnaces.

What is more, the sequence is often cut off from the very outset
by "grudging" philosophers, and so the third Work fails, without
the operator's understanding why. It is for this reason that we are
now abandoning Cyliani, when he declares: "Here begins the first
stage, that is called the Regimen of Saturn"—which shows that from
this point onward his treatise gives misleading information. As far
as I am aware, only a single Philosopher has been sufficiently "generous" to give the true sequence of the Work, and that is Philalethes,
who probably thought he had been "grudging" enough in the course
of his treatise to venture to tell a part of the truth towards the end.
We shall therefore now follow this Master, beginning from Chapter
23 of his *Open Door into the Secret Palace of the King*.

"Know then that in the whole of our Work we have only a single
direct progression, which is purely a matter of cooking and
digesting. Yet this process includes a number of others, which
'grudging' writers have concealed by giving them many different
names and by referring to them as though they were separate
operations. Since I have promised to be truthful and sincere, I
shall be more candid; so that you will be obliged to admit that in
this I am more straightforward than anyone else; for it is not our
custom to speak openly on a matter of such importance.

"*Chapter 24.*
"*Of the first Regimen of the Work, which is that of Philosophic
Mercury.*
"I shall begin with the Regimen of Mercury, a secret of which not
one of the Philosophers has ever spoken. Remember that all of

them have begun with the second part, that is to say with the Regimen of Saturn, and they have given no light to a beginner in the Art to tell him what happens before the *blackness* appears that is one of the principal signs in the Work. Not even the good Bernard of Treviso said anything; for in his parable he teaches that when the King comes to the Fountain, having left behind outsiders, he goes alone to the Bath, wearing a cloak of cloth of gold, which he removes and hands to Saturn who, in return, gives him a garment of black velvet. But he does not say how long it is before the King takes off that golden robe, and so he passes over in silence a whole stage, which may last for forty days or even fifty. During this time, the unfortunate apprentice flounders in confusion over experiments that he does not understand. When once the blackness begins to appear, the fresh signs that show in the vessel every day give great satisfaction to the Artist; but it must be admitted that it is disheartening to remain in a state of such uncertainty for fifty days, with no guide and no sign for reassurance.

"I say therefore that from the time when the compost (*that is, the rebis plus the philosophic mercury*) begins to react to the fire in the furnace and until the blackness appears, Mercury is in the ascendant, which means philosophic mercury, working alone for the whole period; its companion (*natural gold, the metal contained in the rebis*) being inanimate for a certain length of time; and this is what no one before me has disclosed.

"So, when you have united the substances, that is to say gold and our mercury, do not imagine, as alchemists commonly do, that the Occident (or dissolution) of the Gold must follow immediately. No, I assure you that that is not the way it comes. I waited a long time before peace and quiet were established between fire and water. And of this, 'grudging' alchemists have given only a single word when in the first part of the Work they call their substance the *rebis*, that is to say a thing that is made of two things. . . .

"Take the substance that I have indicated, natural gold I mean, and put it into the water of our *sea* that never loses the heat it has acquired by being manipulated for many months: keep on softening the gold with a fire that will produce a continuous rise and fall of mist and dew drops by day and by night. This alternation causes the mercury to rise to its natural height, and the body remains at the bottom of the vessel, as is its nature, until after quite a long time the body begins to absorb a certain amount of water, and thus solid and liquid acquire something of each other's characteristics, which means that the body communicates its fixity to the water, and the water shares its volatility with the body.

". . . Thus, through the mediation of the soul, the spirit is reconciled with the body, and the two are united in the blackness; this occurs after at most fifty days. This operation is called the Regimen of Mercury because, in the alternation, it is raised high, while the gold is boiled in the same mercury at the bottom of the vessel. And during this operation the body is passive until the colours appear, which begin to show by about the twentieth day, provided that ebullition proceeds continuously, with no interruption nor slackening. Thereafter the colours become stronger and more diversified, changing and merging until they end in the deepest black, which happens on about the fiftieth day, if the fates are kind.

"Chapter 25.
"Of the Second Regimen of the Work, which is that of Saturn or Lead.

"The Regimen of Mercury being ended (which may be recognized because its object is to divest the King—that is, the Gold—of his golden robe, to attack and exhaust the Lion in a series of battles until he is at the last extremity), it is succeeded by the Regimen of Saturn.

". . . And this reign is strict as regards heat, because in it only a single colour is seen, which is a very deep black; but there is no wind nor vapour nor any sign or indication of imperfection, and nothing else is noticeable, except that the mixture seems at times to be quite dry, and at others it boils like melted pitch—which is a terrible thing to see. This, as it were, is a representation of eternal death, the epitome of physical nullity; yet it will bring joy to the the Artist who watches the process. For it is no ordinary blackness that is seen here, but is of so tremendous a depth that by the very fact of being black it appears shining and resplendent. And if at any time you see the matter thickening to a paste in the bottom of the vessel, rejoice, for this tells you that a quickening spirit is at work that will give new life to the dead substances when God Almighty wills.

"At this point I must remind you above all things to look to your fire, which you should tend and regulate with exceeding great care. For I warn you that if at this stage you sublimate any part of your substance by over-heating, all your labour will be irrevocably lost. Be content, like the Good Trevisan, to be kept in prison for forty days and forty nights, and leave the matter, which is still fragile, at the bottom of the vessel that is the womb where conception will take place. . . .

"Ordinary gold, being sublimated and glorified by the power of our mercury, manifests in turns all possible metallic stages that exist in it and thus becomes philosophic Gold, vital and life-giving.

"*Chapter 26.*
"*Of the Third Regimen, which is that of Jupiter or Tin.*
"Black Saturn is succeeded by Jupiter, who is of a different colour. For after the matter has duly undergone putrefaction and dissolution and conception has taken place in the bottom of the vessel, you will, please God, see once again ever-changing colours and obtain a new sublimation. This Regimen is not a long one, lasting for not more than three weeks. During this time colours of unimaginable beauty and variety will appear, for no manifest reason. From day to day they will be more splendid; and in the end, after all these things that are most wonderful to see, a whiteness will develop on the inner sides of the vessel in the form of little filaments or hairs (Nicholas Flamel calls it capillary whiteness). When you see this, rejoice! It is a sign that you have successfully passed through the Regimen of Jupiter. . . .

"*Chapter 27.*
"*Of the Fourth Regimen, which is that of the Moon or Philosophic Silver.*
"The Regimen of Jupiter being completed towards the end of the fourth month, you will see the sign of the crescent Moon, and you will know that the whole of the Regimen of Jupiter was occupied in cleansing the Laton (*another name for the rebis at this stage*).

The spirit composing this *lotion* or lavation is white and pure, but the matter that is to be cleansed is of a particularly dense black on account of its impurities; in its passage from black to white all intermediate colours will be seen and, as they fade, everything becomes white—though not perfectly white from the very first day; but from being just white, it will become a dazzling white, little by little, gradually.

"During this Regimen, you must know, the whole mass will come to look like liquid quicksilver, and this stage is called 'enshrining the mother in the womb of the child she has herself borne'.

"But before this Regimen ends, the substance will assume a thousand different forms. Waves will ebb and flow before any coagulation takes place, the mass will liquefy and coagulate a hundred times a day. . . . At the end you will be left with some very small, very white granules like motes in the sun, and more beautiful than anything anyone has ever seen.

"Let us everlastingly give thanks to God, through whose Goodness the Work has been brought to this state of perfection. For indeed this is the true and perfect white tincture, although it is as yet far short of the potency and efficacy, of the glorious power it will acquire if the process is repeated from the second stage.

"*Chapter 28.*
"*Of the Fifth Regimen, which is that of Venus or Copper.*

"Here you must take particular care in tending your fire; for it is a fact permitting of no doubt that the Stone, to be perfect, must be fusible. Hence, if you give it a hotter fire than it should have, your matter will vitrify and, when it is melted, it will cling to the sides of your vessel and you will not be able to do anything further with it, nor bring it to any higher state of perfection. . . . This may occur from the middle of the Regimen of the Moon until the seventh or tenth day of the Regimen of Venus.

"The heat of the fire must therefore be increased only slightly so that it is not sufficient to vitrify the substance, that is, to make it liquid like molten glass. The heat must be gentle, because in this way the matter will dissolve and swell of itself, and by the Grace of God it will receive a winged spirit that will ascend, carrying the

Stone with it; and it will produce and bring into being new colours. The first of these will be the verdure of Venus, which will persist for a long time, and will not wholly disappear until after twenty days. Next will come azure, then a livid or leaden colour, and for the end of the Regimen of Venus, a pale, nebulous purple. . . .

"When you see the verdancy, you will know that it contains within it the power of germination. Take great care at this point that the charming green is not changed to an ugly black by making the heat too fierce, but tend your fire with circumspection, and so the whole of the Regimen will come to an end in forty days, and you will find in it all the vital forces of regeneration and fructification.

"*Chapter 29.*
"*Of the Sixth Regimen, which is that of Mars or Iron.*
". . . The dominant colour in this Regimen is a kind of indefinite orange mixture, shading into yellow and brownish lemon; and thereafter all the colours of the rainbow and of a peacock's tail will be seen; but they are only passing.

"During this Regimen, the consistency of the matter is drier, and it seems as though it took pleasure in disguising itself under different forms. . . .

"Know that, in this final stage, *our virgin earth* receives the seed of the Sun, that is of Gold, so that it may conceive and be fruitful. You must, therefore, always keep up a good heat, and towards the thirtieth day of this Regimen you will assuredly see the orange tinge beginning to show which, two weeks after its first appearance, will colour the whole of your substance.

"*Chapter 30.*
"*Of the Seventh Regimen, which is that of the Sun or Philosophic Gold.*
"You are now very near to the end of the Work, and you have almost consummated it. Everything in the vessel appears as though it were the finest gold, and the Virgin's Milk that covers it, in which you have been steeping and soaking the substance, has turned to a deep orange. . . .

"Remember that you have been waiting for nearly seven months, and that it would be foolish now to destroy and lose all in less than an hour. You must therefore continue to take every precaution, all the more since you are so near to the end and the perfecting of your Work. . . .

"After waiting for twelve or fourteen days, you will observe that in this Regimen of the Sun, or Philosophic Gold, the greater part of your matter will become moist, one might almost say sodden; yet it will still be wholly *carried in the belly of the wind* (*an allusion to the Emerald Table*).

"At last, on about the twenty-sixth day of this Regimen, it will begin to dry out, then liquefy; will become fluid, then congeal; and it will continue to liquefy a hundred times a day until it becomes gritty, and the whole substance appears to split up into tiny granules. After this it will reform into a single mass, and from one day to the next it will go through a thousand different phases; this will continue for two weeks or thereabouts.

"Finally, at the Command of God, the light in your Matter will emit rays of such brilliance as you can hardly imagine. When you see this light, you may expect the end of your work to be near, for, three days later, you will see the completion for which you have striven, when the Matter will break up into granules minute as motes in sunlight and its colour will be of so dark a red that it looks black, like the congealed blood of a healthy man. You would never have expected the Art to give such a colour to the Elixir, which is an admirable creation and has not its like in the whole of Nature; indeed there is nothing in the whole world to equal it."

*

Multiplication

Eirenaeus Philalethes' explanations are so clear that they need no commentary. After the end of the seventh Regimen, therefore, and if God or Fate has willed it, we have the "incombustible red sulphur" that really is the Philosopher's Stone, though not yet fully perfected. It has still to be multiplied, that is, it must again go through the whole cycle of operations to which the prime matter was subjected.

In his Chapter 31, Philalethes says: "But when you come to this point, do not imagine that you are at the end of the Work and that there is nothing more for you to do; you still have to continue, to repeat, to turn the wheel a second time (that is, to do over again the operations you have just completed), so that you may extract the elixir from the incombustible sulphur." All philosophers tell you this, but they show themselves to be "grudging" here, in that they do not say whether the operations have to be restarted from the first Work or only from the second or third. My own view is that the Stone must go through the whole cycle described by Philalethes; that is to say, it must play the part of the *rebis* from the time when it is submitted to the joint action of philosophic mercury and the external fire.

Once this new coction is completed, the fortunate alchemist is in possession of the real panacea, a homoeopathic dose of which becomes his elixir of life. As we saw at the beginning of this book, our new Adept will also have fermented his Stone with gold—in the proportion of one part of the Stone to four parts of gold—in order to obtain the precipitate powder required for any attempt at transmutation.

The method of creating the Stone that we have just examined is that of the Humid Way, which is to all intents and purposes the only one touched on in alchemical treatises. Yet, in his *Le Mystère des Cathédrales*, Fulcanelli writes:

"Few alchemists admit the possibility that there may be two Ways—one short and easy, known as the Dry Way, the other longer and more arduous, called the Humid Way. This may be due to the fact that many authors treat exclusively with the longer process, either because they do not know of the other or because they prefer to keep silence rather than to teach its principles."

Farther on he adds: "In this (the Dry Way) it is necessary to cook the celestial salt, which is the philosophers' mercury, with some terrestrial metallic body, in a crucible and over an open fire, for four days."

Once again we are faced with the usual chaos of Hermetic texts. Fulcanelli seems to accept the idea of two Ways, but he suggests that the Dry Way is the easier, while every other philosopher has said that it is the more difficult. Moreover, he gives an exact time—which does not mean much, since there is no absolute standard of comparison.

255

I have carefully collated texts, ancient and modern, that refer to the subject, and I have managed to extract from them the following principles: there are neither one nor two Ways, but three in which to create the Stone. These are: the *Humid Way*, the one described above, in which the operations continue for about three years, always supposing that they succeed at the first attempt; the *Dry Way*, which needs only a few weeks' work, and is carried out in an open crucible, the secret fire playing a larger part than in the preceding method. For a Philosopher who is thoroughly familiar with the practical work of the Hermetic Art, this Way is easier than the first, as Fulcanelli says, but for a beginner it is very difficult, in fact really pretty well impossible. Finally, there is the *Short Way* that lasts three or four days, and in which the Work is done in an open crucible at very high temperatures. This last method is extremely dangerous because of the risk of explosions, and is reserved only for higher Adepts. It may perhaps be useful to emphasise once again the fact that the chemical substances corresponding to the secret fire, Virgin's Milk, and philosophic mercury are not identical in the three methods.

Three years, therefore, is the minimum time in which the Great Work can be carried out, but we must not forget that Denis Zachaire, Bernard of Treviso, Nicholas Flamel and many another struggled for over twenty years before reaching the end of their labours. In this second half of the twentieth century, Armand Barbault took over twelve years before obtaining his first solution of drinkable gold, another six years to bring the medicine to the second degree, and there is nothing to show that it will not be just as long before he makes the Stone—if he ever does. So, now as always, one must reckon on twenty years as the necessary minimum for the Great Work, five of them spent in study and the rest in practical work in a laboratory. We have seen also that constant attention is needed, especially during the third stage. Nor must it be forgotten that to equip a laboratory is expensive nowadays, and that the ore from which the prime matter is extracted is far from being as cheap now as it was in the Middle Ages. Unfortunately, it is clear that only a very wealthy person can undertake to carry out the Work and to devote the necessary twenty or thirty years to it.

The great Adepts who made the Stone were very rich people,

equivalent to millionaires today: Raymond Lully, Denis Zachaire, Bernard of Treviso, all had large family fortunes; Albertus Magnus had a considerable personal fortune and was permitted by his Order to enjoy the use of it throughout his life. Arnold of Villanova was a fashionable physician, who was paid high fees. Nicholas Flamel, on the other hand, who had no more than a modest competence, found great difficulty in carrying on the Work; and Paracelsus, who was a poor man, got nowhere. I am stressing the point, because if this book should encourage anyone to take up alchemy, I would wish him to realise that he will need a minimum of twenty years of financial independence. In addition he should have a good knowledge of the chemistry of minerals before opening a laboratory—not of modern chemistry, which is no longer akin to alchemy, but that of, say, the eighteenth century, which was still sufficiently closely descended from the operations of Puffers who were familiar with the principles of the Hermetic Art. They describe exactly how to carry out the different operations—sublimation, calcination, dissolution, etc.— which are required in the course of the three stages of the Work.

I can think of no better way of ending this practical study of the Work than by quoting Basil Valentine's final words in his *Revelation of the Mysteries of the Tinctures of the Seven Metals*:

"What my eyes have seen, what my hands have touched, and what my mind has fully accepted, nothing can prevent me from believing and from recognising the results in this life, save only death, by which all things are changed.

"After such proofs of divine love, I am inspired to show that I love my neighbour as myself; also that I wish only good to my enemies and persecutors, and to those who speak ill of this divine science, so that I may heap coals of fire upon their heads.

"In third place, I hope that all adversaries and opponents may come to know one who has erred greatly, but who has revealed the greatest number of the secrets of nature. I may deserve to be blamed and others to be praised, but I write so that this mighty secret may not be lost in the mists of time, nor perish in the torrents of the years; but that it may shine with the rays of the true light, far from shipwreck and from the multiplicity of fools. And that, as a result of the publication of a true and honest exposition, there may come to be many witnesses and irreproachable authorities to prove the truth of what I have written."

Conclusion: The Royal Art

I think I have sufficiently demonstrated the truth of alchemy in the course of the preceding pages to convince the most sceptical. Yet I know that the spurious scientific spirit inherited from the nineteenth century will never admit a truth that it finds embarrassing. That is an attitude of mind common to many, hedged in as they are by habits of thought defined as early as 1758 by Dom Joseph Pernety in the preface to his *Mytho-Hermetic Dictionary*:

"It is a great mistake to treat Hermetic philosophers as fools. Is one not really making a fool of oneself by deciding obstinately to treat the subject of a science as chimerical either because one cannot understand it or because one knows nothing at all about it? It is like a blind man trying to distinguish between colours. What sort of notice can intelligent people take of the opinion of some critic whose only qualification is to have a few catchwords, under cover of which he hides his ignorance, and which he parades to impress stupid readers who are always ready to applaud? Do such writers deserve that anyone should go to the trouble of replying to them? No—all one need do is to send them back to school. Not being puffed up with pride and ignorance nor blinded by prejudice like these men, Solomon himself regarded hieroglyphics and proverbs, the parables and enigmas of philosophers, as things deserving serious attention and profound study by a wise and thoughtful man."

Some people will no doubt object that the proofs I have advanced are based upon human witness, and that such testimony is fallible. True enough; but it all boils down to a case of simple statistics: if I had given only two or three stories of transmutation, it would not have been possible to argue anything from them; but in fact the number of times the phenomenon occurred was considerable, and the number of witnesses even greater. I might add that in this book I have reported scarcely half the cases of transmutation that are historically verified. I think this would be a good place to re-read some words written by a great contemporary scientist, Camille Flammarion: "The number of such reports—leaving out of account illusions, mistakes, and possible trickery—is the more worth considering because we should properly allow for the average of human mentality, for its intellectual slavery, its cowardice, its meanness." (*Haunted Houses.*)

Camille Flammarion, who himself struggled against the lack of a scientific spirit among his colleagues, magnificently proved his point about aeroliths—stones that fall from the skies and that were for many years not recognised by science. The particulars he gives are doubly interesting, first because they are applicable to the transmutation of metals, and then because they introduce the French chemist Lavoisier, who was the prime mover in the rejection of alchemy by official science.

According to Camille Flammarion, a certain Abbé Bachelay saw a stone fall from the sky at his feet, quite a normal occurrence and one that is acknowledged as such in these days. The Abbé sent details about it to the French Academy of Science. His letter was submitted to Lavoisier as an expert, who reported on it as follows:

"M. Fongeroux, M. Cadet and I have been asked to give an account to the Academy of an observation communicated by M. Bachelay about a stone that is said to have fallen from the sky during a storm.

"There is probably no kind of stone that has as widely disseminated a history as the 'thunderbolt', if one were to collect all that has been written on the subject. One may judge of it by the great number of substances that are called by this name. Nevertheless, despite opinions accepted in olden times, true physicists have always regarded the existence of such stones as extremely doubtful. A memorandum on this point by M. Lémery, published by the Academy in the year 1700, may be consulted.

"If the existence of thunderbolts was regarded as suspect in days when physicists had barely an idea of the nature of thunderstorms, they must appear even more doubtful today, when modern scientists have discovered that the power of a meteor is equivalent to that of electricity. However that may be, we are quoting M. Bachelay's statement in full, and we shall then examine what conclusions may be drawn from it. (*The Abbé's statement is omitted, as it is of no particular interest here.*) . . .

"We may therefore conclude, taking into account only the analysis and omitting a large number of other arguments not worth particularising, that the stone sent to us by M. Bachelay did not originate in thunder, *that it did not fall from the sky*, that it was not formed by mineral substances fused by the heat of the thunder, as might have been presumed; that, in fact, the stone is nothing but a kind of pyritic sandstone, that has nothing peculiar about it except for a *hepatic* smell that was given off during its dissolution by marine acid (*hydrochloric acid*), a phenomenon that does not occur in the dissolution of ordinary pyrites. The view that appears to us to be the most probable, and that accords best with accepted principles of physics, with the facts reported by M. Bachelay and with our own tests, is that the stone, which may have lain hidden under a light covering of earth or grass, was struck by lightning and so brought into view; the heat might have been great enough to melt the surface that was struck, but did not continue for long enough to penetrate to the interior, which explains why the stone was not disintegrated."

And Camille Flammarion comes to the conclusion:

"This report from Lavoisier to the Academy of Science inspires thoughts directly associated with the researches with which we are concerned here. *Witnesses saw the stone fall*, in open country, in broad daylight on 13th September 1768. It was examined, and the conclusion arrived at was . . . that it did not fall from the sky! Preconceived ideas prevent people from recognising a truth. Popular opinion that associated such stones with thunder was wrong; but it never seems to have occurred to anyone to examine the theory and to suppose that there might be some other explanation.

The evidence was considered immaterial and, even in our own day, a certain school of thought continues paradoxically to teach that witnesses, whoever they may be, have no determinative value."

It is this same form of intellectual dishonesty that induced certain modern scientific writers to insist that van Helmont and Helvetius were alchemists because their evidence was irrefutable; but we must not allow ourselves to be distracted by rearguard actions fought by sophists. The transmutation of metals is a fact, and that is a point that may be considered to have been established.

On the other hand, it is interesting to find that the scientist chosen by Camille Flammarion to illustrate a good example of the *un*scientific spirit should chance to be Lavoisier, the man who revolutionised chemistry and relegated the Hermetic Art to the limbo of mediaeval superstitions. How did that happen? Actually, it was more or less on the same lines as his invalidation of stones falling from heaven. He took one of Lémery's hypotheses about simple, homogeneous bodies—the very same Lémery whom he cited in his memorandum to the Academy—and transformed this hypothesis into a tenet of the chemical faith: "A homogeneous body is one that cannot be resolved into a variety of elements by any means known at present." Hence, just as the Abbé Bachelay could not have seen a stone fall from the sky because there are no stones in the sky, so metals cannot be transmuted because they are homogeneous bodies that cannot be broken down. That is definite enough—but Arnold of Villanova was no less dogmatic when he wrote in his *Path to the Way*:

"Every body is made up of elements into which it may be resolved. Let us take an example that is impossible to refute and easy to understand: ice, with the help of fire, can be resolved into water; therefore ice is water. Now, all metals can be resolved into mercury, therefore mercury is the prime matter of all metals. At a later stage I shall demonstrate how this transmutation may be carried out, thereby refuting the opinion of those who claim that the composition of metals cannot be changed. They would be right if it were impossible to reduce metals to their prime matter;

but I shall show that reduction to prime matter is easy, and that transmutation is possible and practicable."

Modern scientists have decided against Lavoisier, but they have not yet accepted the opinion of Master Arnold and the other Adepts. They still agree with the eighteenth-century chemist that it is impossible for a parallel science to exist, with different principles that have so far passed them by. If modern chemists have entirely reversed Lavoisier's ideas, they have none the less preserved his doctrine that the transmutation of metals by alchemical means is impossible; yet we know that transmutation has taken place, and that it is still taking place. I am absolutely certain that some day, probably quite soon, the reality of alchemical Work will be recognised by official science, just as stones falling from heaven, denied by Lavoisier, are now admitted to be factual.

*

This study is essentially concerned with the practical, tangible aspect of alchemy, in order to demonstrate its material reality. Meanwhile, a certain number of writers, after studying alchemical texts and concluding, quite properly, that the transmutation of metals was an aim unworthy of Adepts, deduced from this that an alchemist sought only spiritual transmutation and was describing symbolically the stages of a psychical quest in the Work, a quest in which the human body was at once the prime matter and the athanor. They therefore termed it *spiritual alchemy*; but this is a misunderstanding resulting from insufficient study of the texts. Having reached the preliminary level of recognising that a Hermetic Philosopher was not simply a maker of gold, they never managed to reach the second level that would have given them the real key to the Great Work.

At the same time, the symbolic aspect of the texts and of Hermetic operations must not be overlooked. There is room for a very important study to be carried out on this subject, but one which goes far beyond the framework of the present book; I shall do no more than point out that each phase of the Work may be interpreted on several levels: first from the practical view-point, then as the interaction between the operations and the manipulator, and finally to show

263

the Artist's part in the harmony of the Great Work. For example, in Cyliani's text, where he describes the operations in the second Work, we have seen that the matter must be steeped in astral spirit, the synonym of which is Virgin's Milk. This means, on the material level, that the prime matter must literally be steeped in the saline solution referred to, but on another level it must be remembered that the Virgin's Milk is symbolically that of the Virgin Mary, the Mother of God (although this does not imply that it is necessary to be a Christian rather than a member of some other religious faith in order to practice alchemy), and that the operator should be in a "state of grace" as regards the divine attributes symbolised by her; and finally that, in the third stage, the time comes when divine intervention is necessary to ensure that the activity in the philosophic egg passes from the chemical sphere to the alchemical.

There are plenty of other subjects that might be touched upon in this book, some of them most mysterious and generally alluded to in veiled terms, either because the writer has no information about them or because the political and economic implications are too serious to be made public. For example, the Ministry of Industry and Commerce has a department that studies the movements of gold all over the world. A member of this department once told a friend of mine that two countries were selling abnormally large quantities of gold, far beyond what they could extract from their mines or their Bank reserves. . . . Besides, without bringing up legends about the Nine Unknown Superiors who control the world without its knowledge, there are persistent rumours, sometimes actual statements, about a small group of immortals said to be living among us and trying to brain-wash our society into their way of thinking. These Nine are understood to have the power to move in Time, as well as space. Someone I know went unexpectedly one day to see an alchemist of his acquaintance, one of the real alchemists who live and work in secret, and found him talking to a man dressed in seventeenth-century clothes. The alchemist appeared to be very much embarrassed and ushered his visitor out, although he happened to be a close friend. Would he have done this if the man discovered in his rooms had simply been on his way to or from a fancy-dress party —which anyhow would have been surprising in the middle of the day? Of all this, and of a good many other things too, I will say nothing, for the simple reason that I know nothing for certain.

What I do know, however, is that—today as in the past—alchemy is the expression of a perennial truth. So we come back to the question: where did it originate? Now that we have reached this stage in our inquiries, the legend of Hermes can no longer satisfy us. How could so much scientific knowledge, well in advance of official science, have managed to develop in civilisations in which technique was embryonic and theories of matter non-existent? I believe the answer is given by the atomic physicist Frederick Soddy, who was awarded the Nobel Prize for his discovery of isotopes. In his book *Radium—an Interpretation of Radioactivity*, he writes:

"It is curious to think, for example, of the remarkable legend of the Philosopher's Stone, which is one of the oldest and most widespread, and of which the origins, so far as we are able to penetrate into the past, cannot with any certainty be traced to their ultimate source. To the Philosopher's Stone was attributed not only the power of transmuting metals, but also that of acting as the elixir of life. Whatever may have been the origin of this apparently absurd association of ideas, it actually proves to be a very accurate, hardly allegorical, expression of our present mode of thought. It does not require any great effort of the imagination to see Energy as the very life of the universe; and it is known today that it is as a result of transmutation that life first came into being in the physical universe. Is this ancient approximation between the power of transmutation and the elixir of life no more than pure coincidence? I prefer to believe that it may well be an echo from one of the many ages when, in prehistoric times, men followed the same path that our feet tread today. But that past is probably so far behind us that the atoms that were contemporary with it have had time to disintegrate completely. . . .

"Let us for a moment allow our imaginations to wander freely in those ideal regions. Let us suppose that this hypothesis, which seems to have evolved of itself, is true, and that we may have confidence in the slender foundations established by traditions and superstitions transmitted to us from prehistoric times. Might we not see in them a certain justification for the belief that men of some vanished and forgotten race attained not only the knowledge we have so recently acquired, but also potentialities that are not yet ours?"

That, I believe, is the real answer to our enquiry: alchemy is a relic of the science of a race that trod the earth well before the Flood. The argument advanced by palæontologists, that no human fossils or other remains of such a civilisation have been discovered—by which they attempt to justify their refusal to admit the possibility— is valid only within a very brief span of time. Once beyond the primeval era, no verification of any kind is possible, because no fossils have survived. It is, therefore, quite reasonable to postulate an ante-Cambrian civilisation that might have survived across the geological ages in quite small ethnic groups, probably in submarine cities, keeping alive the memory of the catastrophe that destroyed their civilisation—possibly an atomic war—and also the knowledge of certain scientific achievements of their great epoch. Alchemy and its twin sister astrology would then be simply a residuum, little scraps of a lost knowledge, buried in the collective unconscious of the race, and capable of coming to life again through certain individuals under divine inspiration.

As we come towards the end of the twentieth century, and are once more on the eve of a catastrophe on a planetary scale, the Work of alchemy becomes a matter of primary importance, for it is one of humanity's few sheet anchors. At this present time man is particularly seriously threatened, when a materialist, mechanistic, atheistical civilisation is doing its utmost to drive him mad and to destroy him. The machines that he makes with his hands are gradually reducing him to slavery, and we are steering towards a robot civilisation in which the real power will rest with gigantic automata that man has created to be his masters. Certain Asian peoples, Indians in particular, have a chance of escaping from this hell, thanks to yoga and some other techniques of mental concentration; but the implanting of such techniques in the West—due to despair—is of no avail, because they are ill-adapted to our type of mind. The alchemical way, on the contrary, gives us the chance to raise our-

'Subterranean Physics' by Becher (17th century) from *Bibliotheca Esoterica*.

selves to a state of awareness, to a state in which we shall no longer be the playthings, the marionettes, of external circumstances, but shall learn to master them. Alchemy also gives us the means to emancipate ourselves from terrestrial contingencies, to free ourselves from our obsession with illness, and to prolong our lives beyond the absurdly short span originally assigned to them.

Faced with threats of war, with atomic hazards, with the noise and unrest of modern life, with the mechanical civilisation of the near future, I can see only two possibilities—prayer or the Great Work.

I have bought an agate mortar.

Appendix

Whatever anyone may think about the Elixir of Life, there can be no doubt about the medicinal value of the Stone. The following table shows the ages reached by some who possessed the Stone, excluding those who were murdered (Zachaire, Kelly, the Cosmopolite) and some whose birth-dates are not known (Basil Valentine, Lascaris, Sehfeld).

Albertus Magnus	1193–1280	..	87
Roger Bacon	1214–1294	..	80
Raymond Lully	1235–1315	..	80
Arnold of Villanova	1240–1313	..	73
Nicholas Flamel	1330–1418	..	88
Bernard of Treviso	1406–1490	..	84
John Dee	1527–1607	..	80
Michael Sendivogius	1566–1646	..	80
Saint-Germain	End of 17th cent.–1784	..	86, at least.

This gives an average age of 82, over a period when the general average was not more than about thirty-eight.

Glossary

A Glossary of the principal Proper Names and Alchemical
Terms used in this book

A

ABRAHAM THE JEW: Author of the book seen in a dream by Nicholas Flamel.

ADEPT: Alchemist believed to have achieved the Philosopher's Stone.

AGRICOLA: Sixteenth-century alchemist.

AGRIPPA, Henry Cornelius: Sixteenth-century magician and Puffer.

ALBERTUS Magnus (Saint): Thirteenth-century Adept, scientist and philosopher.

ALCHEMIST: Anyone who works in a laboratory, in search of the Stone, but who may not yet have achieved it.

ALEMBIC: Distilling apparatus.

ALKAHEST: Name invented by Paracelsus for the universal solvent.

ALTUS: Pseudonym (and anagram) of Jacob Sulat, author of the *Mutus Liber*.

AMATEUR: Anyone initiated into alchemy, but who does not work in a laboratory. A "Lover of the Science".

ANDROGYNE: Name for prime matter containing the male and female principles—that is, philosophers' sulphur and mercury. Also called hermaphrodite.

AQUINAS, (Saint) Thomas: Theologian, philosopher and "amateur" (q.v.) of the science of alchemy.

ARCHIMIST: A chemist seeking to carry out transmutation of metals by non-Hermetic means.

ARIADNE'S thread: Any means to help students find their way through the mazes of philosophic writings. It is hoped that the present book may act as such.

ARNOLD of Villanova: Thirteenth-century Adept and physician.

ARSENIC: In the older, pre-sixteenth century, treatises this word is used to denote philosophers' salt.

ARTEPHIUS: Adept who probably lived in the twelfth century.

271

Glossary

ARTIST: Adept; one who has mastered the Art of Alchemy.

ASCH MEZAREPH: Book of Abraham the Jew.

ASTRAL Spirit: See Virgin's Milk.

ATHANOR: Furnace used in alchemical work.

B

BACON, Roger: Thirteenth-century English Adept; a Franciscan monk.

BATH of the King: Liquid composed of a solution of Virgin's Milk (q.v.) and philosophic mercury (q.v.), in which the prime matter is bathed when it has reached the *rebis* stage (q.v.).

BARBAULT, Armand: Contemporary alchemist.

BASIL Valentine: Fifteenth-century Adept; a Benedictine monk.

BERGIER, Jacques: Contemporary scientific writer.

BERIGARD of Pisa: Seventeenth-century Italian philosopher.

BERNARD of Treviso: Fifteenth-century Adept. Count of the March of Treviso.

BÖTTGER, Johann-Friedrich: Seventeenth-century alchemist who, instead of the Stone, discovered the secret of making Dresden china.

BOYLE, Robert: Seventeenth-century British physicist and chemist.

C

CARO, Roger: Contemporary alchemist.

CHAMPAGNE, Jean-Julien: Illustrator of Fulcanelli's books. Died 1932.

CHAOS: Prime matter when first extracted from the mine.

CINNABAR: Sulphide of mercury; often mistakenly believed to be the prime matter.

COCTION: Cooking.

COHOBATION: Successive distillations by which to concentrate a product.

COMPOST: Mixture contained in the philosophic egg.

COSMOPOLITE, The: Sixteenth-century Adept, whose real name was Alexander Seton.

CYLIANI: Nineteenth-century alchemist.

CHEMICAL Marriage: Union of sulphur and Philosophers' mercury in the philosophic egg.

D

DEE, John: Sixteenth-century British occultist, magician, and Puffer.

DEWS of May: Ordinary dew, to be gathered in March and April for use in May.

272

Glossary

DIGBY, Sir Kenelm: Seventeenth-century Puffer.

DRAGON: In general the word is used to designate philosophers' sulphur, but when used in compound with other words may have other meanings. For example, the "scaly dragon" means the ore from which the prime matter is extracted.

DUJOLS, Pierre: Kept a book shop in Paris, specialising in Hermetic works at the beginning of this century. Wrote several Studies on alchemy under the pseudonym Magophon.

DRY WATER "that does not wet one's hands": Synonym for the secret fire, but occasionally used to mean philosophic mercury.

E

EAGLE: Synonym for sublimation, as used by Philalethes.

EARTH: To alchemists all solids are "an earth", but "our earth" generally means the prime matter.

EGG, The philosophic: Glass vessel containing the philosophic substance for the final coction.

ELIXIR of Life: The Philosophic Stone in a homoeopathic dose.

EMERALD Table: Earliest known description of alchemy; said to have been carved on an emerald tablet by Hermes Trismegistus.

F

FIRE, Natural: The principle of heat contained in matter.

FIRE, Secret: A dual salt prepared by the Artist. Also known as prime agent.

FIRE, Unnatural: Fire depending on coal, gas, or electricity.

FIGUIER, Louis: Nineteenth-century French scientific writer.

FLAMEL, Nicholas: Fourteenth-century French Adept and Public Scrivener.

FLAMMARION, Camille: French astronomer and scientist; died 1925.

FULCANELLI: Contemporary Adept.

G

"GENEROUS": Expression used to designate an alchemist who gives true information.

"GRUDGING": Designates an alchemist who gives false or misleading information.

GERBERT: Tenth-century French alchemist, born at Aurillac, who became Pope Sylvester II.

Glossary

GLAUBER, Rudolph: Seventeenth-century German alchemist.

GOLD, drinkable: A medicine discovered by Paracelsus, in his search for the Stone.

GOLD, Hermetic: Any metal transmuted to gold; indistinguishable from natural gold because it contains only a single stable isotope.

GOLD, ordinary or natural: The commercial article.

GOLD, philosophic: In general means prime matter or one of its components. Occasionally used for the sulphur in prime matter.

GREAT WORK: The final goal of alchemical operations, the first stage of which is the creation of the Philosophic Stone.

H

HELVETIUS, Johann Friedrich: Seventeenth-century Dutch physician, whose real name was Schweitzer.

HERMAPHRODITE: see Androgyne.

HERMES TRISMEGISTUS: Greek god, to whom legend attributes the foundation of alchemy.

HERMETIC: Adjective describing anything or anyone to do with Hermes.

HERMETIC Philosopher: May be an alchemist or an Adept.

HUSSON, Bernard: Twentieth-century "amateur" of alchemy; has also worked in a laboratory.

J

JABIR: Eighth-century Arab Adept. Also known as Geber.

JOHN XXII: Fourteenth-century Pope, who fulminated in a Bull against alchemists, although he had himself written a treatise on the transmutation of metals, and at his death left an enormous fortune that was believed by everyone to be alchemical in origin.

JOLIVET-CASTELOT: Early twentieth-century archimist.

JUPITER: Synonym for tin.

K

KELLY, Edward: Sixteenth-century British Puffer, whose real name was Talbot.

KERMES: A variety of oak (quercus coccifera). A name used in alchemy for kermesite, a red mineral (antimony oxysulphide), akin to stibium (antimony).

KHALID: Caliph or Sultan, probably eleventh-century; believed to have been an alchemist.

KUNRUTH, Heinrich: Seventeenth-century German alchemist.

L

LASCARIS: Seventeenth-century Adept.

LAVOISIER, Antoine-Laurent de: Eighteenth-century French chemist.

LEIBNITZ, Gottfried Wilhelm: Seventeenth-century German philosopher and mathematician. Died 1716.

LENGLET du Fresnoy, Nicolas: Eighteenth-century French priest and historian. Was himself an alchemist and worked in a laboratory. Died an octogenarian, by falling into a fire when in a state of exhaustion.

LIMOJON de Saint-Didier: Eighteenth-century French alchemist.

LULLY, Raymond: Thirteenth-century Adept, born at Palma in Majorca.

M

MAGOPHON: See Dujols.

MANGET, Jean-Jacques: Seventeenth-century Swiss doctor and "amateur" of alchemy. Editor of *Bibliotheca Chemica Curiosa*.

MARY the Jewess: Fourth-century female alchemist of Alexandria.

MARS: Synonym for iron.

MATTER, Prime: Natural ore, containing philosophers' sulphur, mercury and salt. According to the Cosmopolite (q.v.), it includes a vein of "stinking sulphur" (not to be confused with philosophers' sulphur), that must be eliminated before the substance is used for the Work.

MATRASS: A long-necked chemical flask.

MEDICINE, The universal: A dilution of the Philosopher's Stone, also known as the panacea. If the Work is carried only as far as the "White" stage, a less potent medicine is obtained.

MERCURY: Commercial quicksilver. The expression "our mercury" may be used to mean almost anything from mercury contained in the prime matter to philosophic mercury.

MERCURY, Philosophers': The female principle in prime matter.

MERCURY, philosophic: The salt extracted from the prime matter by the action of the secret fire.

MOON: Synonym for silver. May also represent one of the two principles contained in prime matter, when used conjointly with the word Sun.

MORHOFF, Georges: Seventeenth-century physician, writer, and "amateur" of alchemy.

MORIEN, the Philosopher: Roman alchemist from Alexandria; believed to have lived in the tenth or eleventh century. The book containing his conversations with King Khalid is still regarded as authoritative; but it does not prove the existence of either.

MULTIPLICATION: Last stage of the Master Work, which increases the potency of the Stone. It requires the whole process to be repeated.

MUTUS LIBER (Silent Book): by Jacob Sulat.

MYSTERY, The: Another name for the Great Work or Master Work.

N

NITRE: Synonym for saltpetre (potassium nitrate).

O

OAK: Usually means the natural tree. One component of the secret fire is extracted from its embers. See also Kermes.

ORPIMENT: A yellow mineral, arsenic tri-sulphide, often mistakenly believed to be the prime matter of the Work.

OUROBOROS: The serpent biting its own tail, symbol of the Great Work.

P

PANACEA: The universal medicine obtained from the Stone; believed to be a cure for all human ills.

PELICAN: An alembic with beaks that lead back to the body. Used for continuous distillation.

PERNETY, Dom Antoine Joseph: Eighteenth-century French monk, and historical writer.

PERRENELLE: Christian name of Nicholas Flamel's wife.

PHILALETHES, Eirenaeus Philoponos: Seventeenth-century British Adept.

PARACELSUS, Aureole Philip Theophrastus Bombastes ab Hohenheim: Sixteenth-century German-Swiss physician and alchemist.

POISSON, Albert: Alchemist and writer who lived at the end of the nineteenth century.

PROJECTION: Synonym for transmutation of metal. The powder used to accomplish it is made by fermenting the Stone with a piece of the metal it is hoped to obtain—usually gold.

PYRITES, Iron: Natural sulphide of iron.

PUFFER: A pretended alchemist, who tries to transmute metals to gold

276

by any and every means and in the sole hope of profit. Modern chemistry was born of the researches of Puffers which, though unorganised, led to the discovery of numerous new substances.

Q

QUICKSILVER: Old name for mercury.

QUINTESSENCE: A word with several meanings. It may designate the metallic principle obtained after dissolution; it may be used as a synonym for the "red" stage of the Work; or it may be applied to a red substance that appears during coction.

R

RABELAIS, François: Sixteenth-century French writer, who was a Benedictine monk, a doctor, Professor of anatomy and parish priest at Meudon, but also an alchemist, or at any rate an "amateur" of the science.

RHASES: Arab physician and alchemist, who lived about the tenth century.

REBIS: The dual substance created by the two first parts of the Work, which is cooked in the philosophic egg in the third part.

REGIMEN of Philalethes: The name given to each of the seven stages of temperature which must be applied to the philosophic egg during coction.

RETORT: A vessel in which substances are placed for distillation; usually with a long, bent-back neck.

ROSE-CROIX: Secret society founded by the more or less legendary Christian Rosenkreutz.

ROSENKREUTZ, Christian: Supposed to have lived in the fourteenth century, attained Adepthood and acquired immortality. He has by some been identified with Philalethes and Saint-Germain.

S

SAINT-GERMAIN, Count de: Eighteenth-century alchemist, and possibly an Adept. He is one of the oddest historical enigmas. At the present time he is supposed to be living in a mansion in Venice!

SALMON, Guillaume: Alchemist and writer; lived in the seventeenth and the beginning of the eighteenth centuries.

SALT: The means whereby sulphur is united with Philosophers' mercury.

Before the days of Basil Valentine and Paracelsus this salt was often called arsenic, or else not mentioned at all.

SALTPETRE: Potassium nitrate; formula NO_3K.

SATURN: Synonym for lead.

SCHMIEDER, Karl-Christof: Nineteenth-century German professor and historian. His *History of Alchemy* was published in 1832.

SEAL, Hermetic: Air-tight closure.

SEHFELD: Eighteenth-century Austrian alchemist.

SENDIVOGIUS, Michael: Eighteenth-century Moravian alchemist who collected the works of the Cosmopolite, married his wife, and adopted his identity.

SETON, Alexander: See Cosmopolite.

SOLVE ET COAGULA: Latin words that summarise the greater part of the manipulations used in the Great Work, because in the course of the first two parts of the Work the solid bodies are dissolved, and the volatile spirits are coagulated.

SPAGIRISM: A word, probably coined by Paracelsus, to describe the art of making chemical or medicinal preparations by alchemical methods.

SPINOZA, Benedict: Seventeenth-century Dutch philosopher.

STARKEY, George: Seventeenth-century British chemist who knew Philalethes in America.

STIBNITE: Native antimony trisulphide.

SUBLIMATION: The act of transforming a solid body into vapour without passing through the liquid stage.

SULPHUR: The male principle in prime matter.

SUN: Synonym for gold. When used with the Moon, they usually designate the two components of prime matter.

SYLVESTER II, POPE: See Gerbert.

T

TARTAR: Cream of tartar is purified argol, the hard crust formed on the sides of wine casks.

TIFFEREAU: French Archimist who lived at the beginning of the nineteenth century.

TRANSMUTATION: An alchemical operation which consisted in changing one metal into another, and which can be done in present-day science only by physical methods.

U

UNIVERSAL SOLVENT: This liquid (or alkahest) is the solvent used in all three parts of the Work. Its name does *not* mean that it can be used to dissolve anything and everything.

V

VAN HELMONT, JEAN-BAPTISTE: Seventeenth-century Belgian doctor and chemist.

VENUS: Synonym for copper.

VITRIOL: No connection with the chemical acid of that name. The word was used by Basil Valentine for the philosophic solvent.

VIRGIN'S MILK: Salt obtained through the action of the Dews of May.

W

WAY: There are three ways of accomplishing the Great Work, known respectively as the Short Way, the Humid Way, and the Dry Way. They vary in the length of time needed, in the difficulty of execution, and in the methods used in carrying them out.

WATER: To an alchemist every liquid is a form of water.

Z

ZACHAIRE, DENIS: Sixteenth-century French Adept.

ZOZIMOS THE PANAPOLITAN: Third- or fourth-century Adept, living in Alexandria.

Index

Index